FOUNDERS OF NEW JERSEY

First Settlements, Colonists and Biographies by Descendants

Evelyn Hunt Ogden

and

The Descendants of Founders

of New Jersey

Third Edition 2016

Acknowledgements

We wish to thank Diana Robinson for editing the manuscript; Jennifer Carter for design, editing technical assistance and layout throughout the writing process; Roseann Jessel for cover design; Kurt Jessel and Jennifer Johnson for technical support and Janet Jessel for photography.

Descendants of Founders of New Jersey

www.njfounders.org.

FOUNDERS OF NEW JERSEY:

First Settlements, Colonists and Biographies by Descendants

Descendants of Founders of New Jersey

www.njfounders.org

First Edition 2006 incorporating earlier published
Books I, II, and II of biographies

Second Edition 2011

Third Edition 2016

ISBN-13: 978-0692814819

ISBN-10: 0692814817

Founders of New Jersey:
First Settlements, Colonists and Biographies by Descendants

Member Authors

Paul Woolman Adams, Jr.
Mary Ellen Ezzell Ahlstrom
Annie Looper Alien
Reba Baglio
Lucy Hazen Barnes
Michael T. Bates
Kathryn Marie Marten Beck
Taylor Marie Beck
Patricia W. Blakely
Matthew Bowdish
Margaret A. Brann
Clifton Rowland Brooks, M.D.
Richard Charles Budd
Daniel Byram Bush
James Reed Campbell Jr
Esther Burdge Capestro
Michael Charles
Warren R. Clayton
Eva Lomerson Collins
Mirabah L. LeJambre Combs
Lynda and James Condon
Lynn D. Constan
David Hand Coward
Susan Bakley Coxe
James L. Dennis
Ronald DePue
Margaret Dill
Theodore Matthew Duay III
Julia VanRiper Dumdey
Lester Robert Dunham
Laura Carolina Jennings Fafeita
David Richard Finch
Timothy Christopher Finton
Harol Douglas Ford
Michael Garey
Sally Graham
David Lawrence Grinnell

Steven Guy
Craig Hamilton
William Hampton
Robert J. Hardie, Sr.
James Paul Hess
Steve Hollands
Mary Jamia Case Jacobsen
Edsall Riley Johnston, Jr.
Elaine E. Johnston
John Edward Lary Jr
Guy Franklin Leighton
Marian L. LoPresti
Constan Trimmer Lucy
Michael Sayre Maiden, Jr.
Donna Lee Wilkenson Malek
Douglas W. McFarlane Marshall
Alan Russell Matlack
Amy Adele Matlack
Nancy Elise Matlack
Dorothy J. Maxon
Robert D. McPherson
Teresa Carroll Medlinsky
Jeffrey A. Meyer
Mary McCall Middleton
Don Charles Nearpass
Beverly Nelson
Evelyn Hunt Ogden
Sharon Patton
Ross Gamble Perry
Evelyn Ogden from Petrov
Clarence Mott Pickard
William Young Pryor
Arthur D. Quackenbush, Jr.
David R. Reading
George L. Reeves
Dallas John Riedesel
Byron David Rolfe

Brandon Rowley
Helen L. Schanck
Deanna May Scherrer
Marjorie Barber Schuster
Judy Scovronsky
Sara Frasier Sellgren
James A Shepherd
Barbara Carver Smith
Marian L. Smith
Martha Sullivan Smith
Myron Crenshaw Smith
George E. Spaulding, Jr.
Heather Elizabeth Welty Speas
Charlotte Van Horn Squarcy
Earl Gorden Stannard III
Jacqueline Frank Strickland
David Strungfellow
Harriet Stryker-Rodda
Kenn Stryker-Rodda
Frank S. Sutherland-Hall
Margaret Drody Thompson
James L. Tichenor, Esq.
James Tunison
L. George Van Syckle
Robert Vivian
Kathleen Bastedo Walter
Robertson D. Ward
Craig Hamilton Weaver
Jay Pernell Wells
Janice Crowell Wheeler
William Gammons White
Florence S. Whitehead
Kenneth Winans
Karen Hand Wolzanski
Helen Grey Henning Wright

Introduction to the 2016 Edition

Descendants of founders of New Jersey reside within the state, across the nation and around the world. ***FOUNDERS OF NEW JERSEY: First Settlements, Colonists and Biographies by Descendants*** explores the lives and motivations of the men and women who colonized the state; through 138 biographies by descendants who provide interesting insights into the early culture, settlements and development of the state.

Family historians, genealogists, historical researchers and current and prospective members of DFNJ should find useful the documentation of over 2000 17th and early 18th century settlers, events, settlements, grantors, grantees, deed holders, signers of patents, ship passengers and Native American sellers of land.

Descendants of Founders of New Jersey is an organization dedicated to the origins and heritage of New Jersey. The book contains a list of over 300 "Qualified Founders" who have been documented as founders of the state by the members as a basis for membership. However, there are many many other individuals and families who settled, encouraged and/or financed New Jersey prior to 1702.

We hope this book inspires descendants and those whose ancestors have already been documented by their distant relatives to join with us as members of Descendants of Founders of New Jersey (www.njfounders.org) and to continue to memorialize their New Jersey roots.

Table of Contents

Introduction to the 2016 Edition 5

DESCENDANTS OF FOUNDERS OF NEW JERSEY 15

    1676 Division of New Jersey – the East-West Boundary 16

    Qualifying New Jersey Ancestors – As of June 2016 17

THE HISTORY AND FOUNDING OF NEW JERSEY 21

Historical Timeline of Early New Jersey 22

    The Native New Jerseyans 24

    Early Exploration of New Jersey 24

    The Dutch Period in Albania - 1616 25

    English Colonies of Connecticut and Long Island – 1636 26

    New Netherlands falls to the English and the Founding of New Jersey - 1664 27

    Lord John Berkeley, Sir George Carteret and the Concessions and Agreements 27

THE FIRST ENGLISH SETTLEMENTS IN NEW JERSEY 29

The Founding of Elizabethtown - 1664 30

    The First English Purchase of Land in New Jersey 30

    Arrival of the First English Settlers – 1664 32

    The Elizabethtown Associates 33

    Elizabethtown - The First Capital of New Jersey 34

    Elizabethtown – the First English Church 35

    Elizabethtown – First in Education 36

    Elizabethtown – The first Elected Assembly and Code of Laws 37

The Founding of Shrewsbury and Middletown - 1665 38

    The Monmouth Patent and Patentees 39

    The Growth of the Settlement 40

The Founding of Woodbridge - 1666 46

THE GROWTH OF THE SETTLEMENT	46
EARLY SETTLERS OF WOODBRIDGE	47
FIRST PRESBYTERIAN CHURCH WOODBRIDGE AND CEMETERY OF WOODBRIDGE	48

The Founding of Piscataway - 1666 49

THE GROWTH OF THE SETTLEMENT	49
EARLY SETTLERS OF PISCATAWAY	50

The Founding of Newark - 1666 52

THE GROWTH OF THE SETTLEMENT	54
EARLY SETTLERS OF NEWARK	55
THE FORTY-ONE GUILFORD, MILFORD AND NEW HAVEN MEN WHO SIGNED THE FUNDAMENTAL AGREEMENTS:	55

The Founding of Salem and the Fenwick Colony - 1665 58

EARLY SETTLERS OF FENWICK'S COLONY	59
THE GROWTH OF THE SETTLEMENT	60

BIOGRAPHIES OF FOUNDERS OF NEW JERSEY 63

ABRAHAM ACKERMAN (1656/59 - AFT. 1723)	64
DAVID ACKERMAN (1653 – 1710/24)	65
THOMAS ALGER (AB.1638 - 1687)	66
JOHN ALLEN (C.1625 – 1702/3)	67
BARTHOLOMEW APPLEGATE (C 1625 – AFT 1674)	68
ELIZABETH AUSTIN (1669-1753)	69
OBADIAH AYERS (1636 - 1694)	70
GUILIAM BERTHOLF (1656 - ABT. 1726)	71
WIILLIAM (1630-1712) AND SARAH BIDDLE (1634-1709)	72
JOHN BISHOP SR. (1621-1684)	73
THOMAS BLOOMFIELD SR. (16XX - 1685)	74
ROBERT BOND (1596 – 1677)	75

NATHANIEL BONNELL (1636-1711) 76

RICHARD BORDEN (1595/6 – 1671) 78

JAMES BOWNE (1636 - 1695) 79

ALEXANDER/SANDER BOYER (1618-1661) 80

JOHN BROCKETT (BEF. 1620 – 1689/90) 81

TIMOTHY BROOKS SR. (1634-1712) 82

GEORGE BROWN (16XX -1717/8) 83

JAMES BROWN (1656-1715/6) 84

OBADIAH BRUEN (1606 – BEF. 1690) 85

JAN CORNELIS BUYS (1629 -1689/90) 87

MATTHEW CAMFIELD (1604 - 1673) 88

CALEB CARMAN (1644/5 – 1693) 89

ROBERT CARR (1614 - 1681) 90

JOHN CHAMBERLIN (1687-1739) 91

RICHARD CLARK (C. 1613 - 1697) 92

WILLIAM CLAYTON (1632 - 1689) 93

ROBERT CLEMENTS, JR (C 1634-C 1714) 94

SAMUEL CLIFT (ABT. 1610-1683) 95

THOMAS CLIFTON (ABT. 1606-1681) 96

FRANCIS COLLINS (1635 – 1720) 97

JOHN CONGER (C 1645-1712) 98

HENRY COOK (C. 1671-1723) 99

CORNELIS WILLEMSE COUWENHOVEN (1672-1736) 100

THOMAS COX (1620 - 1681) 101

DR. DANIEL COXE (1640-1730) 102

First Settlers, Colonists, and Biographies by Descendants

JASPER CRANE (1605 - 1681) 103

JAMES DAVIS (1675 – 1769) 104

DAVID DEMAREST (1620 – 1693) 105

ROBERT DENNIS (c. 1619 - 1683+) 106

DANIEL DOD (1649-1701/1714) 107

CORNELIS DOREMUS (c 1655-1715) 108

SAMUEL DOTY (1643-1715) 108

GAVINE DRUMMOND (1659-1724) 110

SARAH DUBOIS (1664-1726) 111

JONATHAN DUNHAM (1639/40 – 1702) 112

NICHOLAS DUPUI (1634-1691) 113

JACOB DU TRIEUX (abt. 1645-1709) 114

JOHN ELLISON (abt. 1695–abt. 1775) 115

JOSHUA ELY (16xx– 1702) 116

JOSEPH ENGLISH II (16xx -1725) 117

DAVID FALCONER (1630-1713) 118

EDWARD FITZ-RANDOLPH (c.1607 - 1675/6) 119

JOSEPH FRAZEE (1635–1713) 120

THOMAS FRENCH (1639 – 1699) 121

HANNAH FULLER (1636 - aft.1686) 122

HANANIAH GAUNTT (1647 – 1721) 123

WILLIAM GIFFORD (1615-1687) 124

MATTHEW GRACEY (GRACIE) (16xx-1715) 126

JOHN GREGORY (1612/15 – 1689) 127

JAMES GROVER (16xx - 1686) 128

First Settlers, Colonists, and Biographies by Descendants

SAMUEL HALE (1639/40-1709)	129
JOHN HAMPTON (1640 – 1702)	130
THOMAS HAND (c. 1646-1714)	131
THOMAS HARDING (c 1635-1708)	132
RICHARD HARTSHORNE (1641 – 1722)	133
MATTHIAS HATFIELD (16xx - 1687)	134
JOHN HAVENS (c. 1635 - c. 1687)	135
RICHARD HIGGINS (abt. 1609– aft. 1674)	136
REV. OBADIAH HOLMES (1606/7 – 1682)	137
THOMAS HOWELL (abt. 1659–1687)	138
HENRY JACQUES (c. 1618-1687)	139
JEFFERY JONES (c.1643 - 1717)	141
ISAAC KINGSLAND (1648 – 1698)	142
JOHN LIMING (16xx-aft. 1697)	143
FRANCIS LINLE (LINDSLEY/LINDLEY) (16xx – 1704)	144
HENRY LYON (16xx - 1703)	145
SAMUEL MARSH (c.1620 - 1683)	146
WILLIAM MATLACK (1648-1738)	147
WILLIAM MEEKER (16xx - 1690)	148
JEAN PIERRE MELLOT (1658–1704)	149
SAMUEL MOORE (c.1630 - 1688)	150
LEWIS MORRIS (c.1660-1696)	151
THOMAS MORRIS (16xx -1673)	152
SAMUEL NICHOLSON [1634 – 1685]	153
JOHN OGDEN (1609 – 1682)	155

First Settlers, Colonists, and Biographies by Descendants

GEORGE PACK (c. 1634-1704) 158

JOHN PANCOAST (PANCKHURST) (c. 1630 – 1694) 159

REV. ABRAHAM PIERSON (1611-1678) 161

JOHN PIKE (1613 - 1689/90) 162

RICHARD PITTENGER (PEWTINGER) (ABT 1645 - 17XX) 163

ELIZABETH POWELL (1677 – 1714) 164

BENJAMIN PRICE (1621-1712) 165

JOHN PRIDMORE (PREDMORE) (1661-1702) 166

JOHN READING (1657-1717) 167

WALTER REEVE (1650/57 - 1698) 168

EDWARD RIGGS (c. 1614 - 1668) 169

JOSEPH ROBINS (1670/71- 1709) 170

MOSES ROLFE (1681-1746) 171

RICHARD ROUNSAVELL (1658-1703) 172

THOMAS SCATTERGOOD (16XX – 1697) 173

JOHN SCHENCK (1670-1753) 174

THOMAS SCHOOLEY (1650 – 1724) 175

ANDERS SINNICKSON (c. 1651 -1699) 176

GILES SLOCUM (c. 1623 – 1681) 178

JOHN SMALLEY (1613–1692) 179

JOHN SOMERS (1623/24-1723) 180

JAMES STEELMAN (JONS MANSSON) (1660/70 - 1734/35) 181

ROBERT STILES (1655-1728) 182

RICHARD STOUT (c. 1615 - c. 1705) 183

CAPTAIN SAMUEL SWAINE (SWAYNE) (c. 1620 - 1685) 184

JOHN THROCKMORTON (1601 – 1684)	187
MARTIN TICHENOR (c.1615 – 1681)	188
JOHN TILTON (1613 - 1688)	189
ROBERT TREAT (1622/24 – 1710)	190
CORNELIUS (TEUNISSEN) TUNISON (1694 - 1775)	191
JAN TUNISEN (1654 - 1723)	192
JOHANNES UPDIKE (OPDYKE) (1651 - 1729)	193
LUBBERT GYSBERTSEN VAN BLARICUM (c.1601 - c.1655)	194
JACOB VAN DOORN (BEF. 1655–ABT. 1720)	195
BALTUS BARENTS VAN KLEECK (1645-ABT.1717)	196
PETER VAN NEST (c 1625 - AFT. 1709)	197
PENELOPE VAN PRINCIS (KENT, STOUT) (c. 1622 –1732)	198
CLAES JANSEN VAN PURMERENT (ABT. 1655- AFT. 1690)	200
CORNELIS VAN VOORST (c. 1580 – 1638)	201
WALING JACOBSE VAN WINKLE (c.1650 - c.1729)	202
HARTMAN (MICKIELSEN) VREELAND (1651 1707)	203
JOHN WARD (16xx - 1684)	204
JOHN WARD SR. (c. 1625 – 1694)	205
THOMAS WARNE (c. 1652 - 1722)	206
BARTHOLOMEW WEST (16xx - c.1674)	208
JOHN WINANS (WYNANTS) (1640 - 1694)	209
BARNABAS WINES (1628 – 1715)	210
JOSEPH WOODRUFF (1676-1742)	211
WILLIAM WOOLMAN (c.1625 – 1692)	212
JOSHUA WRIGHT (BEFORE 1633-1695)	213

ROBERT ZANE (1642-1694) 214

APPENDIX A 215

Concessions and Agreements 215

Genealogical Index of Names 219

Over 2000 names linked with settlement of New Jersey during the Proprietory Period 219

DESCENDANTS OF FOUNDERS OF NEW JERSEY

Descendants of founders of New Jersey reside within the state, across the nation and around the world. The stories of the lives and contributions of their ancestors in settling New Jersey three or more centuries ago may have been chronicled, but many have been lost in time.

Thirty-five years ago a group of descendants of early New Jersey colonists joined together to form Descendants of Founders of New Jersey; a society of those associated with the earliest development of our state. Membership includes those descendants who remained in New Jersey and those who have fanned out across the nation. Today Descendants of Founders of New Jersey is an active society with over 425 members.

Among the objectives of Descendants of Founders of New Jersey are: to establish, preserve and publish information concerning the founders of New Jersey and to provide assistance to those who advocate the preservation of the history of the State.

We welcome in membership any adult, 18 years of age or older, who provides documentation of their descent from a founder who resided in or contributed to the settlement of New Jersey prior to 17 April, 1702, and who subscribes to the objectives of the society.

The date of 17 April, 1702 was chosen because that was the date on which East Jersey and West Jersey were merged to create the single entity of New Jersey. By that date basic settlement had been accomplished in the areas that now make up the state.

More information about the Descendants of Founders of New Jersey and an application form can be found online at www.njfounders.org.

Evelyn Hunt Ogden, Ed.D.
Registrar General
Descendants of Founders of New Jersey

1676 Division of New Jersey – the East-West Boundary

Berkeley and Carteret held undivided joint interests in New Jersey as granted by the Duke of York in 1664. In 1676, after seven towns in East Jersey had been established and John Fenwick had founded Salem in West Jersey, an East-West division line was projected to divide New Jersey between Sir George Carteret and Lord Berkeley. In 1687, the original line was surveyed and the following year the northern boundary of New Jersey was settled. In 1702, New Jersey became one state.

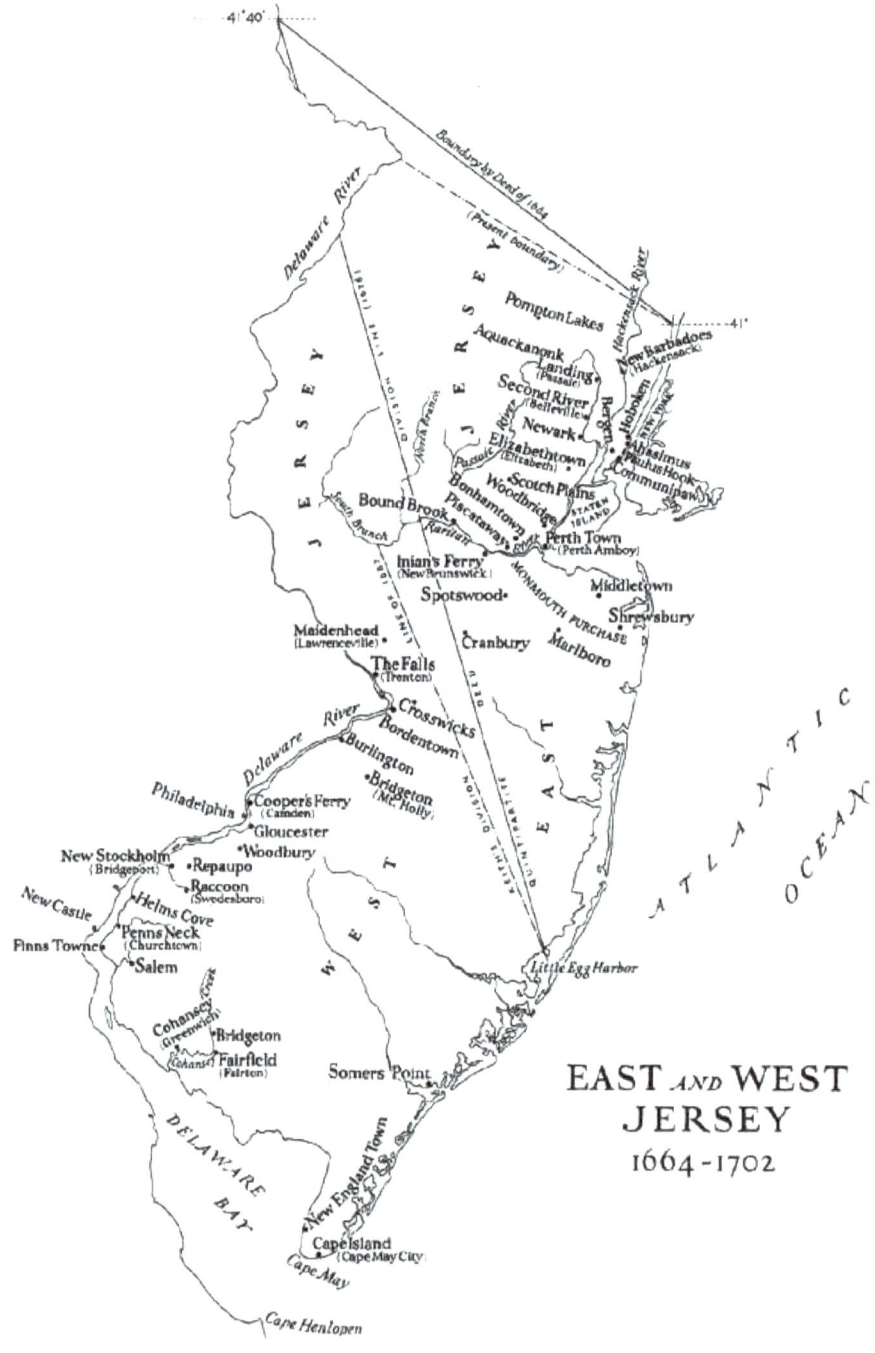

Descendants of Founders of New Jersey

Qualifying New Jersey Ancestors – As of June 2016

The following founders have been submitted and approved as a basis for membership by Descendants of Founders of New Jersey. However, in no way does this list include all those individuals who prior to 1702 settled or contributed to the settling of New Jersey and from whom thousands of descendants reside within the state, across the nation and around the world (See the Index of Names for references to over 1800 other settlers who would qualify as founders. Names in bold type have associated biographies in this volume.

Abraham Ackerman
David Ackerman
Laurents Ackerman
Thomas Alger
Jedediah Allen
John Allen
Joachim Andres
Bartholomew Applegate
Thomas Applegate
Rev. James Ashton
Elizabeth Austin
Obadiah Ayers
John Bainbridge
John Baird
Benjamin Baldwin
John Baldwin Sr.
Edward Ball
Epke Jacobse Banta
Rev. Guiliam Bertholf
William Biddle
John Bishop Sr.
Thomas Blatchley
Thomas Bloomfield
Robert Bond
Nathaniel Bonnell
Jan Cornelisse Boombaert (Bogert)
Richard Borden
Ann (___) Bowne
James Bowne
Mary Stout Bowne
Samuel Bowne
William Bowne
Alexander/Sander Boyer

Edward Bradbury
Hendrick Brinkerhoff
John Brockett
Timothy Brooks, Sr.
Abraham Brown
George Brown
James Brown of Burlington County
Nicholas Brown of Monmouth County
Obadiah Bruen
William Budd
Jan Cornelis Buys
Matthew Camfield
Caleb Carman
Robert Carr
John Chamberlin
John Clark
Richard Clark
Richard Clark Jr.
James Clarkson
William Clayton Jr.
Robert Clements
Samuel Clift
Thomas Clifton
John Coddington
Samuel Cole(s)
Francis Collins
William Compton
John Condit
John Conger (Belconger)
Henry Cook
George Corlies

Cornelius Willemse Couwenhover
Thomas Cox
Dr. Daniel Coxe
Deacon Azariah Crane
Andrew Craig Sr.
Jasper Crane
Joseph Crane
Stephen Crane
Oele Dahlbo (William Dalbo)
James Davis
David Demarest
David. Demarest Jr.
Maria (DeRuine) Demarest
Rachel (Cresson) Demarest
Samuel Demarest
Robert Dennis
Samuel Dennis
Nicholas deVaux
John Dille Sr.
Daniel Dod
Cornelis Doremus
James Dorset
Samuel Doty
Capt. Francis Drake
Gavine Drummond
Sarah DuBois
Rev. Thomas Dungan
Jonathan Dunham
Hugh Dunn
Nicholas DuPui/DePuy
Jacob duTrieux

First Settlers, Colonists, and Biographies by Descendants

Thomas Eaton	George Hulit	John Pancoast
John Ellison	Benjamin Hull	George Parker
Joshua Ely	Thomas Huntington	Edward Patterson
Joseph English II	**Henry Jacques**	John Patterson
Thomas Eves	Jenti Jeppes	George Peck
David Falconer	**Jeffrey Jones**	Roger Perdrick
Edward Fitz Randolph	**Isaac Kingsland**	Daniel Perrin
Nathaniel Fitz-Randolph	John Kinsey	**Abraham Pierson**
Thomas Fouike	Robert Kitchell	Thomas Pierson Sr.
William Frampton	Samuel Kitchell	**John Pike**
Joseph Frazee	Edmond LaFetra	**Richard Pittenger**
Thomas French	William Lawrence	Samuel Potter
Hannah Fuller	Thomas Leeds	Thomas Potter
Hananiah Gauntt	Henry Leonard	John Pound
Jeremiah Genung	**John Liming**	Paul Poulson (Powelson)
William Gifford	**Francis Lindsley (Linle)**	**Elizabeth Powell**
Charles Gordon	Remembrance Lippincott	**Benjamin Price**
Matthew Gracey	Richard Lippincott	**John Pridmore**
John Gregory	Henry Lyon	**John Reading**
James Grover	**Samuel Marsh**	Sarah Reape
Rebecca (___) Grover	Benjamin Martin	William Reape
Safety Grover	John Martin Sr.	**Walter Reeve**
John Haines	Joseph Martin	James Reid
William Hains	Clement Masters	**Edward Riggs**
Samuel Hale	Francis Masters	**Joseph Robins**
William Hall	**William Matlack**	**Moses Rolfe**
John Hampton	**William Meeker**	George Ross
John Hance	**Jean Pierre Mellot**	**Richard Rounsavell**
John Hancock	John Mifflin Sr.	John Ruckman
Thomas Hand	**Samuel Moore**	Joseph Sayre
Thomas Harding	Thomas Morford	**Thomas Scattergood**
Richard Harrison	**Lewis Morris of Passage Point**	**John Schenck**
Richard Hartshorne		**Thomas Scholey**
Matthias Hatfield	Lewis Morris of Newark	**(Schooley) Scholey**
John Havens	Thomas Morris	Robert Seeley
Samuel Hale	George Mount	William Shattuck
Richard Heritage	Matthias Mount	John Shinn Sr.
William Hibbs	Richard Mount	Abraham Shotwell
Richard Higgins	John Nesmith	**Anders Sinnickson**
William Hixson	**Samuel Nicholson**	**(Andrew Senecke)**
William Hoge	Henry Norris	Thomas Skillman
Thomas Holland	Dahlbo Oele	**Giles Slocum**
Rev. Obadiah Holmes	**John Ogden**	Nathaniel Slocum
Christopher Hooglandt	Caleb Osborne	**John Smalley**
Thomas Howell	**George Pack**	Rev. John Smith

Thomas Smith
John Somers
Humphrey Spinning
James Steelman (Mansson)
Casper Steynmets (Steinmets)
Robert Stiles
Richard Stout
Dirck Straatemaacker
William Sutton
Samuel Swaine
Nathaniel Sylvester
Douwe Harmense Tallman
Edward Taylor
Albert Albertse Terhund
Andrew Thompson
Hur Thompson
Job Throckmorton
John Throckmorton
Martin Tichenor
John Tilton Sr.
Peter Tilton
Robert Treat
William Trotter
Jan Tunisen
Cornelius Tunison
Johannes Updike (Opdyck)
Divertje Cornelis VanBlaricom
Jan Lubbertsen VanBlaricom
Lubbert Gysbertsen VanBlaricom

Magdaleentje Theunis VanBlaricom
Jannetje (Jans) (Van Horn) VanBoskerk
Lourens Andriessen VanBuskirk
Walling Jacobse VanDoorn
Barent Christian VanHorn
Cornelius Christiansen VanHorn
Jannetje Van Horn
Helmigh Roelofs VanHouten
Klaes VanHouten
Roeloff Cornelissen VanHouten
Theunis Van Houten
Baltus Barents VanKleeck
Adrian VanLaer
Pieter VanNest Jr.,
Penelope VanPrincis
Claes Jansen VanPurmerent (Cuyper)
Jurian Thomassee VanRiper
Albert Stevense VanVoorhees
Cornelius VanVoorst
Lubbert Lubbertson VanWestervelt
Jacob Waling VanWinkle
Waling Jacobse VanWinkle

Abraham Isaacsen VerPlanck
Hartman (Michielsen) Vreeland
Michiel Jansen Vreeland
William Waddington
Garret Wall Sr.
Walter Wall
John Ward (sergeant)
John Ward (a turner)
Eliakim Wardell
Thomas Warne
Luke Watson, Sr.
Bartholomew West
Nathaniel West Jr.
Christopher Wetherill (Whetherill)
Peter White
Isaac Whitehead
Thomas Whitlock
Robert Willson
John Winans (Wynants)
Barnabas Wines
John Wood
Joseph Woodruff
Timothy Woodruff
Emmanuel Woolley
John Woolley
Willman Woolman
William Worth
John Worthley
Joshua Wright
Albert Zabriskie
Robert Zane

THE HISTORY AND FOUNDING OF NEW JERSEY

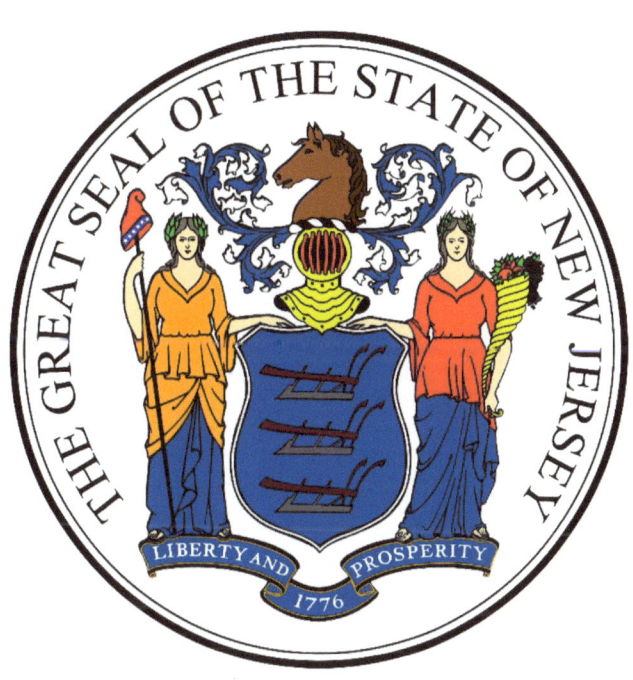

Historical Timeline of Early New Jersey

	Native Jersey Residents – Lenni Lenape or Delaware Indians of the Eastern Algonquin Confederacy
1524	Giovanni da Verrazzano, under French flag explored eastern coast of New Jersey and New York Bay
1609	Henry Hudson and John Colman, Dutch West India Company, explored Hudson River and the west side of Staten Island and discovered Newark Bay and the Passaic and Hackensack Rivers
1610	Sir Argall, governor of Virginia, explored Delaware Bay and named it after Baron De la Warr
1614	Dutch captain Cornelis Mey explored lower Delaware and names it Cape May
1618	Dutch fortification on site of Jersey City
1624	Dutch settlement of Fort Nassau
1626	Dutch settlement of New Amsterdam
1630	Dutch settlement of Pavonia
1638	New Sweden founded
1642	Swedesboro (Raccoon)
1643	Swedish settlement of Fort Elfsborg (near Salem)
1655	Dutch conquest of New Sweden
1660	Dutch settlement of Bergen
1664	James, Duke of York, granted proprietary of New York (Maine to St. Croix) by Charles II
June 1664	James, Duke of York gifts New Jersey to Lord John Berkeley and Sir George Carteret
Aug/Sept 1664	James' small fleet forces the surrender of New Netherlands to England
Sep. 1664	Richard Nicolls, having sailed with the fleet becomes James's appointed Governor
1664-1702	Proprietary Rule by English
30 Sep. 1664	Governor Nicolls grants petition to Associates to purchase lands beyond the Hudson (site of the Elizabeth Colony)
28 Oct. 1664	The Associates (Elizabeth Colony) purchase all the lands between the Raritan and Passaic Rivers from the Indians
Nov 1664	Settlement of Elizabethtown, the first English town in New Jersey
8 April 1665	Governor Richard Nicolls signs the grant known as the Monmouth Patent, for lands which includes what is now Monmouth County and parts of Ocean and Middlesex Counties
10 Feb. 1665	Concessions of Agreement signed by Proprietors Lord John Berkeley and Sir Geroge Carteret
29 July 1665	Arrival of Philip Carteret, first Proprietary Governor of the Providence of New Jersey or Nova Caesarea. He makes Elizabethtown his capital
1665	Settlement of Shrewsbury – part of the Monmouth Patent

The History and Founding of New Jersey

1665	Settlement of Middletown – part of the Monmouth Patent
1666	Settlement of Woodbridge – Purchase of roughly half of the Elizabethtown Patent - Town charter June 1669
1666	Settlement of Piscataway – Purchase of 40,000 acres from a Woodbridge associate Daniel Pierce
1666	Settlement of Newark
1675	Settlement of Salem – Fenwick's Colony
1677	Settlement of Burlington
29 May 1668	First meeting of the first General Assembly of New Jersey at Elizabethtown
1673	Dutch recapture New York and New Jersey
1674	Cession of New Netherlands to England – Treaty of Westminster
1676 and 1687	Formal division into East and West Jersey
3 Mar. 1677	Laws, *Concessions and Agreements* by William Penn, West Jersey
1679	Settlement of Trenton
1680	First meeting of Assembly at Burlington – West Jersey
1680	Lady Elizabeth Carteret proprietor of East Jersey
1682	Settlement of Gloucester
1683	Settlement of Greenwich
1683	Settlement of Woodbury
1683	Settlement of Perth Amboy (capital of East Jersey 1686)
1693	Settlement of Freehold
1682	Settlement of Bordentown
1682	Settlement of Moorestown
1685	Settlement of Town Bank
1702	Union of East and West Jersey under one governor with capitals at Perth Amboy and Burlington

References:

New Jersey History Committee. *Outline History of New Jersey*, Rutgers University Press, New Brunswick, NJ 1950.

Lurie, Maxine N. and Marc Happen. Editors. *Encyclopedia of New Jersey*, Rutgers University Press, New Brunswick, New Jersey, 2004.

The Native New Jerseyans

Evidence discovered along the Musconetcong River in Warren County confirms the presence of human inhabitants in New Jersey as long as 12,000 years ago. The more modern day native peoples known as the Lenape migrated from the west to the area about 3000 years ago. The Lenape were part of the Algonquin language group. They were divided into three clans: the Minci in the north, the Unami in the central area and the Unilachtigo in the south of New Jersey. The Lenape were peaceable farmers, fisherman and hunters. They lived in scattered permanent villages where they planted crops. In the summer they moved to areas along the shore where they ate the abundant fish, clams, oysters and mussels.

Indian Artifacts-The Warne Museum, Old Bridge   Early Pre-New Jersey Map

Early Exploration of New Jersey

The Vikings voyaged along the coast by way of Greenland and Iceland to possibly as far south as Virginia. Leif Ericson is believed to have passed the shores of New Jersey around A.D. 985. Explorer John Cabot, sailing for King Henry VII of England in 1497, may have been the first European to set foot on the land. In 1524, Giovanni daVerrazzano, sailing for the French King Francois I, aboard the Dauphine, entered Raritan Bay.

Verrazzano was followed in 1609 by an Englishman, Henry Hudson, sailing for the Dutch East Indian Company and searching for the "northwest passage" to India. He sailed along the coast from Maine to Virginia. Finding no large enough rivers to the south he turned back north. On September 2, 1609 his ship anchored off shore near what was later called Barnegat inlet and bay. Firstmate Robert Juet recorded in the ships log the following description of the Jersey coast:

> *When the sun rose we steered north again and saw land from the west by northwest, all alike, broken island. The course along the land we found to the norest by north. From the land, which we first had sight of, until we came to a great lake of water, as we could judge it to be, having drowned land, which made it rise like islands, which was in length ten leagues. The mouth of the lake had many shoals, and the sea breaks upon them as it is cast out of the mouth of it. And from the lake or bay the land lies north by east, and we had a great stream out the bay... This was a very good land to fall in with, and a pleasant land to see.*

(Reprinted in *Down Barnegat Bay* by Robert Jahn, Plexus Publishing, 2000)

Continuing north, the Half Moon entered and anchored in Raritan Bay near Sandy Hook. The ship was soon visited by friendly natives who brought green tobacco to exchange for knives and beads. Hudson observed that they had plenty of maize and made very good bread. The following day Hudson sent out a boat, which most likely landed on the Jersey Shore. The crew was kindly received by the natives who gave them more tobacco. Several of the natives, reportedly dressed in "mantles of feathers and fine furs," accompanied the sailors back to the Half Moon bringing presents of dried currants. The  following day a boat was sent up the north side of the bay to explore and take soundings of the river. The crew passed through the narrows between Staten Island and Bergen Neck. They described the land as covered with trees, grass and flowers and filled with delightful fragrance. Unfortunately, on the return trip they were attacked by natives in canoes, and John Colman, who had accompanied Hudson on an earlier trip, was killed and two others wounded. Colman was carried ashore and buried. This was the only negative encounter the Hudson expedition had with natives. Hudson explored New York Bay and probably the Raritan River, as well as many miles up the great river which would bear his name, claiming the lands for the Dutch.

The Dutch Period in Albania - 1616

Dutch explorers in Albania

The Dutch claim in the new world, including the territory they called Albania (now New Jersey) emanated from Henry Hudson's explorations of the area in 1609. As early as 1613 there was a small trading post at the tip of Manhattan Island. In 1616 Peter Minuit was appointed the West Indian Company Director of New Netherlands Company with a mission to establish a fort and port on the southern tip of Manhattan. The major interest of the Dutch in the new world was the lucrative fur trade which they conducted with the Indians up and down the Hudson River. By 1640 New Amsterdam was still a small settlement with a multi-lingual and culturally diverse population engaged in supporting trade. This was the Golden Age of the Netherlands, the wealthiest and most liberal country in the world in the 17th Century, and there was little interest among its population to leave home to colonize far away Dutch territories. Land grants encouraged some Dutch Patroons to establish large farms north of New Amsterdam and on Staten Island. In 1644, the Dutch even granted an association of Englishmen the right to establish a settlement at Hempstead, Long Island, close to New Amsterdam, in return for promising to bring 100 families there within five years.

The New Amsterdam Farm and Stone Church c. 1645

The Dutch did even less to develop or explore their territory west of the Hudson. A few Dutch "plantations" were settled across the river at Pavonia, Hoboken, Bayonne, and Hackensack. In 1643 the Dutch accused the Raritan Indians of crimes and sent eighty Dutch soldiers across the Hudson murdering native men, women and children as they slept. The natives retaliated, destroying homes and the small Dutch settlements. Kief's War, as it would later be known, raged up and down the west bank of the Hudson laying waste to settler's homes forcing most of the Dutch to retreat to the east side of the Hudson. A flimsy treaty was signed in 1643 with the seven tribes, chiefly with the Lenni Lenape.

A second and last war, known as the Peach Tree War (1655-1660), involved the Hackensacks. A farmer near Hoboken resolved to stop the pilfering of Indians from his fruit trees. When he saw someone approaching the orchard he fired and killed an Indian girl. The Indians built beacon fires and swarmed the west side of the Hudson. Soon the whole series of little settlements from Weehawken to Staten Island were in flames and over 100 whites were killed, one hundred and fifty taken captive, and three hundred left homeless. The Dutch paid a ransom for twenty-eight of the captives. After the peace in 1660, the Dutch established a small settlement on the west side of the Hudson River at Bergen.

English Colonies of Connecticut and Long Island – 1636

Unlike the Dutch, English immigrants to New England came with the purpose of establishing permanent settlements where they could practice their religion, own land, pursue financial opportunity and manage their own affairs. They left a land where they were persecuted for their Puritan religious and societal beliefs and which offered little opportunity. Because the English kings were anxious for colonization of the lands they claimed, they were willing to grant charters with liberal "concessions" to colonists for self-management of local affairs and practice of their religion. Two groups of Puritans who came from England settled in the area around Long Island Sound, not very far from New Amsterdam. In 1636 sixty men, women, and children resettling from Massachusetts

organized the Connecticut Colony along the Connecticut River at Windsor, Wethersfield, and Hartford, as a haven for "Puritan gentleman" and their families. In 1638 the independent colony of New Haven was founded by the Puritan minister John Davenport and his congregation at a point of land with a good harbor at the mouth of the Quinnipiac River. New Haven soon became a trading center and several affiliated communities were created in the area, including Milford, Guilford, and Stamford in what is now Connecticut, and on the south side of Long Island Sound at Jamaica, Southold, Northampton, and South Hampton. These settlements were in areas claimed by the Dutch as well as the English, however, the Dutch had little appetite or interest in defending their claims.

New Netherlands falls to the English and the Founding of New Jersey - 1664

In April 1661, after the defeat of Oliver Cromwell, Charles II was returned to the English throne. In March 1664 he granted his brother the Duke of York, Lord High Admiral of the King's Navy (and later James II), vast territories in the New World including all of New Netherlands. The Duke outfitted four ships and charged his commander John Carr with the mission to take over the lucrative Dutch trade and territory. At New Amsterdam the Dutch Governor Stuyvesant surrendered the colony without any bloodshed. Carr was accompanied by Colonel Richard Nicolls, the Duke's new deputy governor for his conquest.

When the English took possession of what had been Dutch New Netherlands in 1664, the land west of the Hudson was still a vast, nearly empty wilderness. A few Dutch farms were sprinkled in the Passaic and Hackensack valleys, a small settlement was located at Bergen on the Hudson River, and along the Delaware were a scattering of small Dutch and Swedish farms. It is estimated that even the native population numbered fewer than 2000, living in small groups mainly inland and coming only to the coast to fish.

Lord John Berkeley, Sir George Carteret and the Concessions and Agreements

On June 24, 1664, only three months after being granted the lands in the New World, the Duke of York gave the land that would eventually be known as New Jersey to Lord John Berkeley and Sir George Carteret, two friends and supporters of the king during the English Civil War. Their intent was to make a profit from their new acquisition by renting all of the land to settlers they would recruit from England.

The Act of Uniformity passed in 1662 prescribed the form of public prayer, administration of the sacraments, and the rites of the Established Church of England. Adherence to these rites was required to hold office in the government or the church in England. Berkeley and Sir George Carteret saw this as an opportunity to entice dissatisfied Englishman to emigrate to the New World to populate their colony. They wrote *The Concessions and Agreements*, which guaranteed prospective settlers certain freedoms and rights that they could not enjoy in England such as freedom of religion, freedom from persecution for religious beliefs, land, and the right to manage their own affairs.

However, their plan to profit from the land was foiled for two reasons. First, the new Governor of New York who had arrived with the Duke of York's fleet, had already granted a half a million acres of the land, known as the Elizabeth Town Purchase, to settlers from Long Island and Connecticut. When Philip Carteret, cousin of Sir George Carteret and the appointed representative of Carteret and Berkeley, arrived in New Jersey he was met by settlers already in possession of the land. A second obstacle to Berkeley and Carteret's rent scheme was the impracticality of collecting rents in the vast unsurveyed territory.

While the *Concessions and Agreements* were not an effective enticement for immigration from England, they were a major incentive for an influx of settlers from New England and Long Island where many, such as Quakers, had experienced religious persecution. Others were desirous of new lands and opportunities. In return for swearing Allegiance to the King and faithfulness to the interests of the Lord Proprietors, the Concessions provided settlers the status of freeman, guaranteed freedom from being molested, punished, disquieted or called in question for any difference in opinion or practice in matters of Religious concernments; the right to choose representatives from among themselves for an Assembly charged with making laws, establishing fair courts, laying out of towns and other divisions; and levying equal taxes on the lands to support the "public charge" of the Province; constitute a military from within the Province for security; and receive clear recorded title to land after seven years. Future settlers were to be seen as naturalized, with all the rights provided by the Concessions, by swearing allegiance to the King and faithfulness to the interests of the Lord Proprietors.

Signed in 1665, *Concessions and Agreements* was an extremely important document which established a representative form of self-government, set civic responsibilities and guaranteed personal freedoms in New Jersey 110 years before the Revolution. A key provision of the Concessions provided that taxes could only be levied by the representative Assembly of the New Jersey for the sole use to support the Province. This provision became of central importance in the next century when King George's attempt to levy taxes for the support of England and the Crown was viewed by colonists as taxation without representation. This clear and direct violation of the Concessions contributed to revolutionary furor in New Jersey (see Appendix A- Excepts from the *Concessions and Agreements*).

References:

Cleveland, Henry R. "Henry Hudson Explores the Hudson River," A project by History World International. (Internet archive).

De Angelo, Walter A. "The Hitchhiker's Guide to Middlesex County," Middlesex County Board of Freeholders, 2008. (Internet archive).

Jahn, Robert. *Down Barnegat Bay: A Noreaster Midnight Reader*, Plexus Publishing Inc., Medford, NJ, 2000.

THE FIRST ENGLISH SETTLEMENTS IN NEW JERSEY

They sailed up the river past vast salt hay meadows.
Rich land rose above the tide line on both sides of the river, beyond lay forests.
Fish, oysters, clams and scallops were plentiful; birds and other wildlife were in abundance.
The perfect location for the new settlement had been found.

The Founding of Elizabethtown - 1664

Celebrating the Many Accomplishments of Elizabethtown:

The First English Settlers

The First English Town

The First Capital

The First State Government

The First English Language Bible

The First English Church

The First School & College

The First English Purchase of Land in New Jersey

Within days of the bloodless transfer of New Netherlands from the Dutch to the English in 1664, the Duke of York's new deputy governor Colonel Richard Nicolls was waited upon by a delegation of six men from towns in Connecticut and Long Island who represented an association wishing to colonize lands in what was then known by the Dutch name Albania; shortly to be renamed New Jersey. The petition, dated September 26, 1664, sought permission to purchase from the Indians *Achter Kol*, the name given to land west of the *Achter Kull*, the narrow channel separating Staten Island from the mainland. Governor Richard Nicolls immediately consented to the proposal and encouraged them in "such good work".

On October 28, 1664, Association representatives John Bailey, Daniel Denton, Luke Watson and with John Baker acting as interpreter, met in the wigwam of Mattano on Staten Island and purchased 500,000 acres of

New Jersey (what is now Union, Somerset, Middlesex, Morris, Essex, Counties); land bounded by the Achter Kull, the Passaic River in the north, the Raritan River in the South, and extending to the west thirty-four miles.

The purchasers bound themselves to pay the Indians in two payments of wampum and goods or the equivalent of about 154 English pounds for what became known as the Elizabethtown Purchase. The deed was signed by the representatives of the Association and for the Indians, Mattano and Seuakhenos.

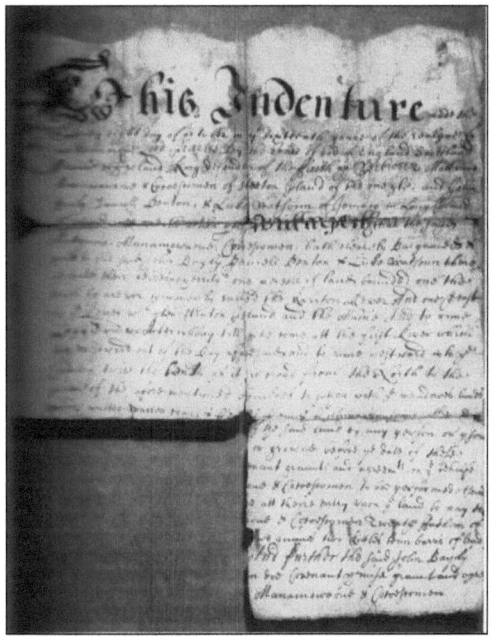

For which bargain and sale, covenants, grants and agreements in the behalf of the said MATTANO, MANAMOWAONE and COWESCOMEN, to be performed observed and done the aforesaid Parties are at their entry upon the said Land, to pay to the said MATTANO, MANAMOWAONE, and COWESCOMEN, Twenty Fathoms of Trading Cloth, two made Coats, two Guns, two Kettles, Ten Bars of Lead, Twenty Handfuls of Powder. And, further the said JOHN BAILY, DANIEL DENTON, and LUKE WATSON, do covenant, promise grant, and agree to and with the said MATTANO, MANAMOWAONE, and COWESCOMEN the aforesaid Indians, four Hundred Fathom of white Wampum after a Years Expiration from the Day of the said JOHN BAILY, DANIEL DENTON, and LUKE WATSON'S entry upon the said Lands. In Witness whereof we have hereunto put our Hands and Seals the Day and Year aforesaid.

The Mark of MATTANO

The Mark of SEUAKHENOS

On December 1, Governor Nicolls confirmed the Association's title:

Governor Richard Nicolls, by virtue of the Power and Authority vested in him by James (then) Duke of York & Did thereby Grant Bargain Sell and Confirm unto Capt. John Baker (then) of New York, John Ogden (then) of North-Hampton, and John Bayle and Luke Watson.

The principals in the Association were men from Long Island: John Ogden, John Bailey (his share subsequently sold to Governor Carteret), Nathaniel Denton (his share was subsequently sold to John Ogden), Thomas Benedick, John Foster, John Baker and Luke Watson. All felt that Long Island was getting overcrowded and thus sought better quality land and greater opportunities. It was never the intent of the principals in the venture to occupy all of the purchased lands themselves; they envisioned not only the growth of the original settlement but multiple new communities over time.

Under the agreement any freeman was entitled to purchase, for 4£ payable in beaver pelts, a full land share in the enterprise and become an Associate. The maximum number of shareholders for the new settlement was set at eighty men (later increased to 100). Most of the settlers came from Long Island or towns in Connecticut. Most knew each other; as many had been associates in the founding of other towns.

Arrival of the First English Settlers – 1664

In November, 1664, a few of the new owners sailed across the Achter Kull, up the Elizabeth River about two miles, past vast salt hay meadows, to the end of navigable waters where there was a fall; an ideal place for building water driven mills. Rich land rose above the tide line on both sides of the river; beyond lay forests. Fish, oysters, clams and scallops were plentiful. Birds and other wildlife were in abundance. The perfect location for the new settlement had been found.

Anxious to get on the land, a few Associates built huts and stayed the winter (memorialized on the official seal of the City of Elizabeth) to fell trees to season for houses, clear land for spring crops, and prepare for the main body of settlers to arrive. Those that came that fall took the opportunity to trade with the Indians for furs, which they had previously taken to the Dutch.

In the spring, families with their possessions and animals sailed to Achter Kol. Land was surveyed and the town laid out with "town-lots" of approximately 264 feet by 750-900 feet for each associate. A town lot was set aside for a minister and, with the exception of John Ogden, John Baily and Luke Watson, all of the other associates drew lots for their plots. In addition to a town lot, additional land beyond the town was awarded each associate based on his investment. First-Lot Right men each received a minimum of 60-70 acres; Second-Lot Right men received twice that of the First-Right men and the Third-Lot men received three times the land as First-Lot Right men.

It was imperative that the families who settled Archter Kol be self-sufficient; able to build their own homes, farm, hunt, spin thread, weave cloth and in general provide for the needs of their family. Early houses were small with low ceilings and large fireplaces, and surrounded by fences in order to keep wild and roaming domestic animals out. While each family had to possess all the basic skills to build and sustain their lives in the wilderness; settlers also possessed specialized skills of value to the community as a whole. John Ogden and his sons were skilled brick makers and stone masons who built the sawmill and grist mill, set up a whaling company and a tannery. Peter Wolverson, a Dutchman with long experience as a brewer, set up a brewery and tavern. Francis Barber and William Cramer were carpenters, William Hill and the Whiteheads were cobblers, and Matthias Hatfield and John Wilants were weavers. In November 1665, the final payment was made to the Indians, minus the cost of Luke Watson's ox that had been accidentally shot by an Indian.

The Elizabethtown Associates

Following is the list of Elizabethtown Associates as listed in the *Elizabeth Book B* and reprinted in *Church of the Founding Fathers of New Jersey, First Presbyterian Church 1664-1964*:

Third-Lot Right Men	**Two-Lot Right Men**	**First-Lot Right Men**
John Ogden	Isaac Whitehead	Jonathan Ogden
John Baily	Joseph Meeker	Abraham Shotwell
John Baker	Humphry Spinning (Spinage)	David Ogden
Luke Watson	Jeffrey Jones (Joanes)	Nathanael Tuttell
Thomas Young	George Ross	Benjamin Price, Jr. (son of Benjamin Price)
Benjamin Price	Joseph Bond	Robert Lambert
John Woodruff	Matthias Hetfield (Hatfield)	Abraham Lawrence
Philip Carteret	Barnabas Winds	John Hindes (Haynes)
Robert Bond	Robert White (Wines)	Thomas Moor (More)
Sealy Chamlain (transferred to Benjamin Parkhurst)	Peter Morss (Morse, Mosse)	Joseph Frazee (Phrasie)
William Meeker	John Winans (Waynes)	Yokum Andross
Thomas Thompson	Joseph Sayre	Denis White
Samuel Marsh	Richard Beach	Nathaniel Norton (since transferred to Henry Norris)
Town lot for Minister	Moses Thompson	Great John Willson
William Piles	John Gray	Hur Thompson
Peter Couenhoven	William Johnson	Benjamin Oman
John Bollen	John Brockett, Jr.,	Henry Lyon
Jacob Melyen	Simon Rouse	John Parker
Nicholas Carter	William Trotter	John Ogden (for John Dickenson)
Jeremiah Peck	John Ogden.	Leonard Headley
Robert Bond	Jonas Wood	Nathaniel Bonnell
John Brockett (trans. to Samuel Hopkins)	Robert Morss	George Morris
	Mr. Leprary	Joseph Osborn
	Caleb Carwithe (Carwitty)	Pardey (trans. to Henry Norris)
	William Pardon	George Pack
	Stephen Osbourne	John Pope
		Francis Barber
		William Oliver
		Richard Painter
		Charles Tooker (Tucker)
		Evan Salsburry
		Little John Wilson
		Stephen Crane

In addition to the Associates named in *Town Book B*, the following settlers were listed as taking the Oath of Allegiance on February 19th, 1665:

William Cramer	Zackery Graues	Benjamin Concklin
Peter Wooluerson*	Christopher Young	Jeremy Osbourne
Michael Simpkin	Joseph Young	Roderick Powell
Thomas Skillman	Moses Peterson	Robert Vanquellin
Jacob Clais	Brockett Sr.	Daniel Harris

*Wooluerson was a brewer and tavern owner who came with the first group of settlers.

Some of these individuals may have been relatives who came with associates but who did not own a share in the Association as well as others such as servants and day laborers who were ineligible to be Associates and possibly persons accidently excluded from the Associates recorded list.

Elizabethtown - The First Capital of New Jersey

Unbeknownst to Governor Nicolls when he approved the purchase of the lands by the Associates, the Duke of York who was indebted to Lord John Berkeley and Sir George Carteret had granted to them his lands between the Connecticut and the Hudson and Delaware Rivers. Berkeley and Carteret named their new possession New Jersey, drafted the *Concessions* and *Agreements* to encourage colonization and appointed Philip Carteret, a fourth cousin of Sir George, Governor of Province. The new governor sailed in April from the Isle of Jersey where he was born with a party of about thirty men and women, eighteen of whom were servants. Arriving in New York in late July he then crossed the bay and landed at Achter Kol in August 1665. He was met by the already established Achter Kol colonists gathered at the landing.

Carteret's Landing in Achter Kol, c. 1665

Carteret read his commission naming him governor of Nova Caesarea or New Jersey and explained to those gathered that New Jersey had been granted to Berkeley and Carteret. He was also pleased to grant the inhabitants of New Jersey a liberal charter, called the *Concessions and Agreements*, guaranteeing them, among other provisions, the rights of freeman of England. He went on to explain the proprietors role in the new colony. John Ogden, representing the interests of the Associates, in turn explained to Carteret how the land had been purchased from the Indians and the deed confirmed by Governor Nicolls.

Governor Carteret acknowledged the rights and land deeds of the Associates and a month later he purchased a Three-Lot right in the Association as a planter. Favorably impressed with the developing settlement he wrote that he "determined to locate himself with the Ogden Company and make their plantation the seat of his government" and thus Elizabethtown became the first capital of New Jersey. He changed the name of the town, which had been referred to as Achter Kol, to Elizabethtown in honor of the wife of a Sir George Carteret. He appointed John Ogden as the first Justice of the Peace.

The first town meeting in New Jersey took place on February 19, 1666, when sixty-five male residents took the Oath of Allegiance and Fidelity to "our Sovereign Lord King Charles the Second and his Successors..." Not all of the signers were Associates, a few may have been servants or day laborers who were not permitted to "enjoy a Town-Lott" or were non-land owning family members of associates. The fact that there were only 65 signers of the oath suggests that many of the Associates had not arrived by February 1665.

In addition to signing the Oath it was determined that those associates who had not yet arrived would forfeit their rights if they were not on their land by April 15, 1665 in which case other associates would then be given the first opportunity to buy their shares. The number of associates was also raised from 80 to 100.

Elizabethtown – the First English Church

The founders of Elizabethtown were Puritans, described in a letter of the time as being of "moderate religious views." Membership in the church was not required in order to own land or vote. However, religion was important to the community and land was assigned for a minister and a meetinghouse. Services were held in private houses or outside until a church/meeting house could be built.

John Ogden was an experienced church builder. With his sons, he built the first meetinghouse in the same place where the First Presbyterian Church of Elizabeth stands today. The building, as was the Puritan tradition, served as meeting house, church and school. It was probably about 36 feet square, with only a few high windows and a cupola. Inside were benches and a pulpit. Services could last several hours. A burial ground was set aside next to the meeting house.

The Cemetary of First Presbyterian Church of Elizabeth with the graves of the founders (www.fpcenj.org)

John Ogden brought with him, probably the first English language Bible in New Jersey.[1] It was a Geneva Bible, printed in Amsterdam in English about 1600, a socially as well as religiously significant translation from early Hebrew texts. This version of the Bible laid the groundwork for today's democratic societies, the right of self-government, and equality of all persons. It was meant for common people to read; annotations in the margins commented and interpreted the meaning for the reader. These annotations challenged the divine right of kings and even translated king from the Hebrew as tyrant. King James I banned the Geneva Bible in England and ordered a new official translation without the Calvinist commentary. At the time of the American Revolution, the Geneva Bible was used to justify and gain support for action against the king. Coded messages written in the Bible date to the Revolutionary period. The bible continues to be associated with the First Presbyterian Church in Elizabeth to the current day.

The Bible of John Ogden, printed 1599

Elizabethtown – First in Education

Essential to Puritan beliefs was that every individual could read the Bible for themselves. Parents were the first source of providing enough education to enable their children to read, write a little, and handle simple arithmetic. If the family couldn't provide instruction, housewives conducted "Dame Schools" in their homes for a small fee, as did preachers to supplement their income. However, by 1681 Elizabethtown had a regular

---

[1] The Bible was returned to Old First Church by John Ogden descendant Jack Harpster in 2013 and was restored by Evelyn Ogden, his 7th great granddaughter, in 2014.

schoolmaster, John Inquehart, a Quaker. A college-educated Scotsman, he would have included Greek and Latin in the boys' education.

With the expansion of the community there was a need and interest in secondary education and in the 1750's the church leaders built the "Academy" across the churchyard. Aaron Burr, Alexander Hamilton, Jonathan Dayton (the youngest signer of the Declaration of Independence), and Henry Brockholst Livingston were among the alumni. The Academy was one of the most celebrated in the Colonies. Now named the Snyder Academy it has been restored by the Old Historic Trust of Elizabethtown and continues to serve the community.

In 1746, the Province of New Jersey granted a unique charter for the College of New Jersey in Elizabeth, specifying that "any person of religious Denomination whatsoever" might attend. Classes met in the parlor of Rev. Jonathan Dickenson in Elizabeth. The college moved with the president, first to Newark, then New Brunswick and in 1756, to Nassau Hall in Princeton and in 1896, changed its name to Princeton College.

Alexander Hamilton, Aaron Burr, Jonathan Dayton, and Henry Brockholst Livingston (pictured left to right above) attended Elizabethtown's Snyder Academy

Elizabethtown – The first Elected Assembly and Code of Laws

The meetinghouse was completed by May 25, 1668, the date the first meeting of the New Jersey General Assembly, which met at Elizabethtown. The legislature was in session for five days and passed the first series of laws for New Jersey, later referred to as "The Elizabethtown Code of Laws."

By 1680 Elizabethtown's population had grown to about 700 and the towns of Woodbridge, Piscataway and Newark had been established with the borders of the original Elizabethtown Purchase.

References:

First Presbyterian Church of Elizabeth. *Church of the Founding Fathers of New Jersey: A History of the First Presbyterian Church of Elizabeth, Elizabeth, New Jersey 1664-1664*, Carbrook Press, Maine, 1964.

Hatfield, Rev. Edwin F. *History of Elizabeth, New Jersey*, Carlton and Lanahan, New York, 1868. (Internet archive).

Thayer, Theodore. *As We Were: the Story of Old Elizabethtown*, Published for the New Jersey Historical Society by Grassmann Publishing Co. Elizabeth, New Jersey, 1964.

The Founding of Shrewsbury and Middletown - 1665

Penelope Van Princis is considered the first white woman in New Jersey. The daughter of Baron Van Princis (a.k.a. Van Prinzen), she was born in Amsterdam, the Netherlands, in 1622. After her marriage to John Kent c.1640, bride and groom set sail for New Amsterdam. Near the end of the journey their ship ran aground near what is now Highlands in Monmouth County.

Penelope with her husband and others made it to shore, however, her husband was too ill to travel with the rest of the survivors who headed on foot toward New Amsterdam. She and her husband stayed behind in the Navesink woods where they were attacked by hostile Indians. John was killed and Penelope left for dead. She survived for a week before she was found by two friendly Indians who took her to their camp. She lived with the Indians until she recovered and eventually made it to New Amsterdam.

In 1644, Penelope married Richard Stout. Richard had left Nottingham, England, to serve in the British navy. At the end of his seven-year enlistment he left his ship in New Amsterdam. The Stouts settled a plantation at Gravesend, Long Island.

The beach in Monmouth

Penelope is credited with being instrumental in the decision by a group of Long Islanders to seek land in New Jersey. Early in 1665 several residents of Gravesend, Long Island made an expedition to the Monmouth area of New Jersey, secured the friendship of the Indians and made treaties. The first deed from the Indians was dated the 25th of January 1664. This was for land at Navesink, secured from Sachem Popomora, and agreed to by his brother Misgacoing. The Indians were given in exchange for the land *118 fathoms seawamp, 68 fathoms of which were to be white and 50 black seawamp, 5 coats, 1 gun, 1 clout capp, 1 shirt, 12 lbs tobacco and 1 anker wine; acknowledged as received with an addition 82 fathoms of seawamp to be paid twelve months later.*

On April 7, 1665, Popomora and Misgacoing went to New York and acknowledged the deed before Governor Nicolls. Two other deeds were also recorded. On 8 April 1665, at Fort James in New York, Governor Nicolls granted to the Patentees a triangular tract of *land extending from Sandy Hook to the mouth of the Raritan River, up the river twenty-five miles, then southward to Barnegat Bay.* A condition of the grant was that the Patentees and their associates settle one hundred families within three years.

The Monmouth Patent and Patentees

I Richard Nicolls Esq., Governor under his Royal Highness the Duke of York of all his territories in America send greeting. Whereas there is a certain tract or parcel hath been with my consent and approbation bought by some of the inhabitants of Gravesend upon Long Island of the Sachems (chief proprietors thereof) who before me have acknowledged to have received satisfaction for the same, to the end that the said land may be planted, manured and inhabited, and for divers other goods causes and consideration, I have thought fit to give, confirm, and grant, and by these presents do confirm and grant unto WIILIAM GOULDING, SAMUEL SPICER, RICJARD GIBBONS, RICHARD STOUT, JAMES GROVER JOHN BROWN, JOHN TILTON, NATHANIEL SYLVESTER, WILLIAM REAPE, WALTER CLARK ,NICHOLAS DAVIS , OBADIAH HOLMES, , patentees and their associates, their heirs, successors, and assigns, all that tract and part of the mainland , beginning at a certain place commonly called or known by the name of Sandy Point and so running along the bay West North West, till it comes to the mouth of the Raritan River, from thence going along said river to the westernmost part of a certain marsh land which divides the river into two parts, and from that part to run in a direct south-west line into the woods twelve miles, and thence to turn away south-east and by south, until it fails into the main ocean; together will all lands, soils, rivers, creeks, harbors, mines, minerals (Royal mines excepted,) quarries, woods, meadows, pastures, marshes, waters, lakes, fishing, hawkings, huntings and fowling, and all other profits, commodities and hereditaments to said lands….. said patentees and their associates, their heirs or assigns shall within the space of three years, beginning from the day of the date hereof, manure and plant the aforesaid land and premises and settle one hundred families at the least; in consideration whereof I do promise and grant that the patentees … shall enjoy the said land…free from any rents, customs, excise tax or levy whatsoever. But after the expiration of the said seven years, the persons in possession thereof, shall pay after the same rate which others within this his Royal Highness' territories shall be obliged unto… Given under my hand and seal… Richard Nichols.

The men named in the Monmouth Patent were each allowed 500 acres; then each man and wife 120 acres each; then allowances for children, and also for servants (servants after completing their years of indenture were to receive 60 acres in their own right).

In addition to those named as patentees there was a list of men who contributed monetarily to the purchase:

Christopher Almy, Job Almy, John Allen and Robert Taylor, Stephen Arnold, John Bowne, James Bowne, William Bowne, Gerrard Bourne, Richard Borden, Benjamin Borden and George Mount, Nicholas Browne, Francis Brinley, Henry Bull, John Conklin, Walter Clarke, Robert Carr, John Coggeshall, Joshua Coggeshall and Daniel Gould, William Coddington, Thomas Clifton, John Cooke, George Chutte, Thomas Cox, Joseph Coleman, Nicholas Davis, Roger Ellis and son, Peter Easton, James Grover, Richard Gibbons, Zachary Gauntt, William Goulding, Ralph Goldsmith, Daniel Gould, Samuel Holliman, John Horabin, Obadiah Holmes, Jonathan Holmes, Tobias Handson, John Hance, William James, John Jenkins, William Shadduck, Edmund Lafetra, Henry Lippitt, Richard Lippencott, Thomas Moor, Francis Masters, George Mount, Thomas Potter, Edward Pattison, John Ruckman, Richard Richardson, Samuel Spicer, Richard, Stout, Nathaniel Sylvester, Thaomas Saddock, William Shaddock and George Webb, Edward Smith, Robert Story, William Shaberly, Richard Sussell, John Tilton, John Throckmorton, John Townsend, Edward Thurston, Nathan Tomkins, Edward Tartt, Robert Taylor, Emanuel Woolley, Thomas Winterton, Edward Wharton, Eliakim Wardell, Bartholomew West, Robert West, Walter Wall, John Wall, John Wilson, John Wood.

Thirty-six men were allotted lots in Middletown:

John Ruckman, Edward Tartte, John Wilson, Walter Wall, John Smith, Richard Stout, Richard Gibbons, Thomas Cox, Jonathan Holmes, George Mount, William Cheeseman, Anthony Page, Samuel Holeman, William Laiton, William Compton, James Grover, Steven Arnold, Samuel Spicer, John Stout, Obadiah Holmes, Benjamin Denell, Job Throckmorton, James Ashton, John Throckmorton, William Goulding, William Reape, Edward Smith, John Bowne, Benjamin Burden, Samuel Spicer, William Lawrence, Daniel Estell, Robert Jones, Thomas Whitlock, Richard Sadler, James Grover.

Out-lots were also surveyed, numbered and granted to the settlers and the lots given to each one entered in the Town Book.

The lots at Portland Point, at or near Highlands, were awarded in regular order as follows:

John Horaben, James Bowne, Richard Richardson, Randall Huet, Henry Percy, John Bird, Randall Huet, Jr., William Bowne, William Shackerly. (N. Y. Col. Hist. vol. 1, p.360)

The following list includes men who records show bought property before the expiration of the three-year provision:

James Ashton, Joseph Bryce, John Bird, Abraham Brown, William Cheeseman, William Compton, Jacob Cole, Benjamin Deuell, Thomas Dungan, Daniel Estell, Gideon Freeborn, William Gifford, James Grover, Jr., Thomas Hart, John Hall, Robert Hazard, James Heard, Randall Huet, John Hawes, Joseph Huet, George Hulett, John Havens, John Jobs, Robert Jones, Gabriel Kirk, Bartholomew Lippincott, William Layton, William Lawrence, James Leonard, Lewis Mattox, William Newman, Joseph Parker, Peter Parker, Anthony Page, Henry Percey, William Rogers, William Reape, John Slocum, Samuel Shaddock, William Shearman, John Smith, John Stout, Richard Sadler, Bartholomew Shamquesque, John Tomson, Job Throckmorton, Peter Tilton, Thomas Wansick, Robert West, Jr., Thomas Whitlock.

During the first few years of settlement, many small sloops shuttled back and forth from Gravesend, Newport, and elsewhere bringing colonists and household goods. Lots and tracts of land were selected, and log houses and few more pretentious dwellings erected. Land was cleared and fences constructed. As many as eighty families arrived in the first year. Purchasers at Middletown and Shrewsbury paid £3 or £4 for 120 acres, with additional increments allowed for wives and children, and 60 acres for each servant.

The Growth of the Settlement

The new settlers were mostly Baptists and Quakers; drawn to New Jersey by the liberal provisions of the *Concessions and Agreements*, particularly the guarantee of religious freedom of expression. Among the settlers were Quakers who had been the victims of severe persecution in New England. While the Puritans of New England had emigrated across the ocean to escape strict religious rule of the Crown and the established Church of England, they became the worse persecutors of those they deemed different than themselves. Quakers were not part of the Puritan movement and held different religious and social views. Quakers in Massachusetts were tried for heresy, whipped, jailed, and in some cases, hanged. Rhode Island, New Netherlands (before the fall to England) and Long Island were slightly less intolerant.

The First English Settlements in New Jersey

The Quakers among the settlers founded the Shrewsbury Meeting in 1665. It is considered the oldest continuously existing rural religious group and the oldest Quaker meeting in New Jersey. Early meetings took place in the homes of members. The first meeting house was built in 1672 and was visited by George Fox, the founder of Quakerism.

The Baptists among the settlers organized the first Baptist Church in New Jersey in 1668. For twenty years they met at homes of members until a log church could be built.

Quakers began meeting in Shrewsbury in 1665 in the homes of Friends. The first meeting house was constructed in 1672. The current meeting house was constructed in 1816. The meeting house is of the two-cell form, affording women and men equal space. Division walls were closed for business meetings and left open for worship and other functions.

In 1667 the work of building settlements had advanced to the point where attention turned to establishing a local government. Under the terms of the Nicolls patent, the colonists had the right to elect by vote the major part of the inhabitants; five or seven persons of their ablest and most discreet inhabitants to make such laws to govern their affairs. The first town-elected delegate Assembly in New Jersey met on 14 December 1667, in Shrewsbury. Richard Richardson was chosen as its secretary and appointed to record acts, orders and deeds.

By 1682, the European population of Middletown was about 500 (100 families) and Shrewsbury 400 (80 families). At the first General Assembly of New Jersey at Elizabethtown in March 1682, the Province was officially divided into four counties: Bergen, Essex, Middlesex and Monmouth. The bounds of Monmouth were given as:

> *Monmouth County to begin at the Westward Bounds of Middlesex County, containing Middletown and Shrewsbury and so extend Westward, Southward, and Northward to the extreme Bounds of the Province. Provided this distinction of the Province into Counties, do not extend to the infringement of any Liberty in any Charter already granted.*

The name Monmouth was given to the county through the influence of Colonel Lewis, a member of the Governor's Council and a large landowner. On 25 October 1676 Lewis purchased 3540 acres where, in 1680, he located *his iron mills, his Manors, and diverse other buildings for his servants and dependents; together with 60 or 70 negroes about the Mill and Husbandry which he named Tintern (corrupted afterwards to Tinton) after an estate which belonged to the family in Monmouthshire, England.*

First Settlements, Colonists, and Biographies by Descendants

Following are several lists of some of the earliest settlers who claimed land ownership under the *Grants and Concessions*. The records were taken from the Proprietors Records at Perth Amboy and reprinted in *Historical and Genealogical Miscellany: Data Relating to the Settlement and Settlers of New York and New Jersey* by John E. Stillwell M.D., New York, 1906.

1675: *Richard Stout, of Middletown, brings for his rights for himself, his wife, his two sons John and Richard, 120 acres each, 430 acres. For his sons and daughters that are to come of age since the year 1667: James, Peter, Mary, Alice and Sarah, each 60 acres — 300 acres, total 780 acres.*

John Stout, of Middletown, for himself and wife, 240 acres; Richard Stout in his own right, Shrewsbury, 120 acres, James Stout in his own right, 60 acres, Peter Stout in his own right, 60 acres, Sarah Stout in her own right, 60 acres; James Bound (Bowne) in right of himself and wife, Mary Stout, 240 acres; John Throckmorton in right of himself and wife, Alice Stout, 240 acres.

Thomas Whitlook, of Middletown, for his rights from the year 1664 for himself, wife and three sons, Thomas, William and John, in all five persons, at 120 per head, 600 acres. Katherine Brown, the widow of Bartholomew West, of Shrewsbury, in right of herself and deceased husband, from 1666, 90 acres each — 180 acres, and for her two sons and daughter, Stephen, William and Audry West, 60 each — 180 acres; Nicholas Brown in his own right from 1665, 120 acres, and his wife's from 1666, 90 acres -210 acres

Captain John Bowne, of Middletown, for his rights, 18th March, 1675, 500 acres, as being a first purchaser — 500 acres. For rights of himself and wife, his father, mother, and for William Compton and his wife from first year, 120 acres each, 780 acres; three servants at 60 acres each, 180 acres,

Jonathan Holmes demands for his 500 acres, given by the Lords Proprietors as being one of the Patentees under first purchase at Navesink, and in right of self and wife, 240 acres —740 acres.

Edward Smith, Middletown, self, 120 acres; James Ashton, self and wife, 240 acres; Thomas Cox, self and wife, 240 acres; John Throckmorton and wife from first year, 240 acres; and in right of his father, John, 240 acres; Job Throckmorton, self, 120 acres; Charles Hynes (Haynes?) and wife, 240 acres; Joseph Huet in right of Randall Huet and wife, 240 acres.

Sarah Reape demands for her rights, in right of Benjamin Speare, Shrewsbury, 240 acres; John Homdell, Shrewsbury, 240 acres; Thomas Dungan, Shrewsbury, 240 acres; James Leonard, Shrewsbury, 240 acres, Marmaduke Ward, Shrewsbury, 240 acres, William James, half share, Shrewsbury, 120 acres, Self and husband, Shrewsbury, 240 acres;, Self and husband, Middletown, 240 acres; Samuel Borden, three-fourth share, Shrewsbury, 90 acres; Joseph Bryer, 120 acres — 2010 acres.

Christopher Allmey demands for his rights, for himself and wife and three servants in the year 1665, at 120 acres a head, which is in part in fence, 600 acres; in right of John Hall, who came same year, 120 acres; in right of Henry Bull, one of the first purchasers, 120 acres; in right of Henry Pdersie and wife from the year 1666, 180 acres; man servant, 60 acres — 1080 acres.

Jonathan Holmes as being a first purchaser, 500 acres; and for self and wife, 240 acres; Obadiah Holmes and wife, 240 acres; Edward Smith,120 acres; James Ashton and wife, 240 acres; Thomas Cox and wife, 240 acres; John Throckmorton and wife, 240 acres; John Throckmorton for his father, John, 240 acres; Job Throckmorton, self 120 acres.

Warrants for tracts of land to be subsequently located and surveyed, were issued by the Proprietors to the following among other persons – 1675-1697:

1675: *Nicholas Brown, 210 acres; Thomas Wainright and wife 180 acres; Katherine Brown, late widow of Bartholomew West, in right of her deceased husband, 180 acres, Stephen; William and Audry West, 60 acres each, 180 acres; Edward Lafetra and wife, 180 acres; Robert West, 120 acres; Abraham Brown and wife, 120 acres.*

Joseph Parker and wife, 240 acres; Richard Stout Jr., and wife, 120 acres; Richard Stout Sr., and wife, 780 acres; John Stout, 120 acres, James, Peter and Mary Stout, 60 each, 180 acres; Richard Hartshorne, 200 acres; Peter Parker, 180 acres; Francis Le Maistre, 240 acres; Clement and Pauline Masters, 120 acres; Thomas Wright, self and wife, 180 acres; Gabriel Stelle, 120 acres.

John Throckmorton, 480 acres; Job Throckmorton, 120 acres; James Ashton, 240 acres; Thomas Cox, 240 acres; Joseph Huet, 210 acres; James Bowne, 240 acres; Thomas Warne, 240 acres; Stephen Arnold, 360 acres; Hannaniah Gifford and wife, 240 acres; Thomas Leeds, and wife, 120 acres; William Leeds and wife, Dorothea, 120 acres; Daniel Leeds and wife, Anne, 120 acres; Thomas Leeds. Jr., 120 acres; Clement Shinn and Elizabeth wife, 120 acres; George Shinn, 60 acres; Thomas Jacob and wife, 120acres; William Heyden, 60 acres; John Hanoe, 330 acres; Richard Richardson, 150 acres; John Wilson, 240 acres; James Grover, (500 and 360)— 860 acres; Peter Tilton (500 and 570)— 1070 acres; Richard Gibbons, 500 acres; Sarah Reape, 500; Nathaniel Sylvester, 500 acres; Thomes Grover Sr., 400 acres; Henry Leonard, (450 and 360)— 750 acres; Richard Sidler, 240 acres; John Jobs, 120 acres; George Jobs, 120 acres; Francis Hirbert, 120 acres; Thomas Harbert, (132 and 240)— 372 acres; Benjamin Deuell, 250 acres; John Vaughan, 135 acres.

1676: *Thomas Cook, 60 acres; John Champners, 60 acres; William Shattoek, 360 acres; Samuel Spicer, for his rights from Lords Proprietors, 500 acres; Col. Lewis Morris, for iron works, about 3,000 acres. Christopher Allmey in right of self, wife and others, 1080 acres. Sarah Reape in right of ten persons, 2010 acres.*

Walter Wall and wife, 210 acres; William Layton and wife, 240 acres; John Smith and wife, 240 acres; Richard Dans and wife, 120 acres; Daniel Estell and wife, 120 acres; James Dorsett and wife, 240 acres; George Mount and wife, 240 acres; William Cheeseman, 120 acres; Thomas Morford, 120 acres; John Williama and wife, 240 acres; Henry Marsh, 120 acres; William Whitelock, 120 acres; John Whitelock, 120 acres.

Richard Hartshorne, in right of servants that he hath brought, 90 acres each, 270 acres, right of William Goldingand and wife, 240 acres, right of Robert Jones and wife, 240 acres -- 750; William Lawrence, in right of self and sister, Hannah Lawrence, 240 acre; John Havens and wife, 240 acres; William Worth and wife 240 acres; Morris Worth, 120 acres.

Hugh Dikeman, wife and daughter, 360 acres; Abraham Brown and wife, 240 acres, and in right Peter Tilton and wife, 240 acres— 480; Isaac Ouge and wife, 120 acres: John Ruckman and wife, 240 acres; Richard Lippencott, wife and two sons and two servants, 600 acres; John Lippencott and wife, 240 acres; John Woolley and wife, 120 acres; Eliakim Wardell, in right of Nicholas Davis, ten shares, 480 acres; Thomas Ward and wife of, 240 acres; Stephen Arnold and wife, in right Samuel Holeman, 560 acres: George Hillitt and wife, 240 acres; Thomas Barnes, wife and maid servant, 180 acres..

1677: *Caleb Shrife (Shrieve), in right of John Cooke, 240 acres; John Slocum and wife, 240 acres; Benjamin Burden and wife, 240 acres; John Hance, wife and man servant, 360 acres in right of. John Poxall, 240 acres in right of Thorlogh Swiney, 240 acres; Edward Wharton and wife, 240 acres; Francis Borden in right of Nathaniel Tompkins 240 acres; and for self and wife, 240 acres — 480; John Borden and wife, 240 acres; Sarah Reape, in right of Thos. Winterton and wife, 240 acres, also Christopher Frazee and wife, 240 acres, also Gabriel Hicks and wife, 24 acres, also Marmaduke Ward, 240 acres, also William James, 120 acres, also self and husband, 240 acres, also Samuel Borden, 90 acres — 1410.*

Thomas Applegate Sr., 240 acres; Thomas Applegate, Jr., 120 acres; John King, 60 aces; Ebenezer Cottrell, 120 acres; Thomas Williams, 60 acres; Adam Ohanuelhouse, 240 acres; Bestue Lippencott and wife, 240 acres; Peter Easton and wife, 240 acres; Peter Tilton, in right of his brother John and wife, 240 acres; Gideon Freeborn and wife, 240 acres; Jacob Cole and wife, 240 acres; Benjamin Kogers and wife, 120 acres; Remembrance Lippincott and wife, 240 acres; Judah Allen, in right of Annanias Garrett, 240 acres; Judah Allen, in right Daniel Gould, 120 acres; Judah Alien, in right Joshua Coggeshall, 120 acres; Annaniaih Gifford, in right Wm. Gifford, 120 acres.

Eliajam Wardell and wife, 240 acres; Eliaikim Wardell for Robert Story and wife, 240 acres; Samuel Woolcott and wife, 240 acres; Hannah Jay, alias Hannah Cook, 60 acres; Samuel Hatton (no amount).

1678: *Daniel Applegate, 120 acres; Samuel Leonard, 240 acres; Nathaniel Leonard, 120 acres; Thomas Leonard, 120 acres; Henry Leonard Jr., 120 acres; John Leonard, 120 acres; Samuel Willett and wife, 120 acres; Lewis Mattex, three tracts; Cornelius Steenmen, adjoining lands; William Lawrence, in right of original purchaser, for self, wife and son, 360 acres.*

1679: *Roger Ellis, 440 acres; William Compton, 280 acres; Nicholas Serrah, 80 acres; Isaac Bryan, 840 acres; Jacob Triax, (Truex) 120 acres; Peter Parker, George Parker, Stephen West, John Jerson, Christopher Gifford (no amount).*

Jarret Wall and wife, 120 acres; Kandall Huet and wife, 240 acres; Derrick Tinneson and wife, 240 acres; Joshua Silverwood and wife, 120 acres.

Safety Grover and wife, 120 acres; Jacob Triax (Truax), 120 acres; Robert Hamilton, 100 acres; Thomas Potter, wife, son and daughter, at Deale, 500 acres; Francis Jeffrey, at Deale, 120 acres; Isaac Bryan, Poplar Swamp, self, wife, four children and eight servants, 840 acres.

1681: *Patents or confirmations of titles for land were granted to Gideon Freeborn, Hannah Joy, Henry Bowman, Caleb Shrieve, Peter Easton, John Williams, George Parker, Nathaniel Cammaok, Samuel Wolcott, Francis Jeffries, Daniel Leeds, Joseph Wardell, John Chamnis, Kestre Lippencott, Remembrance Lippencott, John Lippencott, Christopher Gifford, Morris Worth, Annanias Gifford, Edward Wharton, Henry Marsh, John Skookum, Nathaniel Slocum, Thomas Potter, Elizabeth Hatton, Job Havens, Samuel Spicer, William Shattock, John Hance, Peter Parker, John Clayton, Stephen West, J. Edmond Lafetra, William West, Francis Parden (Purdaine), John Chambers, Kobert West, Thomas Hilborne, Tobias Hansen, John Borden, John Worthley, Hugh Dickman, Wilham Worth, Eliakim Wardell, John Jerson, Benjamin Bogers.*

1685: *Confirmation of titles to Richard Gardiner, Samuel Colver, Garret Wall and George Corlies.*

1686: *Confirmation of titles to Gershom Bowne, George Mount, Safety Grover, James Grover Jr., Joseph West, George Keith, Robert Hamilton and Francis Jackson.*

1687: *Confirmation of titles to William Shadook, Edward Williams, Thomas Eatone, Jacob Lippencott, Thomas Huet, Abigail Lippencott, Francis Borden, John Borden, Peter White, John Cranford, John Brea (Bray), Samuel White, Job Jenkins and Nathaniel Parker.*

1688: *Mordecai Gibbons in right of his father, Richard Gibbons, had confirmed to him a tract of 540 acres; so called "headlands" were granted to James Paul and Isabel, his wife, 30 acres; Robert and Mary Cole, 30 acres; Archibald Siliver and Christiana, his wife, 30 acres; also patent to Thomas and Richard Hannson, 150 acres.*

1689: *Confirmation of titles to Rebecca Coward, a servant of William Duokura, had a patent for 30 acres, which she transferred to John Bowne.*

1692: Richard Hartshome had patent in right of Walter Clark, of E. I., one of the patentees, 500 acres.

1693: Thomas Webley had patent in right of Stephen and Audry West.

1697: Patents were given to Gershom Mott and John Chamberlain

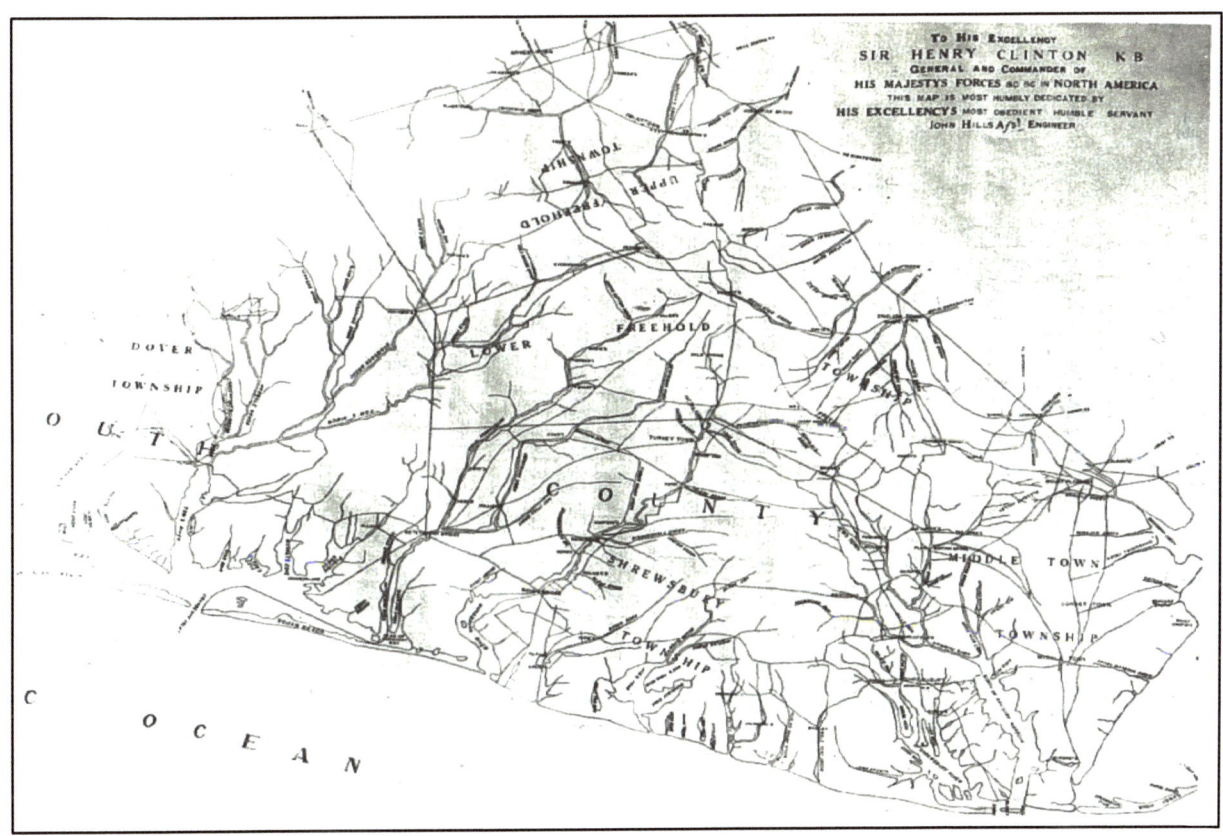

Early Monmouth County map

References:

Regan, Curt. "Quakerism –its Origin, Development, Testimonies and Activities: Friends for Three Hundred Years." (Presentation April 26, 1970, Plainfield, New Jersey).

Kleu, Joseph R. "Using the Records of East and West Jersey Proprietors," New Jersey State Archives, 2014. (Internet archive)

Slater, Edwin. *A History of Monmouth and Ocean Counties Embracing a Genealogical Record of the Earliest Settlers of Monmouth and Ocean Counties and the Descendants. The Indians: Their Language, Manners and Customs*, Bayonne, New Jersey, 1890. (Internet archive)

Stillwell, John D. *Historical and Genealogical Miscellany: Data Relating to the Settlement and Settlers of New York and New Jersey*, NY, 1906. (Internet archive)

The Founding of Woodbridge - 1666

Shortly after Governor Philip Carteret had established himself in Elizabethtown he sent messengers to New England to publicize the liberal provisions of the *Concessions and Agreements* and to invite emigration to New Jersey. The severity of the justice system and intolerance of the New England Puritans made the provisions of the Concessions inducements to relocate to New Jersey where land could be easily acquired, settlers could largely control their own affairs, and where they would be guaranteed the right to exercise their own religious convictions free from persecution (see Appendix A).

> *"No person qualified as a freeman shall be any ways molested or called in question for Any difference in opinion and practice in matters of religious concernment; but all such Persons may from time to time, freely and fully enjoy their judgements and conscience in matters of religion."*

Late in 1666 Daniel Pierce, John Pike, and associates from Newbury, Massachusetts, explored the area southwest of Elizabethtown, found it agreeable, and on 11 December 1666 entered into an agreement with Governor Philip Carteret, John Ogden and Luke Watson (the latter two were original large landowners in the Elizabethtown Patent), for roughly the southern half of the original Elizabethtown Patent lying between the Rahway and Raritan Rivers. The agreement was confirmed by deed on 3 December 1667. Daniel Pierce was immediately commissioned as deputy-surveyor to run the boundary lines and lay out land to the associates: John Pike, Daniel and Joseph Pierce, Obadiah Ayers, Henry Jacques, Thomas Bloomfield, Elisha Parker, Richard Worth, John Whitaker, Jonathan Dunham, Hugh Dunn and Robert Van Quellen. The purchase price was 80£ per share as provided for in the *Concessions and Agreements*. Amboy Point and a thousand acres of upland and meadow were reserved for the Proprietors; this was the one-seventh share stipulated under the Concessions. In addition, land was set aside for the ministry and for maintenance of a school.

The Growth of the Settlement

They called their new territory Woodbridge in honor of Rev. John Woodward, a congregational minister in Newbury, Massachusetts. The deed specified the speedy settlement within the territory. No time was wasted and settlers, mainly from the associates home areas in New England, were invited to purchase and plant farms within the area. Among the new settlers were a blacksmith, joiner, mason, and wheelwright who contributed needed skills to the new community. The original associates were allowed to retain 240 acres of upland and 40 acres of meadow in addition to the regular allotment to each freeholder. The charter stipulated that home lots were to be 10-20 acres with each purchaser entitled to 60 acres of upland and 6 acres of meadow.

In February 1668, thirteen men took the oath of allegiance as required by the Concessions to the King and Proprietors. After five years under the agreement settlers were expected to pay the Proprietors a quit-rent of one half-penny per acre (many settlers refused to pay the rents). On 1 June 1669 the Woodbridge Associates were granted a charter creating a township covering six square miles, comprising not less than sixty families and not exceeding that number unless by special order of the town. In 1670/1 the requisite number of families had not purchased land and made improvements, however the Governor waived any legal objections.

In 1668 Woodbridge sent two representatives to the first General Assembly of New Jersey at Elizabethtown comprised of the Governor, Governor's Council, and the General Assembly. By 1682-84, Governor Barclay's record book estimated the European population of Woodbridge had grown to 120 families, 600 individuals.

The First English Settlements in New Jersey

Early Settlers of Woodbridge

Early settlers and land acres, from the New Jersey Archives, reprinted in Monnette, 1930.
(Note: the following list does not contain all of those who may be considered first settlers)

Settlers	Acres	Settlers	Acres	Settlers	Acres
John Adams	97	George Little	100	In addition, listed as freeholders in the Woodbridge town register	
Ephram Andrews(1673)	98	David Makany	168	Thomas Adams	
Thomas Auger/Alger	167	Hugh March*	320	John Allen "Minister"	97
Obadiah Ayers*	171	Matthew Moore	177	John Averill	
Samuel Baker/Bacon	170	Benjamin Parker "Joiner"	105	William Bingley	186
Joshua Bradley	171	Elisha Parker (1675) *	182	Jonathan Bishop	
John Bishop Sr.	470	John Pike *	308	Capt. Philip Carteret	313
John Bishop Jr *	77	John Pike, Jr	91	James Clauson or Clarkson	
Matthew Bunn "Mariner"	165	Daniel Pierce*	456	Jonathan Dennis	97
Thomas Bloomfield/Blomfield*	326	Joshua/Joseph Pierce*	30	John Ilsley*	
John Conger	170	Daniel Robins	173	John Martin Sr	255
John Cromwell	173	Richard Worth *	172	Thomas Pike	
William Compton	174	John Smith "Wheelwright," *	176	*John Tewman	97
Robert Dennis	448	Abraham Toppan	95.5	Lord Proprietors	1000
John Dennis	107	Isaac Toppan	172	For the Ministry	200
Samuel Dennis	94	John Taylor "Blacksmith"	92	Maintenance of School	100
John Dilly (Dille	94	Israel Thorne (1676)	96		
Hugh Dun *	92	Robert VanQuellen* or La Praire	175	Others who took the oath on 27 February 1667	
Jonathan Dunham (1672) **	213	John Watkins	92	*Samuel Moore	280
John French "Mason"	15	Nathan Webster*	92	*George March	
Rehoboth Gannit	448	John Whitaker *	91	*Marmaduke Potter	
Daniel Grasie	164	Stephen Kent	249	Stephen Kent Jr	104
Samuel Hale	167	Elisha Ilsey*	172	Henry Lessenby*	88
Jonathan Haynes (1673)	97	Henry Jacques* and Henry JacquesJr. *.	368	John Smith "Scotchman"	92
Samuel Smith	103	Stephen Kent	249	Samuel Moore	356
Henry Lessenby	88	Stephen Kent Jr.	104		

*Signed the Oath of Allegiance and Fidelities as Inhabitants of Woodbridge on the 27 February 1667.
**The mother of President Barack Obama, Stanley Ann Dunham, was the seventh great-granddaughter of Jonathan Dunham, born in 1639, and Mary Bloomfield.

Some other Early Settlers of Woodbridge Mentioned in the Records[2] include:

George Brown	John and Hannah Freeman	Ann and Richard Knight
Thomas Cawood	Mary Gilman	Samuel Moore
Robert Clements, Jr.	Thomas and Annabel Gordon	Ephraim Plummer
Stephen Emery	Jasper (Indian Servant of Henry Jacques)	Rebecca Potter
Elizabeth Fawne	Mary Jacques	Mary Turril/Tarville
Mary Kelly		

---

[2] Klett, Joseph R. "Using the Records East and West Jersey Proprietors," New Jersey State Archives, 2014. (Internet archive)

First Settlements, Colonists, and Biographies by Descendants

First Presbyterian Church Woodbridge and Cemetery of Woodbridge

The foundations of the Woodbridge town meetinghouse was laid in 1675 and finished six years later. The building was thirty-foot square and lasted over a hundred years. It was replaced in 1803. The historical colonial cemetery lies adjacent to the present church. The cemetery has been used as a burial ground since the meeting house was built in 1675. The earliest tombstone is dated 1690; however, in all probability there were earlier ones that deteriorated and disappeared.

[3]

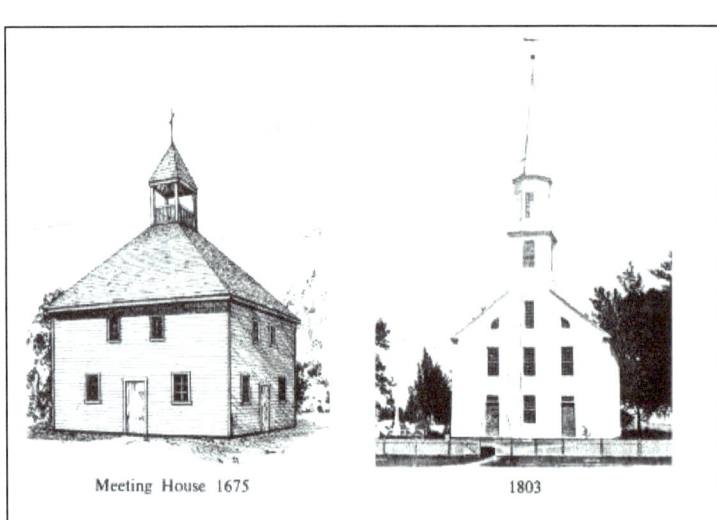

Sketches of early Woodbridge churches; credit: www.fpcwoodbridgenj.org

Earliest gravestone dated 1690

References:

First Presbyterian Church Woodbridge website. www.fpcwoodbridgenj.org

Klett, Joseph R. "Using the Records East and West Jersey Proprietors," New Jersey State Archives, 2014. (Internet archive)

Monnette, Orra Eugene. "New Jersey Archives – First Series Vol. 1 Documents Relating to the Colonial History of the State, 1631-87," reprinted in *First Settlers of Ye Plantations of Piscataway and Woodbridge Olde East Jersey 1664-1714, Part 1*, Leroy Carmen Press, CA, 1930.

---

[3] First Presbyterian Church Woodbridge website. www.fpcwoodbridgenj.org

The Founding of Piscataway - 1666

Hugh Dunn, John Martin, Hopewell Hull and Charles Gilman from New Hampshire answered the call in 1666 to migrate to New Jersey. Traveling from Elizabethtown they explored southwest along Indian paths to the Raritan River, there they found a few log huts on the site of an old Indian village (across the river from what is now New Brunswick). Pleased with the area they purchased 40,000 acres, from Daniel Pierce, on 18 December 1666, a third of his share in his Woodbridge acquisition. On 30 May 1668, John Gillman, Benjamin Hull, Robert Dennis and John Smith were joined by endorsement to the deed as associates. Less than two years later they were joined by Francis and Mary Drake who came from the vicinity of Portsmouth.

Raritan River: Empties near Staten Island in Raritan Bay on the Atlantic Ocean; source: Wikipedia

The Growth of the Settlement

They called their purchase New Piscataqua, after Piscataqua County, an area lying between Maine and New Hampshire. They founded the township of Piscataway for the purpose of colonization and a provision of the deed required the speedy settlement of the territory. In addition to their own families the associates brought numerous other families from Piscataqua, in New Hampshire (now Maine) as well as other areas of New England. In 1677, the area that became the village of Piscataway was purchased from two Indian Sachems, Canackawack and Thingorawis.

Up until the 1680's nearly all the settlers came from New England or from Long Island. After the death of Sir George Carteret and the sale of East Jersey in England by his trustees in 1682, the original settlers began to be joined by those coming directly from the Old World. Most of the new residents were representatives and servants of the 24 new landholder Proprietors, most of who remained in England. The new Proprietors confirmed the same liberal terms granted by Carteret and Berkeley. This migration brought thousands of settlers to the shores of New Jersey.

Early Settlers of Piscataway

Names of those for whom land was surveyed up to 1690 from the New Jersey Archives, reprinted in Monnette, 1930.

(Note: There are many others who were early settlers of Piscataway)

Settlers	Acres	Settlers	Acres	Settlers	Acres
Alexander Adams	150	Rehoboth Gannet	224	Daniel Lepinton/Lippington	129
Thomas Bartlett	70	Henry Greenland	384	Thomas Lowry	70
Simon Brinley/Brindley	90	Charles Gilman	340	John Langstaff	300
Peter Billow	210	John Gilman	300	John Martin	334
Nicholas Bonham	100	Matthew Giles	120	John Jr Martin.	230
Timothy Carter	63	James Giles	280	Joseph Martin	60
Benjamin Clarke	274	James Godfry	34.5	Jefrey Maning (1678)	195
George Drake	424	Thomas Gordon (of Amboy)	110	Ann Maning (his widow (1690)	200
Francis Drake (Capt.)	245	John Hendricks (Jabez)	120	Samuel Moore	280
John Drake	30	Daniel Hendricks	195	John Millison	100
Samuel Doty	252.5	Mary Higgins	254	Nicholas Mundaye	101.5
Hugh Dun	138	Jediah Higgins	80	Joshua Perine	30
Benajah Dunham	103.75	Thomas Higgins	53	Vincent Rognion	154.5
Edmond Dunham	100	George Jewel	95	Walter Robinson	100
John Fitz-Randolph	277	Hopewell Hull	285	Edward Slater	464
Benjamin Fitz-Randolph	130	Benjamin Hull*	498	John Smalley	118.5
Thomas Fitz-Randolph	106	Samuel Hull	144	John Smalley, Jr.	215
				Michael Simmons	104.5
				Richard Smith	164
				William Sutton	249
				Samuel Walker	120
				Andrew Worden	67
				George Winckfield	63
				Robert Wright	86

Original Associates not listed as having land surveyed by 1690 in Piscataway but are listed as landowners in Woodbridge: Robert Dennis and John Smith

Prominent among other citizens and freeholders just before the close of the Proprietary Period (1702)
(Exclusive of those named above)

Daniel Blackford	Thomas Lawrence	John Runyon
Daniel Brinson	Cornelius Longfield	William Runyon
Peter Billieu	Joseph Manning	Michael Simmens
Thomas Blackford	James Manning	Richard Stockton
Samuel Blackford	Benj. Martin	John Steward
Thomas Bartlett	Jonathan Martin	Thomas Wester
Thomas Carle	John Manning	George Windfield
Thomas Claws	Joseph Manning	Robert Wright
Thomas Cawood	Nicholas Mundy Jr.	Joseph Worth
John Doty	Daniel Mc Daniel	Francis Drake
Thomas Farsworth	David Mundie	Francis Drake Jr.
John Field	William Olden	Hugh Dunn Jr.
Henry Gretson	John Pound	Joseph Drake
Thomas Grubs	Ino Pridmore	Samuel Dunn
Benjamin.Griffith	Rene Pyatt	John Lonestaff
John Horner	Walter Robinson	John Liang Jr.
John Harrison	John Royce	Jacob Pyatt
Benj. James	Vincent Runyon	Joseph Smalley Jr.
Benj. Jones	Vincent Runyon Jr.	
William Laing		

The Raritan River was an important resource to new settlers in Piscataway

References:

Monnette, Orra Eugene. "New Jersey Archives – First Series Vol. 1 Documents Relating to the Colonial History of the State, 1631-87," reprinted in *First Settlers of Ye Plantations of Piscataway and Woodbridge Olde East Jersey 1664-1714, Part 1*, Leroy Carmen Press, CA, 1930.

Klett, Joeseph R. "Using the Records East and West Jersey Proprietors," New Jersey State Archives, 2014. (Internet archive)

The Founding of Newark - 1666

Founders Monument, Fairmount Cemetery, Newark

Newark was founded by conservative Puritans, chiefly from three towns in the New Haven Colony. The increasingly tolerant views of religious freedom (especially tolerance for Quakers, whom Puritans were intolerant), and the merger of the New Haven Colony in 1662 with the more religiously tolerant Connecticut Colony, combined with the English ouster of the Dutch in 1664 from New Amsterdam, set the stage for a band of Pilgrims from Branford, Guilford and Milford to seek lands in the new English province of New Jersey.

In 1666, Captain Robert Treat, after scouting several locations, successfully completed arrangements with Governor Carteret to settle a plantation on the Passaic River, in the northern section of what was known as the Elizabethtown purchase. He bore a letter to be presented to the chief Hackensack Indian Sachems; however, when the first settlers arrived they were warned off by the Indians who disputed their claims of ownership. Carteret refused to negotiate with the Indians, claiming that the area had been purchased as part of Elizabethtown.

Left to their own devices, some of the others went up to the Hackensack [the village and headquarters of the local tribe of Lenni Lenape] to treat with the Indian proprietors for the land lying on the West Bank of the Passaic River. Treat, through Samuel Edsal, an interpreter of the Lenni Lenape tongue and land-owner in Bergen Neck, negotiated with the Indian proprietors a deed of sale for the land. The price paid was *fifty double hand of gun powder, one hundred bars of lead, twenty axes, twenty coats, ten guns, twenty pistols, ten kettles, ten swords, four blankets, four barrels of beer, ten pair of breeches, fifty knives, twenty hoes, eight hundred and fifty fathoms of wampum, twenty ankers (about ten gallons of wine) of liquors and ten troopers' coats.*

The First English Settlements in New Jersey

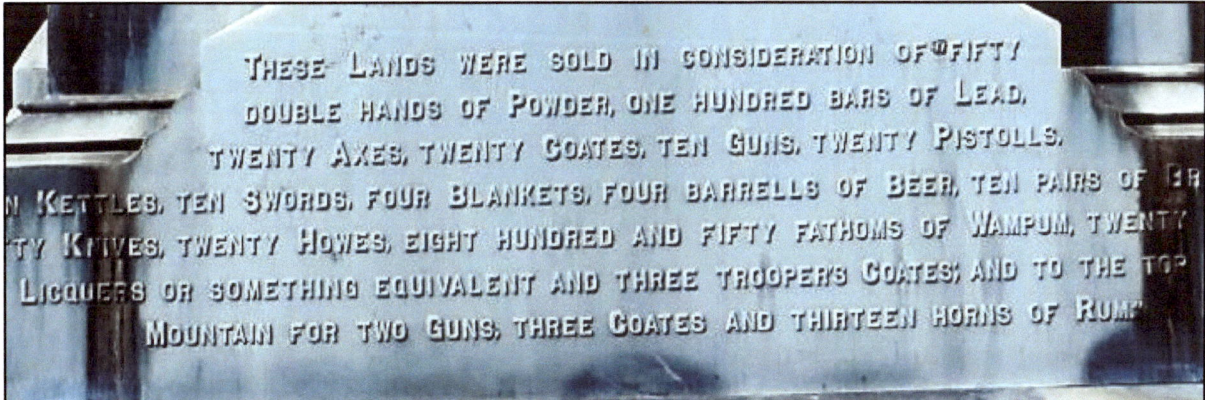

Founder's Monument

The natives who signed the document with marks or individual totems were: Wapamuck, Harish, Captamin, Seasson, Manustome, Peter Wamesane, Wekamuck, Cackmackque and Perawae. The settlers who signed were Michael (Micah) Tompkins, Samuel Kitchell, John Browne and Robert Denison. The natives probably felt this was a good bargain since it provided knives, guns, axes and other goods useful in their lives.

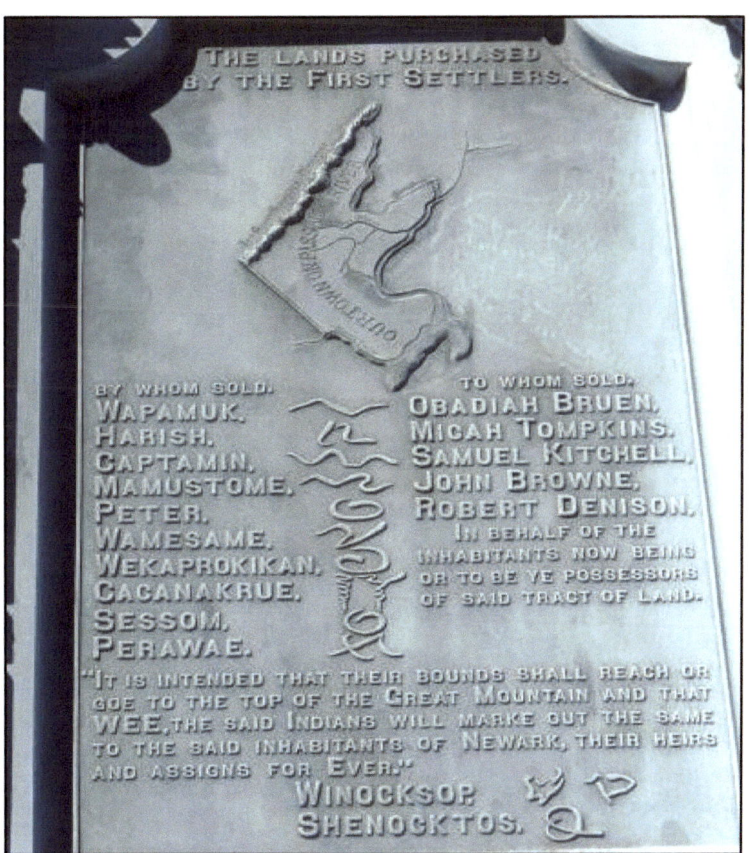

Plaque comemerating the signing by the Native Americans and Associates of the title for Newark - Founders Monument, Fairmount

The Growth of the Settlement

It is storied that Elizabeth Swaine, daughter of Captain Samuel Swain, a leader among the settlers was the first to be assisted to the land in May 1666, by Josiah Ward who she later married. After Ward's death she married David Ogden. The land was described as rich and the river and bay teaming with seafood. Forests of oak, chestnut, hickory, elm, maple (including sugar maple) provided for energy and building material. White cedar swamp occupied much of what are now the Hackensack meadowlands. Fresh water was at hand. Salt hay meadows provided for easy grazing of cattle. Deer, elk, beaver, otters, fox and wolves were plentiful. Wolves were the only animals to cause concern.

The Landing at Newark-Founders Monument, Fairmount Cemetary, Newark

A committee, which included Captain Robert Treat, Samuel Swaine, Samuel Kitchell, Michael Tomkins, Mr. Morris, Sergt. Richard Beckly, Richard Harrison, Thomas Blatchley, Edward Riggs, Stephen Freeman and Thomas Johnson were charged with distribution of home-lots (six acres) and to act on behalf of those who would come by June of the next year. Additional uplands east of the home lots and partition of the marsh or meadow were made in January 1669, with a further division of salt meadow in February 1670, and uplands in May 1673.

Unlike the other early East Jersey settlements, which embraced the freedom and diversity of religion granted in Berkeley and Carteret's *Concessions and Agreements*, the settlers of Newark following the practices from their New Haven towns established Newark as a theocracy, in which the Church (*the Word of God shall be the only Rule attended unto in ordering the affairs of Government*) and State (*that free burgesses shall be chosen from Church members, and they shall choose magistrates and officers among themselves to share the power to transacting all public civil affairs of plantation*). The Branford group led by their pastor, Rev Abraham Pierson, drew up *Fundamental Agreements* setting forth the religious foundation for the town, which was agreed to by each who would join in the venture. Only those who were members of the Congregational Church could own or inherit land, hold office or enjoy civil liberties and privileges. Provision was also made to remove any person from the town who would *subvert us from the true religion*. However, the *Fundamental Agreements* were only rigidly enforced for about fifteen years.

Early Settlers of Newark

Early settlers of Newark as they appear in *A History of Newark, New Jersey* by Urquhart, 1913.

The first signers of the *Fundamental Agreements* were the men from Branford:

Jasper Crane	Josiah Ward	Ebenezer Camfield
Delivered Crane	John Johnson (his mark)	Richard Laurence
Abra Pierson	Samuel Rose	John Ward Sr.
Samuel Swaine	Thomas Pierson	Edward Ball
Laurence Ward	John Warde	John Harrison
Thomas Blatchley	John Catlin	John Crane
Samuel Plum	Richard Harrison	Thomas Huntington
Aaron Blatchley	Thomas Lyon	

The forty-one Guilford, Milford and New Haven men who signed the Fundamental Agreements:

Robert Treat	Francis F. Linle (his mark)	Robert Daglesh
Obadiah Bruen	Daniel Tichenor	Hans Albers
Matthew Camfield	John Bauldwin, Sen.	Thom. Morris
Samuel Kitchell	John Bauldwin Jr,	Hugh Roberts
Jeremiah Pecke	Jona. Tomkins	Eph'm Pennington
Stephen Freeman	George Day	Martin Tichenor
Henry Lyon	Thomas Johnson	John Browne Jr.
John Browne	John Curtis	Jona. Seargeant
John Rogers	Ephram Burwell	Azariah Crane
Stephen Davis	Robert Denison (his mark)	Samuel Lyon
Edward Riggs	Nathaniel Wheeler	Joseph Riggs
Robert Kitchell	Zachariah Burwell	Stephen Bond
J.B. Brooks (his mark)	William Camp	
Robert Lymon (his mark)	Joseph Walters	

It should be noted that only five of the signers could not write. It was a tenet within protestant churches that every person should be able to read the Bible and instruction in reading and at least limited mathematics was provided within the community.

THE ORIGINAL TOWN PLATE

The map given herewith and showing the town lots of the early settlers of Newark is reproduced from the drawing prepared at the time of the bi-centennial celebration of the settlement, in 1866, by Samuel H. Conger and William A. Whitehead, for the New Jersey Historical Society, in Urquhart, 1913.

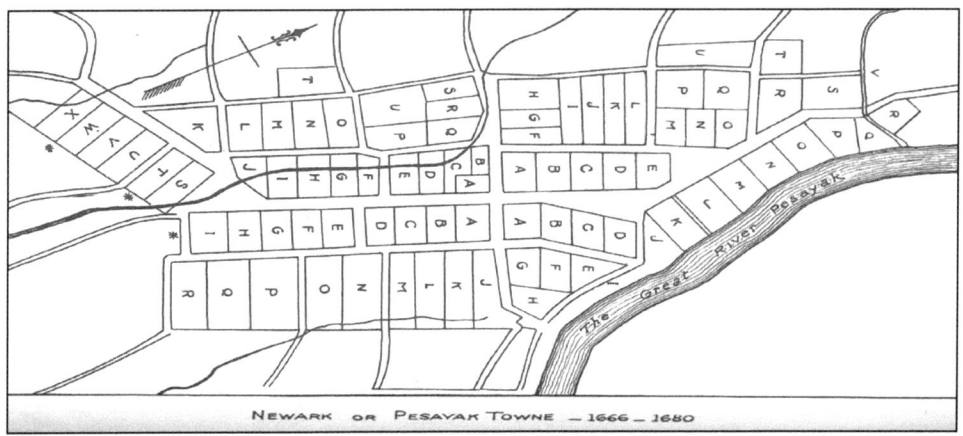

Southeast
A. Robert Treat
B. Abraham Pierson
C. Robert Denison
D. Thomas Johnson
E. George Day
F. Nathaniel Wheeler
G. Joseph Riggs
H. William Camp
I. Martin Tichenor
J. Stephen Freeman
K. John Curtis
L. John Baldwin Sr.
M. Thomas Staples
N. John Baldwin Sr.,
O. Michael Tomkins
P. Jonathan Tomkins
Q. Ephraim Pennington
R. Seth Tomkins
S. The Tailor's Lot
T. Thomas Pierson Jr.
U. Samuel Harrison
V. John. Brown Jr.
W. Edward Riggs
X. Hugh Roberts
Z. Azariah Crane

Southwest
A. Meeting House Lot
B. Treat's Recompense
C. John Johnson
D. Parsonage Home Lot
E. John. Brown Sr.,
F. Stephen Bond
G. Zachariah Burwell
H. Ephram Burwell
I. Thomas Ludington
J. John Brooks
K. Thomas Lyon
L. Joseph Johnson
M. John Treat
N. Samuel Lyon
O. Henry Lyon
P. Joseph Walters
Q. Samuel Camfield
R. Robert Dalglesh
S. Francis Lindsley
T. Mathew Williams

Northeast
A. Laurence Ward.
B. John Catlin
C. Samuel Kitchell
D. Josiah Ward
E. John Rogers
F. Robert Kitchell
G. Jeremiah Peck
H. Jasper Crane
I. Benjamin Baldwin
K. Thomas Ludington
L. Alex Munroe
M. The Elder's Lot
O. Richard Laurence
P. Delivered Crane
Q. Hans Albers
R. Samuel Rose
S. The Miller's Lot
T. Samuel Dod
U. Daniel Dod
V. The Corn Mill

Northwest
A. Samuel Swaine
B. Robert Harrison
C. Edward Ball
D. John Morris
E. John Ward Sr.
F. Matthew Camfield
G. John Gardner
H. Obadiah Bruen
I. The Seaman's Lot
K. John Harrison
L. Aaron Blatchley
M. Stephen Davis
O. John Crane
P. Jonathan Sergeant
Q. Robert Lymon
R. John Davis

Founders Monument at Fairmount Cemetery (markes the graves of the founders of Newark that were moved from the original burial grounds under what is now NJPAC in downtown Newark) image source: www.newarkhistroy.com

References:

The New Jersey Historical Society. *Records of the Town of Newark 1666-1836*, Newark, N.J. Published by the Society, 1864, reprint 1966.

Urquhart, Frank John. *A History of the City of Newark New Jersey: Embracing Practically Two and a Half Centuries 1666-1913*, Volume I., Lewis Historical Publishing Co., 1913. (Internet archive)

The Founding of Salem and the Fenwick Colony - 1665

Assamhockin Creek (Salem Creek)

Salem was founded by Quaker John Fenwick in October 1665; the first English settlement established in West Jersey following the English defeat of the Dutch in 1664 and the first Quaker colony in North America, predating Philadelphia by seven years. At the time, in addition to Native Americans, there were in the area a scattering of descendants of earlier Swedish, English and Finnish settlers. Sweden made a royal claim on the region in the 1640's; but yielded to the Dutch in 1654. However, in 1665 Fenwick's new acquisition was mainly a vast wilderness of forest, bogs, meadows and waterways.

John Fenwick was born at Stanton Manor, England, in 1618, the second son of wealthy and prominent William Fenwick. John was appointed as a captain of Cavalry by Oliver Cromwell and took an active part in the fight against the Crown. About 1648, he married Elizabeth Covert, with whom he had three daughters. Abandoning the Church of England in 1665, he and his wife became members of the Society of Friends.

Example of Finnish log house built between 1638 and 1643

Fenwick was involved in a financial dispute concerning an undivided portion of New Jersey, which Lord Berkeley had sold to Edward Billinge for £1000, in 1675. The final outcome of the dispute was that for financial considerations Fenwick was granted a tenth of West Jersey. Known as the Salem Tenth, it encompassed 350 square miles in the Southwestern part of the state (much of what are Salem and Cumberland Counties today).

Fenwick immediately began to make preparation to emigrate and take possession of his lands in West Jersey and provide inducements to those who would join him. Land was offered at £5 per 100 acres, owners of 1000 to 10,000 acres were to be proprietors or freeholders. However, settlers were mainly Quakers of modest means, generally merchants or craftsman. Farms were generally of medium size from 50 to 300 acres.

The First English Settlements in New Jersey

The settlers set sail from London on the *Griffin*, under Robert Griffin, in September 1665. Arriving in Delaware Bay, they sailed about 50 miles up the Delaware River from Cape May, to the mouth of Assamhockin Creek. Following the stream for about three miles, they arrived at a point near an abandoned Swedish settlement on 5 October 1675. Thinking the site, a suitable location to settle, Fenwick named it New Salem, from the word Shalom meaning peace.

Early Settlers of Fenwick's Colony

Partial list of Passengers on the Griffin 1665:

Fenwick's Extended Family	Fenwick Servants:**
John Fenwick	Robert Turner*
Elizabeth Fenwick Adams	Gewas Bywater
John Adams (husband)	William Wilkenson
Elizabeth, Fenwick and Mary Adams (children)	Joseph Worth
Anne Fenwick (married Samuel Hedge Jr).	Joseph Ware
Samuel Hedge Jr.	Michael Eaton
Priscilla Fenwick Chamneys	Eleanor Geere
Edward Chamney*	Ruth Geere
John and Mary Chamneys (children)	Zachariah Geere
A Few of the other Passengers	Sara Hutchens
John Pledger*	Ann Parsons
Samuel Wade*	
Robert Windham*	**Chamney Servants**
Richard Handcock*	Edward Webb
Isaac Smart (unmarried)	Elizabeth Waiters/Waites
Nathaniel Chambless	Mark Reeves
Nathaniel Chambless Jr.	

*Traveled with unnamed family members. ** Many of those who sailed as servants became prominent in civil and religious affairs of the colony.

Soon after landing, the Proprietors purchased all the land in three separate agreements from the Indian chiefs living in the area securing perpetual peace with the natives. Under provisions of the deed, the Indians reserved certain rights to themselves, including trapping, fishing and the privilege of cutting certain kinds of wood for making baskets, canoes and other items. The third parcel was purchased for the following goods: *4 guns, powder and lead; 10 ½ ankers of rum, equal to about 336 gallons; some shirts, shoes, and stockings; 4 blankets; 16 match-coats; 1 piece of match coating and other English goods.* The early emigrants found the natives to be excellent neighbors and reliable associates; the relations brought about marriages between the immigrants and natives.

Native Chiefs who signed the Agreements of Sale

1st Land Purchase	2nd Land Purchase	3rd Purchase
Tospaininkey	Mahoppony	Shuccotery
Henaminkey	Allways	Mahawskcy
	Necomis and his mother	Mohut
	Myhoppony	Newsego,
	Myhoppony	Chechenaham
		Torucho
		Shacanum

First Settlements, Colonists, and Biographies by Descendants

The Growth of the Settlement

Fenwick established the town of Salem in 1675 and before long other ships with settlers arrived. Quakers were the first to come to Salem and a Friends Meeting was organized in March 1678. They were soon followed by Calvinists from New England and Long Island.

The population grew rapidly with brisk sales of large as well as small tracts of land. Salem City was planned as the "shire town" of the colony. It was set to have 42 purchasers of 16 acre plots. A 90' wide street (West Broadway) was laid out from Salem Creek and intersected another street that began at Fenwick Creek (Market Street). East Broadway was then called Wharf Street and Market was Bridge Street. The extension of Wharf Street was called Fenwick Street, now East Broadway. The office of burgess and other civil offices were established. By 1682 Salem had become a port of entry and a place of foreign trade.

William Hampton erected a saw-mill in 1682 and there were three windmills. A weekly market was established by law to be held on every Tuesday, with fairs to be held on May 1st and 2nd and October 20th and 21st, of each year. In the 1680's a Friends School was built in an Indian village for both Indian and white children. In Fenwick's will dated 1683 he called for a second town to be built on the Cohansey Creek.

Some of the settlers mentioned in historical records of Salem during the Proprietary Period listed in Historical Collections of the State of New Jersey by John Barber and Henry Howe, 1844

Settlers	Settlers	Town of Salem Officers
Richard Guy	David Sheppard	John Worledge (Salem 1st Burgess)
Christopher White	Thomas Abbott	Benjamin Acton (Salem Recorder)
John Smith	Westcott family	John Jeffrey (Salem Bailiff)
Richard Tindal	Bateman family	Richard Johnson (Salem Surveyor)
Daniel Elmer	Richard Whitacar	John Fithian
William Button	Thomas Harding	Jonathan Beere (Salem Burgess 1698)
Rev. John Mills	Harrise family	William Hall (Salem 3rd Burgess)
Edward Wade	William Malster	Richard Johnson (Salem 4th Burgess)
William Waddington	John, Jonathan and Daniel Davis	Thomas Killigsworth (Salem 5th Burgess)
Richard Noble	Benjamin Acton	Hugh Middleton (Salem Sheriff)
Samuel Nicholson	Rebecca Brassey	Reyneer Van Hyst (Justice)
Hypolit Lefevre	John, Richard, William, Sarah Hancock	John Ogden (son of Richard Ogden, Fairfield CT)
Rebecca Cox,	Mary Cooper	Richard Darking (Justice 1698)
Benjamin Griscom	Christiana England	William Rumsey (Justice 1702)
T. Hilliard	Elizabeth Walker	Harrise (Family)
Robert Wade	Isabella Marshall Thompson	Reyneer Van Hyst (Justice)
Benjamin Stratton	John Thompson	Obadiah Holmes (Justice 1699)
James Sheppard	John Maddox	
Samuel & Priscilla Fithian		

The Delaware River; vital for both Native American and white settlements

References:

Shroud, Thomas. *History and Genealogy of Fenwick's Colony* Salem County, Bridgeton NJ, 1876. (Internet archive)

Barber, John W. and Henry Howe. *Historical Collections of the State of New Jersey*, S. Tuttle, NY, 1844.

"Salem New Jersey Monthly Meeting Records" (wikitree/category/Salem_Monthly_Meeting%2c_New Jersey)

BIOGRAPHIES OF FOUNDERS OF NEW JERSEY

The following biographies were written by descendants of founders of New Jersey, who documented their lineage and are members of Descendants of Founders of New Jersey.

Governor Philip Carteret landed at the new English settlement at 1665

Painting in the Hall of Records, Newark

ABRAHAM ACKERMAN (1656/59 - aft. 1723)

Abraham Ackerman was the seventh and youngest child of David and Lysbeth Bellier Ackerman born at Berlicum, Holland on 3 May 1656/59. The family left Amsterdam on 2 Sept 1662 on the ship De Vos ("The Fox"), arriving in New Amsterdam on 14 Nov 1662 after a stormy voyage. The Dutch West India Company ledger of the trip is still preserved at the New York State Archives in Albany. David, the father, probably died on the voyage, but Lysbeth managed to keep her family together settling at New Amsterdam. At her second marriage in 1668 to Kier Wolthers, she moved to his farm at Harlem just north of New York City. Abraham, then nearly twelve, was old enough to help with work on the farm.

Abraham married Aeltie Van Laer, daughter of Adrian Van Laer and Abigael Ver Planken at Flatbush, Long Island, New York on 28 May 1683. Their marriage was recorded at both the New York and Bergen Reformed Dutch Churches. Her father came from Amsterdam with his servant in the ship "Gilded Beaver" in May 1658. Aeltie was born on 14 May 1663, and baptized at Kingston, NY on 26 Apr 1666. Abraham and Aeltie Ackerman had fourteen children; the first two born in New York, and the rest at Bergen, New Jersey.

From the deed dated 10 Mar 1689 transferring land from John Berry to Louwerense Ackerman, brother of Abraham, we learn that Abraham owned a tract of land south of that conveyed to Louwerense, reaching from the Hackensack River to the Saddle River. This location comprises the whole of what is now known as Woodbridge and Hasbrouck Heights, New Jersey.

Abraham Ackerman was received into the Dutch Reformed Church at Hackensack, New Jersey on 3 Oct 1696. His wife Aeltie Van Laer was received on 3 Jan 1697. Among the founders of this Church were two of his brothers, David and Louwerense, and their wives. This Church was also known as the "Church on the Green." Both Abraham and his wife Aeltie were present at the baptism of a grandchild in 1723. The date of Abraham's death is recorded as 4 June 1724. There is a fieldstone marker for his grave at the west side of the Reformed Dutch Church at Hackensack.

John Edward Lary Jr.   #369

References:

Ackerman, Herbert Stewart. *Descendants of David Ackerman of 1662, Volumes I and II*, 1944.

Klett, Joseph R. *Genealogies of New Jersey Families, Volume II, 1996.*

Tobey, Barbara W. *The Ackerman Family, Volumes I and II*, 1980, 1988.

DAVID ACKERMAN (1653 – 1710/24)

David Ackerman was born at Geffen, Holland in September 1653 and baptized 5 October 1653. He was the fourth child of David and Lysbeth Bellier Ackerman. The family, which included six children, left Amsterdam 2 September 1662 on the ship Da Vos. The Dutch West India Company ledger of the trip is preserved at the New York State Archives in Albany. David, the father, probably died on the voyage, but Lysbeth managed to keep her family together, settling at New Amsterdam. At her second marriage in 1668 she moved to Harlem.

David married Hillegont Verplanck, born October 1648 and baptized 1 November at New Amsterdam. He married by license dated 13 March 1680, at New York, Hillegont Verplanck, the daughter of Abraham Isaacsen Verplanck and Maria Vinge. At one time David owned the property at No. 1 Broadway, New York City. From 1680 to 1683 he paid quit rents on 540 acres of land in Essex County, New Jersey, now part of Bergen County, then in 1685 moved his family to Hackensack.

With his wife Hillegont, David was one of the organizers of the Reformed Dutch Church at Hackensack in 1686. His initials are carved in the outside wall of the Church Tower. He was appointed Justice of the Peace in 1699. His will dated 2 October 1710, and proved 4 October 1724, mentions three children who lived to adulthood and his wife who outlived her husband. David died at Hackensack, 4 June 1724.

Elaine Elliot Johnston #174

References:

Tobcy, Barbara W. *The Ackerman Family, Volumes I and II*, 1980, 1988.

George Inness "Hackensack Meadows Sunset" Source: NY Historical Society

First Settlers, Colonists, and Biographies by Descendants

THOMAS ALGER (ab.1638 - 1687)

Thomas Alger was born about 1638. He married Susanna (-) last name unknown. Very little is known concerning the life of Thomas Alger. His name was recorded variously, as "Auger" or "Awger". When the family arrived in this country is not now known; however, he was among the early settlers of Woodbridge, New Jersey, where he received a house-lot of 12 acres, 120 acres of upland and 35 acres of meadows on 18 March 1669/70.

Thomas and Susanna had at least two sons and two daughters, namely Thomas, Jr., William, Susannah, and Mary (or Marie), probably all born before the family arrived at Woodbridge. Thomas' wife Susanna outlived him and was executrix of his will, dated 14 January 1687, which mentions his property as a plantation, a home lot in Woodbridge, and a share in the grist mill owned by John Dennis, valued as £30. Family members mentioned in his will include "son William, daughter Mary Gilman, and grandchild John, son of John Allen of Woodbridge." He died at Woodbridge, New Jersey in 1687.

Elaine Elliot Johnston#174

1st Presbyterian Church of Woodbridge Cemetary founded 1675

References:

Monnette, Orra Eugene, *First Settler of Ye Plantations of Piscataway and Woodbridge, Part IV*, Leroy Carmen Press, CA, 1930.

New Jersey Archives. *New Jersey Archives Will Abstracts, Vol. 1*, 1670-1730 (Internet Archive)

New Jersey Archives. *Calendar of New Jersey Records, First Series, Vol. XXI* (Internet Archive)

Biographies of Founders of New Jersey

JOHN ALLEN (c.1625 – 1702/3)

John Allen's birth place and exact date of birth are unknown. The first mention of John Allen is in 1644, where in the allotment of town lots in Rehoboth, Plymouth Colony he was given, lot no. 42. He then appears in the records at Barnstable, Cape Cod in 1650 and also at Newport, Rhode Island in the same year. He was a Quaker.

John married Elizabeth Bacon on 11 October 1650, at a Friend's Ceremony. They had the following issue:

1. Elizabeth Allen born 1651, married Nathaniel Tompkins
2. Mary Allen born 1653, married Rowland Robinson
3. John Allen born 1654
4. Mercy Allen born 1656
5. Priscilla Allen born 1659
6. Samuel Allen born 1661

John Allen was not among the original patentees in the 8 April 1665 grant by Governor Nicolls known as the Monmouth Patent. However, he contributed monetarily to the purchase and his name appears among purchasers of land in Monmouth County, New Jersey in 1667.

John Allen's stated profession was "cooper of Middlesex County" which refers to a tradesman who makes wooden vessels bound with wooden hoops such as butter churns, barrels and casks. These wooden vessels were primarily used for shipping goods and for storing wines and other assorted liqours. John Allen died 4 January 1702/3, at the home of his son-in-law, Rowland Robinson in Kingstown, Rhode Island.

#366 David Lawrence Grinnell

References:

Colket, Meredith B. Jr. "Founders of Early American Families: Immigrants from Europe 1607-1657" Cleveland, published by The Ohio Society with the authority of The General Court of the Order of the Founders and Patriots of America, 2002.

Austin, John Osborne. *The Genealogical Dictionary of Rhode Island*, Joel Munsell's Sons, Albany, 1887.

Salter, Edwin. *A History of Monmouth and Ocean Counties*, F. Gardner & Son Publishers, Bayonne, 1890.

BARTHOLOMEW APPLEGATE (c 1625 – aft 1674)

Bartholomew Applegate was the eldest son of Thomas Applegate and Elizabeth Morgan, members of the Massachusetts Bay Colony as early as 1635. The family included three other children: John, Helena, and Thomas. The family moved first from Massachusetts to New Amsterdam, second to Flushing, and third to Gravesend, Long Island.

In 1650 Bartholomew married Hannah Annet je Patrick. He was a land owner in Gravesend. On 8 March 1674 he and his brother Thomas Applegate, with Richard Sadler were granted permission to purchase lands from the Indians, near the Navesink, in East Jersey. Bartholomew was not present at the drawing of lots in the new purchase, but was represented by John Rawles. One of the conditions of the purchase was that settlements be made within two years or the land would be forfeited. In 1674, Bartholomew with his family left Gravesend; moving either to Monmouth County, New Jersey or more likely to New England to live. In 1685/86 his rights to 200 acres of land at the fall of the river at New Shrewsbury, New Jersey were vested with Col. Lewis Morris.

Summarized from documents submitted by # 366B David Lawrence Grinnell by Evelyn Ogden

Monmouth county encompasses two distinct ecologies; the ocean to the east and abundant mixed-deciduous forest to the west.

References:

Charles, Robert. *The Great Migration Begins*, Boston 1995.

Stillwell, John. *Historical and Genealogical Miscellany: Early Settlers of New Jersey and Their Descendants*, Vol. III, New York 1914.

Honor, William S. *This Old Monmouth of Ours*, Moreau Bros., Freehold, NJ, 1932

ELIZABETH AUSTIN (1669-1753)

Little is known about Elizabeth Austin's early life, except that she came to this New World from Horsemonden, Kent, England in 1688 with her brother, Francis Austin, who was the progenitor of the Quaker Austin family of Burlington County, New Jersey. Land records show that Francis purchased over the next few years 350 acres in Evesham, Burlington County. Elizabeth undoubtedly lived with her brother until she married Thomas Haines, in Burlington County, New Jersey in 1692.

Thomas was the son of Richard and Margaret Haines, who immigrated from Aynhoe, Northamptonshire England in 1682. He was a farmer and became owner of much valuable property in Burlington and Hunterdon Counties. The Haines had nine children: Daniel, 1694, Ann, 1696; Elizabeth, 1698; Thomas Haines II, 1700, Deborah, 1703, Margaret, 1705, George, abt. 1709, Amos, abt. 1710, Jane, 1712. Thomas's will was probated Aug. 30, 1753 and named his wife Elizabeth as the sole executrix. The date and place of the Elizabeth's death is not known.

Leah L. Samuels #422

Burlington County land was developed for farming, pasturing and fishing in the Delaware river, which borders the county on the western side.

References:

Haines, John Wesley. *Richard Haines and his Descendants: A Quaker Family of Burlington County, New Jersey since 1682*, Carr Publishing Company, Inc., Boyce, VA, 1961.

OBADIAH AYERS (1636 - 1694)

Obadiah Ayers, son of John and Hannah Ayers, was born probably in Salisbury, Massachusetts in 1636 and died in Woodbridge, New Jersey in 1694. He married Hannah Pike, a daughter of Captain John Pike on 19 March 1661 at Haverhill, Massachusetts. She died 30 May 1689, in Woodbridge.

With his father-in-law, John Pike and seven associates, Obadiah purchased a tract of land in New Jersey in 1666, where they founded a settlement that became Woodbridge between 1665 and 1667.

Obadiah is named many times in deeds of the area in those early years. His will of 17 November 1694 left his real and personal estate to his sons Samuel, John, Joseph and Obadiah, and to his daughter Mary. Letters of testament were issued to the witnesses, Ephraim, Andrew and John Pike, all relatives of the deceased wife of Obadiah, and were affixed to the original will.

L. George Van Syckle #C 10

First Presbyterian Church cemetary in Woodbridge established in 1675

References:

Monnette, Orra Eugene. *First Settlers of Ye Plantations of Piscataway and Woodbridge Olde East Jersey 1664-1714, Part 1*, Leroy Carmen Press, CA, 1930.

Hoyt, David. W. *The Old Families of Salisbury and Amesbury, Mass*, R.I, 1897.

Chambers, Theodore.F. *The Early Germans of New Jersey*, Dover, NJ, 1895.

New Jersey Archives, *Calendar of New Jersey Records 1664-1705*, First Series, Vol. XXI (Internet archive).

GUILIAM BERTHOLF (1656 - abt. 1726)

Guiliam Bertholf, the sixth child of Cryn Bertholf and Sara Guiliamse Van Coperen, was baptized in Sluis, Holland on 02 Feb 1656. It is thought he was born no more than a week or two before his baptism, as this was the practice in Holland at the time. He married Martyntje Hendrickse Vermeulen, daughter of William Vermeulen and Martyntje Weymoers, in Sluis on 15 Apr 1676. At least their first three children were born in Sluis with the third child, Elizabeth, being baptized there on 26 Sep 1673. Guiliam Bertholf and his family immigrated to America sometime after Elizabeth's baptism. We know from records of the old Reformed Church of Bergen, NJ the following entry of members received: "October 6, 1684—Guillaume Bertholf and his wife Martyntje Hendrics, with certificate from Dutch Flandres—Sluis in Flandres."

Guiliam Bertholf studied theology in Middletown, Holland. He came to America "to instruct Holland colonists in the Bible and the catechism." Reverend David Cole, in his History of the Reformed Church of Tappan, NY, observes "He was a man of profound spirituality, warm heart, great capacity for teaching, and of an order that day known as 'Voorlesers' and 'Krankbesoekers' (public readers and comforters of the sick)." In 1693 the two Reformed Churches in Hackensack and Aquackanonck (Passaic) joined together to send Guiliam Bertholf back to Holland, to the Classis of Middelburg to become ordained as their pastor. This mission was completed on 16 Sep 1693. He returned to New Jersey, and began his ministry on 24 Feb 1694.

For the next thirty years, Domine Bertholf served his ministry of the Hackensack and Aquackanonck Churches. For the first fifteen years of that ministry, he also was responsible for establishing all new Reformed Churches in New Jersey, as well as those in New York, such as Tarrytown and Port Richmond. Remarkably, Reverend Cole states, "The Tappan and Hackensack books from 1694 to 1724, as kept by Domine Bertholf or under his supervision, are exceedingly valuable as covering almost every Rockland County marriage or baptism that occurred."

The Bertholfs had eight children, whose names were Sara, Maria, Elizabeth, Hendrick, Quirinus (Cryn), Martays, Anna and Jacobus. There is some historical conjecture they may have had as many as thirteen children, but no supporting records have been found.

The last recorded event in Guiliam and Martyntje Bertholf's lives was the signing of a deed on 16 Feb 1726. It is thought they both died sometime later that year. Reverend Cole says, "There is a tradition that his remains were buried under the pulpit of the Hackensack Church".

John Edward Lary Jr. #369A

References:

Cole, D.D. *History of the Reformed Church of Tappan*, NY, 1894.

Dooley, Joseph. "Biography of Guiliaem Bertholf."

Documents Relating to the Colonial History of New Jersey, First Series, Vol. XXX, Calendar of Wills, Vol. II (Internet archive).

The New York Genealogical and Biographical Records, Vol. LV, New York, 1924.

WIILLIAM (1630-1712) AND SARAH BIDDLE (1634-1709)

William Biddle, the second son of an illiterate farmer in rural England, was sent to London as an apprentice to learn to be a shoemaker. He found himself in the midst of a group of people who were among the earliest Quakers in London. He soon became a member of the Religious Society of Friends and experienced the persecution of the Anglican government, serving time in jail for standing firm on his beliefs. He married Sarah Kempe and they began to raise their family in London as a part of the growing Quaker movement there.

The Quakers kept meticulous records in London and in West New Jersey where William and Sarah eventually settled in 1681. The couple was part of the group in England who planned to settle a new territory in America, with a new constitution that would give them the ability to own land, form a government, and practice their religion without fear of arrest or injury. For years members of this Quaker group emigrated from London to Burlington, in West Jersey.

William and Sarah were members of the group and along with their young family migrated to Burlington. From the very beginning of his life in America, William played a leadership role in the government, the court system, in the matters concerning the settling of land and in his Quaker religion. The records for each of these areas confirm the important contributions that William and Sarah made to their new country.

The couple had two children: William who married Lydia Wardell and Sarah who married Clement Plumstead of Philadelphia. Lydia was a descendant of Eliakim Wardell and Lydia Perkins who both fled Massachusetts having been persecuted because they were Quakers. Lydia had been whipped over a dozen times. They settled in Shrewsbury, New Jersey where they were among those who established the first Quaker meeting house in New Jersey, in 1666. The Wardells who remained in Massachusetts were physically harmed and Eliakim's uncle Samuel was hanged. William Biddle's second child Sarah married Clement Plumstead who became Mayor of Philadelphia. Among the guests at their wedding was William Penn Jr, who grew up right across the river from William Biddle's Mount Hope Estate.

William Biddle & Sarah Kempe's grandchildren were William, Elizabeth, Sarah, Penelope, Lydia, Joseph and John. William and John Biddle removed to Philadelphia in the 1720s. Their brother Joseph Biddle remained in Burlington County and his son Arney settled in Salem County, New Jersey where many of his descendants reside today.

372 Brandon Rowley

References:

Biddle, C. Miller. *William & Sarah Biddle 1633-1711: Planting a Seed of Democracy in America*. Private publisher, P.O. Box 714 Moorestown, N.J. 08057. Hardcover, 2011.

JOHN BISHOP SR. (1621-1684)

John Bishop Sr. was born in England c. 1621 and married Rebecca Kent Scullard in New England about 1647. He died between 19 September and 27 November 1684, the dates of his will.

John Bishop was probably both a ship's carpenter and a house carpenter. He was evidently in New England before 1643 as he knew of the building of the ship "Adventure" which sailed from Boston for Glasgow at that time. John was likely one of the crew and was back in London in April 1645 where he testified in court concerning the journeys of this ship. He was then 24 years of age.

Returning to New England in 1647, he married a widow Rebecca Kent Scullard. John and Rebecca lived at Newbury, Massachusetts for several years where their eight children were born 1648-1660. John was a Selectman at Newbury in 1655. The family removed to Nantucket about 1663 and John purchased land there in 1664 from the Indian Sachem. Later that year he joined others to become an Associate in the Woodbridge Patent.

John built a corn mill in the Rahway section of the Patent and was quite a respected man of the area, mentioned in many Woodbridge and vicinity records. He was the first representative to the Assembly in 1668 and was one of Governor Carteret's Council in 1672.

When John's will was written 19 September 1684 and probated 27 November 1684, it did not include his wife; indicating that she probably predeceased her husband. Two of the eight children also predeceased their father: daughter Elizabeth who died in infancy and son David. Six other children outlived their father: Jonathan, John, Noah, Rebecca, Joanna and Ann, known also as Hannah.

Elaine Elliot Johnston #174

References:

Dally, Rev. Joseph. *Woodbridge and Vicinity: the Story of a New Jersey Township*, New Brunswick, NJ, 1873.

Essex Institute Historical Collections, Vol. 63, 1927.

New Jersey Archives, Vol. XXI. (Internet archive)

Savage, James. *A Genealogical Dictionary of the First Settlers of New England*, Boston, 1840.

THOMAS BLOOMFIELD SR. (16xx - 1685)

Thomas Bloomfield, Sr., a carpenter, came to Woodbridge, New Jersey, from Newburyport, Massachusetts, with his wife Mary (-).

Thomas received a patent from Governor Carteret for about 326 acres in and around Woodbridge, on 20 December 1669. Active in local affairs he was made a Freeholder in 1670 and elected a representative from Woodbridge to the General Assembly of New Jersey at Elizabethtown in 1675. He was an Assistant Judge of Woodbridge Corporation Court from 1679 to1680 and Coroner, Middlesex County 1682 to1683.

Thomas he died in 1685, his will of 10 June 1684 was proved 5 March 1685/6. The date of his wife's death is unknown.

Kathleen Bastedo Walter #117

Early map showing Piscataway, Woodbridge, Elizabethtown and Newark

References:

New Jersey Archives, Vol. XXI (Internet archive).

N.Y. Genealogical & Biographical Record Vol. 68 (Internet archive).

Whitehead, William A. *History of Perth Amboy*, D. Appleton & Co., NY, 1856.

ROBERT BOND (1596 – 1677)

Robert Bond was born in Kent County, England in 1596; came to New England about 1639. Bond was a Puritan who probably settled first at Lynn, Massachusetts. He was an educated man, although his occupation was blacksmith. By 1642 he had a daughter Mary by his first wife, whose full name is not now known and there were at least three more children by that marriage.

About 1643 Robert moved his family to Southampton, Long Island, where he was appointed by the General Court of Connecticut to ask each family the amount they would give to scholars at Cambridge College in Massachusetts. Because of a split on this church matter, Robert was one of the 9 men who began the new town of East Hampton, purchasing 31,000 acres from the Indians in 1648. Robert was elected one of four men to run the affairs of the town and was one of the first three judges of the town's General Court. He was also appointed "Magistrate for East Hampton" by the general assembly at Hartford, under whose protection East Hampton was at this time, and represented the town in the General Assembly of the colony at Hartford in 1660, 1661.

In 1665 Bond and his son Joseph became part of the group who purchased the land known as Elizabethtown and signed the oath of allegiance there on 19 February 1665. He was appointed in 1667/8 to Gov. Carteret's Council and an assistant to the Justices. In 1668 he helped define the boundary between Elizabethtown and Newark and was a member of the first General Assembly of New Jersey at Elizabethtown that same year.

Robert Bond married in 1672 for his second wife, at Newark, Mary Calkins, daughter of Hugh Calkins and widow of Hugh Roberts. He is many times mentioned in the Newark records, now being a resident of that place and holding various positions in the town government. He died there in April of 1677, his second wife surviving him until 1700. There was at least one child by his wife Mary Calkins Roberts Bond.

Edsall Riley Johnston, Jr. #175

References:

Cory, Charles Henry. *The Lineal Ancestors of Susan (Mulford) Cory, Vol. III*, 1937.

Hatfield, Rev. Edwin F. *History of Elizabeth, New Jersey*, Carlton & Lanahan, NY, 1868.

The New Jersey Historical Society. *Records of the Town of Newark, 1666-1836*, reprint 1966.

Footnote to History

On 8 Dec. 1651, Lenni Lenape Indians granted a deed to Augustine Herman for land at the mouth of the Raritan, which eventually became the site of Perth Amboy. The first houses were built in 1683 and it became a major point of entry. The capital of East Jersey was transferred from Elizabethtown to Perth Amboy in 1686

NATHANIEL BONNELL (1636-1711)

Nathaniel Bonnell (Bunnell, Bonnell, Bonnel) was born in New Haven Connecticut in 1636 to parents William Bonnell and Ann Wilmont. He married Susanna Whitehead, daughter of Isaac Whitehead and Mary Brown, on 3 Jan 1665 (probably in New Haven).

In September 1664 the Duke of York sent a fleet to drive the Dutch from New Amsterdam. This was accomplished without a single shot being fired and Colonel Nicolls became the first English Governor of the area. A small group of associates from "overcrowded" New England petitioned the new English governor for the right to purchase a large parcel of land west of the Hudson River between the Raritan and Passaic Rivers, and to settle a "plantation" at Achter Kull. Permission was received on the 18 October. A delegation of the Associates met with the Indian Sachems on Staten Island and concluded the negotiations on 28 October. In November 1664 a few of the new owners sailed across the Achter Kull, up the Elizabeth River about two miles, past vast salt hay meadows, to the end of the navigable waters where there were falls, an ideal place for mills and a settlement. So was founded the first settlement in what was now New Jersey. On 1 December Governor Nicolls registered the deed and set forth the "Conditions for New Planters."

In August 1665 Governor Philip Carteret, whose cousin Sir George Carteret, with Lord Berkeley, had been granted land encompassing all of New Jersey, arrived from England. He issued a proclamation confirming the land to the settlers. Carteret changed the name of the settlement from Achter Kol to Elizabethtown, after the wife of the Sir George Carteret. The new governor made Elizabethtown his capital; the first capital of New Jersey.

Among the Elizabethtown Associates in the purchase were Nathaniel Bonnell and Isaac Whitehead (father of Susanna). They signed the "Oath of Allegiance and Fidelity" as inhabitants of Elizabethtown 19 February 1665. Nathaniel was granted a farm of sixteen acres and a six-acre town-house lot in an area with others who had come from Connecticut. Before 1682 he had built a house, which still stands (1045 East Jersey Street; headquarters of New Jersey Society of Sons of the Revolution), in Elizabeth. In 1692 and 1696, Nathaniel was elected a representative to the General Assembly of New Jersey from Elizabeth.

The Bonnells had seven children: Nathaniel II abt. 1670, Isaac l 1673, Samuel 1675, Lydia 1677, Jane 1680, Benjamin 1682, and Mary 1685. Nathaniel died in 1711 and was buried in the First Presbyterian Church of Elizabeth churchyard where his grave is marked with a tombstone which reads *Nathaniel Bonnel who died Sept. 4 1736, in his 67th year of his life*. After his death, Susanna moved to the family farm in the area of Elizabethtown called Connecticut Farms (now Union). In 1730, the followers in the area had tired of traveling four or five miles to the church at Elizabethtown and built the Connecticut Farms Presbyterian Church. Susanna Bonnell died 13 Feb. 1733, and was the second person buried in the cemetery at the new church.

#296B Evelyn Hunt Ogden

The Nathaniel Bonnel House
1045 East Jersey Street
Elizabeth, NJ

Nathaniel Bonnel (Bonnell, Bunnell) was born 1648 in New Haven, CT., and died 1696 in Elizabeth. He was one of the Associates who came to Elizabeth with the John Ogdens, in 1664. He was granted a "first lot Right", consisting of a sixteen-acre farm and a six-acre house lot. About 1670 Nathaniel with his skill as a carpenter and builder erected a residence on his town house lot. He married Suzanna Whitehead, daughter of Isaac Whitehead, another of the original settlers.

References:

Connecticut Farms Presbyterian Church. "Connecticut Farms Church History," (Website - ctfarms.org).

First Presbyterian Church of Elizabeth. *Church of the Founding Fathers of New Jersey: A History., New Jersey 1664-1964*, Carbrook Press, Maine, 1964.

RICHARD BORDEN (1595/6 – 1671)

The Borden (or Burden) name first appears in the fourteenth century Chancery Proceedings of County Kent, England. Richard Borden was baptized at Headcorn, Kent, England on 22 February 1595/6, and married Joane Fowie at Headcorn on 28 September 1625. Joane was the daughter of Richard Fowie of Frittenden and Headcorn. In 1637/8, Richard Borden and family immigrated to New England and eventually settled in Portsmouth, Rhode Island. Richard Borden became a freeman on 16 March 1640/1 and held many public offices in Portsmouth, including: treasurer 1654, 1655; commissioner 1654, 1656, 1657; member of a committee to treat with the Dutch, 18 May 1653; and deputy from Portsmouth to the Rhode Island General Assembly 1667, 1670. The Bordens had twelve children; the first five were born in England while the remaining seven were born in Portsmouth, R.I.

In 1665 residents of Gravesend, Long Island, along with a group of residents from Rhode Island, provided funds to purchase lands in Monmouth County, New Jersey from the Indians. Richard Borden was one of these "first purchasers." He died in Portsmouth on 25 May 1671 and was buried in the Quaker burial ground of the Society of Friends in Portsmouth.

He never lived in New Jersey, but in his will he left his land in New Jersey to his son Francis Borden, who moved to Shrewsbury, Monmouth County, in 1677 and died there in 1703. Another son, Benjamin Borden, had moved to New Jersey by 1670 when he married Abigail Grover at Shrewsbury. They raised a large family, and Benjamin left a large estate at his death about 1728.

Myron Crenshaw Smith #302

Monmouth County

References:

Moriarty, G. Andrews. "The Bordens of Headcorn," Co. Kent, NEHG Register, 1930.

Salter, Edwin. *A History of Monmouth and Ocean Counties*, Bayonne, NJ, 1890.

Austin, John Osborne. *Genealogical Dictionary of Rhode Island*, Albany, NY, 1887.

JAMES BOWNE (1636 - 1695)

James Bowne, eldest son of William and Ann (-) Bowne, was baptized at Salem, Massachusetts on 25 August 1636 and died at Middletown, New Jersey, February 1695. He married on 26 December 1665 Mary Stout, daughter of Richard and Penelope (Van Princis) Stout at Gravesend, Long Island, New York. There were five known sons.

On 14 December 1667 James Bowne was residing at Portland Point, New Jersey. He was elected Deputy to represent Middletown in the General Assembly of New Jersey at Elizabethtown and in 1668, he was made County Clerk. In 1669 and 1671, he was chosen one of the Overseers of Middletown and was also appointed Deputy to the General Court held at Portland Point in May 1669 and July 1670.

In 1671, Bowne was an Indian interpreter at the purchase of Navesink land; in 1675 was elected Magistrate of a monthly Court of Small Causes. He was elected a Deputy to the Council at Woodbridge in 1676 and in 1677 to the Council at Elizabethtown. While he was Town Clerk, 1677 to 1680, he was chosen Deputy to the General Assembly in 1679.

Bowne was one of the Founders of the Baptist Church of Middletown, the first church of that denomination in the colony. At the time of his death, his estate consisted of 500 acres granted to him as one of the original Monmouth Patentees. In total, his holdings were 1520 acres. The inventory of the estate consisted largely of cattle, horses and pigs.

Esther Burdge Capestro #C26

References:

Ellis, Franklin. *History of Monmouth County New Jersey*, Philadelphia, 1885.

Horner, William S. *This Old Monmouth of Ours*, Clearfield Press, 2009.

Reading, Miller K. M.D. *William Bowne and his Descendants*, Flemington, NJ, 1903.

Salter, Edwin & George Beekman. *Old Times in Old Monmouth*, Freehold, NJ, 1887.

Stillwell, John E. *Historical and Genealogical Miscellany*, NY, 1914.

Stout, Herald F. *Stout and Allied Families*, Eagle Press, 1951.

ALEXANDER/SANDER BOYER (1618-1661)

In 1623 Cornelius Mey of Hoorn, Holland built a trading post he named Casimir. In 1638, Swedes, Finns, Dutch, and Walloons settled along the Delaware River. The Queen of Sweden claimed the territory and named it New Sweden. Peter Ridder, a Dutchman working for the Swedes, negotiated with the Indians for the entire side of the Delaware River from Raccoon Creek to Cape May.

In 1646 Governor Stuyvesant sent 320 troops from New Amsterdam to in an attempt to re-establish Dutch control of the area and built Fort Nassau on the east bank of the river, which he later relocated to the west bank to take better advantage of trade with the Indians who lived inland to the west. He called the new fort, "Fort Casimir". Alexander Boyer, a freeman, also called Sander Boyer, arrived with the troops and served as the Dutch quartermaster at Fort Nassau (Gloucester, NJ) from 1646 until the capture of Fort Casimir (New Castle, Delaware).

On Trinity Sunday, 21 May 1654, the Swedes conquered Fort Casimir and renamed it Fort Trinity. They also acquired a new group of settlers, predominately Dutch, but also including a number of Swedish families. In May 1654, Governor Rising reported that Alexander/Sander Boyer was considered a "malicious and hateful man," but since he had a Swedish wife, he was allowed to stay at Fort Trinity. On June 9th, 1654, Sander Boyer signed a Swedish loyalty oath on Tinicum Island. He made purchases from the company store from 6 July 1654, to 10 November 1654, and sold his tobacco crop to the store on 18 May 1655. In 1655, the Dutch reclaimed the area from the Swedes. Sander Boyer returned to Manhattan where his two sons, Samuel and Peter, were baptized on 1 December 1655. However, by the end of that month he had returned to Fort Casimir, where he remained. Governor Stuyvesant granted him a lot near the fort in 1656. He was still living 18 February 1661, when he sought restitution of land sold to Jacob Alrichs, deceased, which had not been paid for. Boyer was survived by one known son, Jan (John) Boyer, and one known daughter, Joseyn.

Harold Douglas Ford #305

Example of Finnish log house built between 1638 and 1643

References:

Craig, Dr. Peter Stebbins, "New Sweden Settlers, 1638-1664", *The Swedish American Genealogist*, 1998.

JOHN BROCKETT (bef. 1620 – 1689/90)

John Brockett was born in England probably before 1620. He was educated and likely to have been of yeoman stock. He sailed from London on the *Hector*, arriving at Boston on 26 June 1637. The following spring, he and others settled in Quinnipiac in Connecticut and renamed it New Haven by 1640. John most likely married in New Haven ca. 1642/3 though the name of his wife is unknown. According to his Will, John had the following children: John, Silence, Samuel, Jabez, Benjamin, and Mary.

John Brockett was prominent in the public affairs of New Haven, especially in the capacity of surveyor. He was frequently employed in laying out lands about the town. He was probably induced to accompany his neighbors to the new town of Elizabethtown New Jersey in order to aid them in laying out their lands. After several of the planters had urged the Governor, Philip Carteret, to have the exact bounds of their several possessions defined, the Governor, on 19 December, 1667 deputized Brockett *to lay out, survey, and bound the said bounds of Elizabeth Towne the planting fields [sic] towne lotts and to lay out every particular man's proportion according to his allotments and the directions of the Governor; for the avoiding of all controversies and disputes hereafter concerning the same, having had certain notice of the good experience, knowledge, skill, and faithfulness of John Brockett in the surveying and laying out of land.* These surveys were superseded by later surveys and have not been preserved.

When the First General Assembly of New Jersey convened in Elizabethtown and was constituted on 26 May 1668, the town chose John Brockett as one of the two men to represent it in the House of Burgesses.

For his services, the town of Elizabethtown made an allotment of land to him. In 1670 the Connecticut General Assembly incorporated the village of Wallingford. That same year Brockett sold his land in Elizabeth in order to relocate to the new Connecticut Farms village to help manage the affairs of the settlement. Brockett died in Wallingford on 12 March 1689/90. The value of his estate was appraised at £372 1s 10p.

Michael T. Bates #368

References:

Bedini, Silvio A. "The History Corner: The Ubiquitous John Brockett," *Professional Surveyor Magazine*, June 2002.

Hatfield, Edwin Francis. *History of Elizabeth, New Jersey*. New York: 1868

Hornstein, Harold "Scholar debunks 'myth' concerning city's planner," *New Haven Register*, 1 November 1981.

"John of New Haven d. 1690", *The Brokett Archive*, <www.brockett.info>, March 2007.

TIMOTHY BROOKS SR. (1634-1712)

Captain Timothy Brooks Sr. was born at Concord, Massachusetts in 1634. He was the son of Henry Brooks and the first of his two wives, name unknown. Henry Brooks, a farmer and clothier, was born in England about 1592 and migrated to Massachusetts as part of the Great Migration in the early 1630's.

Timothy Brooks Sr., moved with his parents to Woburn, Massachusetts about 1648-1649, where he married Mary Russell on 2 December 1659. About 1670, Timothy and Mary moved to Billerica, Massachusetts with their two sons, Timothy Jr. and John . While living in Billerica and later Swansea, they had an additional eight children- all girls. Swansea had been created under the protection of the court of New Plymouth for the purpose of founding a colony for a band of exiled Welsh Baptists who had come to Massachusetts from Swansea, South Wales in 1649. Here they built one of the first Baptist churches in America followed shortly after by the founding of a second church at Rehoboth. Following Mary's death in 1680, Timothy married Mehitable Mowry, widow of Eldad Kinsley, in Swansea, Massachusetts later that year. Timothy and Mehitable had one son, Josiah, born 26 August 1681.

Timothy Brooks Sr. was one of the respected citizens of Swansea during his ten years of residence. In 1689, shortly before migrating to New Jersey, he was elected a representative and on 20 May 1690, he was commissioned a Captain of Militia.

About 1687, a little colony of Baptists migrated from Swansea, Massachusetts to New Jersey, settling along the river called by Indians "The Cohanso." The Cohansey River Settlement (as named by the white settlers) was near the old town of Greenwich that lies near the mouth of the Cohansey River in present-day Cumberland (then Salem) County, New Jersey. During the summer of 1690, an additional group of Welsh Baptists (mostly Seventh-Day worshippers) from Swansea, Massachusetts came to the Cohansey Settlement. Among these were Timothy Brooks Sr., Timothy Brooks Jr., the Bowens, Barretts, and Swinneys. These families moved further inland and settled at Bowentown, Barrett's Run, and Shiloh.

Timothy Brooks died at Cohansey in Salem County, New Jersey in 1712. His will was proved on 7 October 1712 and mentions his wife Mehitable, sons Timothy Jr. and Josiah, and daughters (unnamed).

408 Col. Steven C. Guy, USA (Ret.)

References:

Brooks, Robert Peacock. *Timothy Brooks of Massachusetts and His Descendants*, Pompton Lakes, NJ, pp. 11-17, 20,. 1927.

Nelson, William. Documents Relating to the Colonial History of New Jersey, Vol. 23, Calendar of New Jersey Wills, pp. 62-63, 1901.

Snow, Nora E. "The Snow-Estes Family Ancestry," Vol. 2, *The Estes Family, Vol. 2*, NY, pp. 282-285. 1939.

GEORGE BROWN (16xx -1717/8)

George Brown was born in Scotland, son of Rev. Richard Brown. George and Annabel Gordon (his future wife) were part of a group of Scottish Presbyterians who were imprisoned in Scotland because of the fight for religious liberty. George Scot, at one time a fellow prisoner, had the idea to transport about one hundred and five of these prisoners to New Jersey after reading a pamphlet published in Edinburgh which contained an attractive description of "The Province of East New Jersey". He received permission for a voyage and the prisoners in the "tollbooth" of Leith, including George and Annabel, left there on 5 September 1685. Annabel left a protest of banishment upon removal from Scotland. Many died on this extremely tragic journey, but the survivors arrived during the late fall of 1685. George settled at Woodbridge, near Perth Amboy.

On 13 February 1693 George Brown married Annabel Gordon Knox. She had first married William Knox and was described as "widow" at the second marriage. George and Annabel raised a family of five sons: James, Thomas, William, Grier and Andrew, and one daughter, Christian.

Described as a "tailor" in early records, Brown perhaps had learned that skill in Scotland. He was quite active at the Presbyterian Church of Woodbridge and purchased a number of lots in and around Woodbridge. When he died intestate c. 1717/8, administration of his estate was granted to his widow, Annabel. He was survived by his six children. George and Annabel were buried in the cemetery of the First Presbyterian Church of Woodbridge.

Elaine Elliott Johnston #174

References:

Brown, Charlotte Cowdrey. *The New Jersey Browns*, Milwaukee, WI, 1931.

New Jersey Archives, First Series, Vol. XXI (Internet Archive).

New Jersey Historical Society Proceedings, 1922, 23. (Internet Archive)

Woodrow, Robert. *Sufferings of the Church of Scotland*, *Vol. II*, Glasgow, 1828-31.

First Settlers, Colonists, and Biographies by Descendants

JAMES BROWN (1656-1715/6)

In summer of 1677, two hundred and thirty English Quakers sailed from London aboard the ship *Kent* and arrived on Chygoes Island on the east bank of the Delaware River, about fifty miles north of Salem. Their settlement was named Burlington. Over the next four years five or six additional ships followed, bringing fourteen hundred or more people to Burlington and other new towns in West Jersey. Many of the immigrants were Friends, as is attested by the freeholder census of 1699 which showed more than a third of landholders in the province of West Jersey were Quakers. The highest percentage of Friends was in Burlington County.

Among the passengers of the Kent were William Clayton and a very young man named James Brown. James, the son of Richard Brown, an English Quaker, was born 27 March, 1656 in Puddington, Northamptonshire, England. Records of the first minutes of Burlington Monthly Meeting state that *the said friends in those upper parts have found it needful according to our practice in the place we came from to settle Monthly Meetings for the well ordering of the Affairs of ye Church it was agreed that accordingly it should be done and accordingly it was done the 15th of ye 5th mo 1678.*

The following year, the marriage confirmation of James Brown and Honour Clayton appeared in the minutes of the Burlington Monthly Meeting: *1679, 6, 8 James Brown of Markors Hook, m Honor Clayton, Burlington, Burlington MM, New Jersey.* Honour, the daughter of William Clayton and Prudence Lanckford, was born 29 January, 1662, in Sussex, England. Before his marriage James had moved to Marcus Hook in Pennsylvania. He was active in the affairs of Marcus Hook, sitting on the first jury under British rule on 13 September, 1681, and, later sitting on a jury with his brother William on 1st July, 1684.

Although James became a resident of Marcus Hook before his marriage, he remained in contact with other Quakers of Burlington, New Jersey. James died 1st February, 1715/6 in Nottingham Township, Chester County, Pennsylvania. In his will he describes himself as a 'Yoman.' Honour died later, probably in Chester Pennsylvania.

Jacqueline Frank Strickland #200

References:

Bellarts, James E. *The Descent of Some of Our Quaker Ancestors, Facts, Fiction, Folklore and Fakelore*, 1986.

Hinshaw, William Wade. *Encyclopedia of American Quaker Genealogy, Vol.II*, pp 200,207, 1931.

Everton, George. *The Handy Book for Genealogists, Seventh Edition*, 1982.

National Society Descendants of Early Quakers Plain Language, Vol.3, 1990

Will of James Brown, 15 January 1715/6, Township of Nottingham province of Pennsylvania, Chester County Archives and Records Service..

OBADIAH BRUEN (1606 – bef. 1690)

Obadiah Bruen was the fourth child of John Bruen and his beautiful wife, Anne Fox. Obadiah was born in Bruen-Stapleford, Cheshire, England, and was baptized on 25 December 1606 in St. Andrews Church, Tarvin, Cheshire, England. Bruen's ancestry can be traced to Charlemagne.

On 7 March 1632, Obadiah married Sarah Seeley in Shrewsbury, Shropshire, England. The couple immigrated about 1640 with their children to Gloucester, Massachusetts (three additional children were born in Gloucester). He was a Freeman in Gloucester in 1642 and made a selectman and representative from 1647 to 1651.

Obadiah moved to Pequot (now New London), Connecticut where in 1653 he was the town recorder. In 1660, and again in 1663-1666, he was appointed Deputy Judge. In 1660, he was empowered by the General Court to administer oaths. His name is frequently mentioned in public records, and he filled many positions of public trust. Obadiah was one of nineteen men to petition King Charles II for the Charter of Connecticut and one of the grantees to that instrument on 20 April 1662. The General Court appointed him one of the commissioners to settle the differences between the settlers and the Niantic Indians.

Obadiah became very dissatisfied with the state of affairs in Connecticut, and with other settlers anxious to leave, signed the "Fundamental Agreements" and moved to Newark, New Jersey with their families in 1666-67. At this point in his life he was approaching "old age" and the move was difficult for him make as well as the challenges of leaving all he had accomplished to start anew in a new wilderness.

Obadiah came with the Milford group, which included John Baldwin Jr. who had married his daughter Hannah. Altogether, 63 men are listed as the first settlers of Newark, New Jersey. While the Hackensack Indians made the agreement to sell the lands to the settlers in May 1666, the bill of sale was not signed until 11 July 1667. On that day, the prepared document, which confirmed and enlarged the May 1666 agreement, was read to the assembled tribal elders and explained to them by a Dutch interpreter. The document was then signed first (their marks) by Wapamuk and others for the Indians, and then by Obadiah Bruen, Michael Tomkins, Samuel Kitchell, John Brown and Robert Denison, in that order, for the town, and "with the consent and advice of Philip Carteret, Governor of the Province of New Jersey." The lengthy bill of sale described the lands and defined the boundaries which included most of the present day Essex County and part of Union County and stated the Indian hunting and fishing rights, the settler's rights, etc. The bill of sale provided that the Indians would receive, in consideration for the sale of the lands: *fifty double-hands of powder, one hundred bars of lead, twenty axes, ten guns, twenty pistols, twenty coats, ten kettles, ten swords, four blankets, four barrels of beer, ten pairs of breeches, fifty knives, twenty hoes, 850 fathom of wampum, two "Ankers" of liquor and three trooper's coats.*

In a town meeting, 20 June 1667, highways were agreed upon and land was divided by lot beginning at Obadiah's home-lot at the river spot. He was also required to maintain the second gate next to the great river. In the division of lands, Obadiah drew lot no. 21, which became his home-lot, located on Market Street. He was considered one of the five most important men in the new Newark settlement. The families were very close knit and descendants remained bonded through marriage in later generations.

378   Michael Edwin Garey

Property allotted to Obadiah Bruen

Drawing prepared for the bicentennial of the Newark by Samuel Conger and William Whitehead for the New Jersey Historical Society.

References:

Richardson, Douglas, *Plantagenet Ancestry*, 2004.

Ricord, Frederick W. *Biographical and Genealogical History of the City of Newark and Essex County, New Jersey*, 1898.

Weis, Frederick Lewis, *Ancestral Roots of Certain American Colonists Who Came to America before 1700*, Genealogical Publishing Co., 1992.

Willis, C.E. and F.C. *A History of the Willis Family*, 1917.

JAN CORNELIS BUYS (1629 -1689/90)

Jan Cornelis Buys (alias Damen) was born about 1629 in Bunick, The Netherlands, based on the fact that on 27 August, 1667 he signed a formal statement indicating that he was 38 years old. He emigrated to the New Netherlands in 1648. He was the son of Cornelis Buys and Hendrickje Jans Damen, the sister of the vast landholder Jan Jansen Damen, a member of "The Twelve" and "The Eight." The extensive farm of Jan Jansen Damen was outside the fort wall of Wall Street and included the property on which The World Trade Center was later built. An interesting article on this subject appeared in The New York Times after the destruction of The World Trade Center in 2001. Jan Jansen Damen, along with two others, was responsible for convincing Director Kieft to commence the devastating Indian War of the 1640's.

Jan Cornelis Buys married as his first wife Eybe Lubberts, daughter of Gysbert Lubbertsen. The date of baptism of their first child was 3 November 1652 in the Brooklyn Dutch Church. Eybe Lubberts died prior to 24 August, 1663, at which time Jan married his second wife Femmetje Jans. On 24 April 1668, Jan Cornelis Buys declared in Flatbush that he had five living children by the deceased Eybe Lubberts over whom Jan Vanderbilt and another were declared guardians. Jan Vanderbilt was the progenitor of the Vanderbilt dynasty in America.

On 4 December, 1654, Jan Cornelis Buys was granted a patent for 25 morgens of land on Bergen Neck in what is today the Greenville section of Jersey City. It was near the property of his father-in- law Gysbert Lubbertsen. Jan Cornelis Buys and his mother-in-law survived the Indian uprising of 1655, in which Guysbert was killed, and departed from the west side of the Hudson, never to return to either Bergen Neck or Bergen, New Jersey.

On 1 May 1656, Jan Cornelis and his mother in law Divertje made a petition to open a tavern east of the Hudson. Jan Cornelis Buys resided in the Wallabout and was a member of the Dutch Church of Brooklyn in 1677. He was on the assessment rolls of Brooklyn for 1675, 1676, and 1683. He obtained a patent in 1662 from Gov. Stuyvesant for 28 morgens of land in Flatbush. His third wife was Willemetie Thyssen.

#370B Craig Hamilton Weaver

References:

Zabriskie, George. *Van Blaricum Faimily in New Jersey*, 1968.

The Dutch Church Records of Haarlem (Internet archive).

Van Benthuyson, A.S. *Van Kleek Genealogy*, 1957.

NYGB Record Vol 138 (Internet archive).

"Records of the Bergen Dutch Church in Holland Society Yearbook 1915."

MATTHEW CAMFIELD (1604 - 1673)

Matthew Camfield, son of Gregorie Camfield and Joan of Harlestone, was baptized 27 February 1604 in St. Andrew's Church, Marlton, Northampton, England. Matthew was in Plymouth, Massachusetts by 1637 and in New Haven, Connecticut by 1639, where he was a member of the church in 1642 and signed the Oath of Fidelity 1 July, 1644. He married Sarah Treat, daughter of Richard and Alice Galliart Treat, before 1643 in Connecticut. Richard and Alice Galliard Treat were also the parents of Governor Robert Treat. A year later Matthew was chosen at the General Court in New Haven to collect corn and/or wampum for Yale College.

Camfield removed to Norwalk in 1652, where in 1666, he joined the first group that moved from Connecticut to establish a new colony at Newark, New Jersey. In Newark, he held many positions. In 1667, he and six others were appointed to adjust land values, and as an agent of Newark on 20 May 1668, he signed the agreement that settled the location and division line between Newark and Elizabethtown. In addition, he was chosen Deputy to assist the Magistrate in the town courts and was on a committee to examine the accounts of the Town Treasurer.

On 24 May 1669, Matthew and four others were chosen townsmen and he was one of three chosen magistrates. On 2 January 1670, he was chosen deputy to assist the magistrates. Matthew's home-lot in Newark was on the northwest corner of Washington and Market Streets. His will of 19 March 1672/3, proved 11 June 1673, is on file in Trenton, New Jersey.

Helen Grey Henning Wright #C4

Property allotted to Samuel Camfield

Drawing prepared for the bicentennial of the Newark by Samuel Conger and William Whitehead for the New Jersey Historical Society.

References:

Harlestone Register, England

Norwalk Records (Internet archive).

New Haven Town Records, New Haven, 1917.

Canfield, Frederick A. *Descendants of Thomas Canfield and Matthew Camfield*, 1897.

Jacobus, Donald Lines. *Families of Ancient New Haven*, Rome, NY, 1923.

New Jersey Historical Society. *Records of the Town of Newark 1666-1836*, 1864.

CALEB CARMAN (1644/5 – 1693)

John and Florence (Fordham) Carman arrived in Boston on the ship *Lyon* in 1632. Their son Caleb was born 1 March 1639. John, with other associates, purchased a large tract of land on Long Island from the Indians, under a patent granted by the Governor Wilhelm Kieft of New Amsterdam, 16 November 1644. The Carman family moved to the purchase which became known as Hempstead.

Sometime prior to 1680, Caleb Carman and his eldest sons were among a group of Long Island whale men who shifted their operations to Delaware Bay and lived at what was known as Town Bank during the whaling season. However, by 1685, the family had permanently relocated to West Jersey, since in that year Caleb Carman was commissioned Justice of the Peace for Cape May County, New Jersey.

The Burlington County, West Jersey Court Records of 4 September 1685, include an indictment against a man for stealing a whale, which by rights the judge ruled belonged to Caleb and John Carman. In 1688, Caleb was indicted taking, breaking up, and disposing of a whale on the shore. The whale was purported to have yielded eleven barrels of oil. Carman argued that under license from the Governor all drift whales that came ashore belonged to him. The jury found Carman not guilty.

On 25 March 1688, the governor of the West Jersey gave a seven-year lease to Caleb Carman for 1200 acres of land along Cold Spring Creek, near Cape May, with the right to purchase any of the land for five pounds per 100 acres for 400 acres and ten pounds per acre for the other 700 acres. At the time of his death in 1693, Caleb Carman owned over 1000 acres in Cape May County. He left his entire estate to his wife Elizabeth (Seaman) Carman, with the mention of his sons John and Caleb, Jr. The sons each purchased 250 acres from the estate, as did son-in-law Jonathan Forman; Elizabeth retained 300 acres. Elizabeth later gave 100 acres to her son Jonathan and bequeathed 100 acres to her son Daniel. Elizabeth died some six years after Caleb, but before September 1699.

Teresa Carroll Medlinsky #313

Evelyn Hunt Ogden (Registrar)

References:

Campin, Clifford, Jr. "Caleb Carman Whaler, Millwright and Miller," *The Cape May County Magazine of History and Genealogy,* June 1945.

Nelson, William, Editor. *Patents and Deeds and other Early Records of New Jersey 1664-1703*, Clearfield Co., 2000.

Elliott, Rev. John. *Roxbury Church Records*, Boston, 1884.

ROBERT CARR (1614 - 1681)

Robert Carr, son of Benjamin and Martha Hardington Carr was born c. 1614, probably in the British Isles; He married, but the name of his wife, the date and place are unknown. Robert Carr "taylor", aged twenty-one, and his brother Caleb Carr, aged eleven, embarked in the ship *Elizabeth and Ann* in 1635 from London for New England. Caleb Carr later became a Governor of Rhode Island. Robert was admitted an inhabitant of Portsmouth on 21 February 1639, and was made a freeman of Newport 16 March 1641. Newport became his permanent home where he engaged in trade and thrived, as is attested to by his will which disposed of considerable property. He embraced the religion of the Society of Friends probably about the time of the visit of George Fox to Rhode Island.

Carr's activities included involvement in the purchase of the island of Conanicut (Jamestown) from the Indians, and he became a non-resident shareholder of the Monmouth Patent in New Jersey, the grant by Governor Nicolls on which the patentees and their associates commenced their settlements immediately at Middletown and Shrewsbury before the fall of 1665. The tract of land which was Robert Carr's he sold to Giles Slocum by deeds dated in 1676.

The will of Robert Carr was dated 20 April 1681, he "being bound on a voyage to New York and New Jersey and aged sixty-seven." Having sold his land in New Jersey he devised only his lands in Rhode Island to his children and provided for "my loving wife." He died probably in Newport, Rhode Island between 20 April and 4 October 1681, the dates of his will. His wife died after 20 April 1681, since she was mentioned in her husband's will.

Frank S. Sutherland-Hall #116

References:

New England Historical and Genealogical Register, Vol. 102. pp. 203-205, 1948.

Austin, John O. *The Genealogical Dictionary of Rhode Island*, Clearfield Co., 1887.

Carr, Arthur A. *The Carr Book*, Madison, Wisconsin, 1947.

Carr, Edison I. "The Carr Family Records," *The New England Historical and Genealogical Register Vol. 8*, 1902.

Ellis, Franklin. *History of Monmouth County, New Jersey*, R.T. Peck and Co., Philadelphia, 1885.

JOHN CHAMBERLIN (1687-1739)

John Chamberlin was born in Shrewsbury, Monmouth County, East Jersey on or about 1687. The Quaker records give his birth date as occurring on the 17th day, but the month and year have been completely worn away with the passage of time. John was the son of Henry Chamberlin and Ann West. He married Rebecca Morris, daughter of Col. Lewis Morris and Elizabeth Almy of Passage Point, Monmouth County, on or about 1711 in Monmouth County.

On 1 April 1709, John Chamberlin, calling himself a *singleman*, son and heir of Henry Chamberlin, late of Shrewsbury, deceased, sold 50 acres of land of which he stated: *The same was conveyed to me in the right of my father Henry Chamberlin, deceased, by a papent bearing the date 1 May 1697*. The 50 acres of land was sold to Thomas Layton for 50 pounds of silver, for "this fifty acres of meadow in Freehold." These 50 acres of land was part of the Passaquenecqua Lands that had been jointly purchased by his father and his uncle William Chamberlin. From 1733 to 1737, he paid interest upon a mortgage on the remaining portion of this land, which was bounded east by the sea and west by the land of Henry Chamberlin, his cousin and son of his uncle William Chamberlin.

John Chamberlin was a member of the Grand Jury, 1711-1720 and 1735; Constable in 1716; and Surveyor of Highways in 1729. On 14 September 1714, he was mortgager to John Bowne, merchant. On 28 May 1717, his nephew Henry, petitioned the court to appoint him as his guardian, and on 8 July 1717, letters of guardianship were issued to him.

The records of Christ's Church at Shrewsbury gives 2 Sep 1739 as John Chamberlin's date of death. He was interned near his house at Deal. On 27 Nov 1739, letters of administration were granted to his widow Rebecca; her brother John Morris was appointed her bondsman. On 21 May 1743, Rebecca, together with their son John and his wife Hannah, sold 360 acres of land to Henry Green. This land was described as being located from Whales Pond northward to a line above the site of the famous hotel known as Howlands, and from the sea to Deal and Long Branch Turnpike. Of this tract, three square rods were reserved for the Chamberlin burial plot.

Rebecca Chamberlin was listed in an account, dated 12 June 1751, in the settlement of the estate of George Williams of Shrewsbury. In the same list are named Louis Chamberlin, her son, and William Chamberlin (her nephew), along with many other names.

Harold Douglas Ford #305

References:

Stillwell, John D. *Historical and Genealogical Miscellany Early Settlers of New Jersey and Their Descendants*, New York, 1906.

Nelson, William, Editor. *Patents and Deeds and Other Early Records of New Jersey 1664-1703*, Clearfield Co., 1899.

Christ's Church Records at Shrewsbury (Internet archive).

RICHARD CLARK (c. 1613 - 1697)

Richard Clark was born in England c. 1613 where he later married his wife Elizabeth. In England, Richard Clark was at Southampton, Long Island, New York, in 1650 where he served in the Indian War of 1657. In 1661, he resided in Southold, Long Island where by 1667, he was a whale striker, boat carpenter, ship builder, and planter. On 22 March 1741 his eldest son, Richard Jr., stated in Elizabethtown that he was *aged about four score years (80) ... that he was brought to Elizabeth Town by his father, named Richard Clarke, when he was between sixteen and seventeen years of age.* This statement placed the Clark family in the Town by 1677.

When James Hinds purchased some upland on 1 July 1677, he named Clark's land as a boundary, as also did Jonas Wood in 1679. Richard had purchased land also from Caleb Carwithey at Luke Watson's Point in 1678; it was named as a boundary in a deed of William Oliver of Elizabethtown to John Decent on 12 February 1683/4.

When the lists of Elizabethtown Associates were re-entered in the new Town Book by order of the 1699 Town Meeting, Richard Clark was listed among them and again in the Town Book of 7 June 1735. Richard Clark, Sr., deceased, was recorded as an Associate, and thus had been entitled to a second lot right.

Richard died between 1 April 1687, the date he made his will, and 9 April when the inventory of his estate was taken in Elizabethtown, New Jersey. Elizabeth died intestate in 1724 in Elizabethtown, with administration granted to the eldest son, Richard, on 16 February 1724/5.

Marjorie Barber Schuster #C29

Richard Clark was buried in the First Presbyterian Church cemetary in Elizabeth

References:

Hatfield, Rev. Edwin. *The History of Elizabeth, New Jersey*, New York, 1868.

New Jersey Archives, Documents Relating to the Colonial History of the State of New Jersey, Vol. XXI, First Series (Internet archive).

WILLIAM CLAYTON (1632 - 1689)

William Clayton was baptized 9 December, 1632 at Boxgrove Parish, Sussex, England. His parents married thirteen months earlier on 30 October, 1631. William's four known siblings by his mother, Joan Smith Clayton (buried 27 April, 1644) were also baptized at Boxgrove Parish.

After the English Civil War of 1642-1649, the Clayton family became religious dissenters as early converts to the Quaker faith, sometime around 1655 becoming members of the Lewes and Chichester Monthly Meeting. William came to New Jersey with other Quakers aboard the *Kent*, arriving first in New York on 4 August, 1677, and later setting sail for the mouth of the Delaware River.

The colonists established a settlement on the east bank of the river in what became New Beverly, Bridlington, and finally Burlington, New Jersey. William Clayton's family did not travel with him on the *Kent*, but arrived later. The record of the Burlington Monthly Meeting states *The certificate of the first recorded marriage in the eight month, 6, 1678 was signed by Wm. Clayton, Sr., Wm. Clayton, Jun and Prudence Clayton.*

William Clayton, Sr. was selected by William Markham, Proprietor of the Colony of West Jersey, to serve on a Council of nine men dedicated to the preparation of the 'Holy Experiment of Government.' Acting as Colony Legislature, the Court, held at Burlington, had jurisdiction over legal matters, functioning as the court of appeals for Salem and other towns in West Jersey after 1683.

William Clayton continued his career in the state of Pennsylvania after purchasing land near Marcus Hook, Pennsylvania, from Hans Oelsons in March 1678/9, and moved there from Burlington. He was therefore available when the Council seated in Chester (Upland) County, Pennsylvania began working on a Charter in the fall of 1681.

On 11 September, 1681 William Clayton presided over the first court under the proprietary government at Upland, Chester County, Pennsylvania. He became one of the first two Judges for the City of Philadelphia and was a member of William Penn's council from 1683-85. In 1684 and 1685 he served as Acting Governor of Pennsylvania before his death in 1689 at Chichester, Chester County, Pennsylvania.

Jacqueline Frank Strickland #200

References:

Bellarts, James E. *The Descent of Some of Our Quaker Ancestors*, p 53, 1984.

Everton, George B. *The Handy Book for Genealogists, Seventh Edition*, 1982.

Hinshaw, William Wade. *Encyclopedia of American Quaker Genealogy, Vol.II*, VA, 1950.

The New York Genealogical and Biographical Records, Vol. LV, 1924 (Internet archive).

ROBERT CLEMENTS, JR (c 1634-c 1714)

Robert Clements, Jr. was born in England about 1634, and came with his parents to Haverhill, Massachusetts in 1642. Here he married Elizabeth Fawne on 8 Dec 1652. Elizabeth, probably born in New England, was the daughter of John and Elizabeth Fawne, who came to New England before 13 January 1637.

He was the first cooper in Haverhill. In 1658 he went back to Ireland at the desire of his brother, John, who wished him to come over with his family to act as a guide to John's wife and daughters. Probate papers of John's estate tell of the voyage, the capture by the Spaniards, the going to Ireland and the subsequent return to New England. The settling of John's estate also shows the strong affection and sense of justice among the brothers and sisters, for they all wished John's estate to be given to Robert to recompense him for his losses caused by compliance with John's request. After his return to New England, Robert continued to live at Haverhill for the rest of his long life.

While there are no records of Robert Clements, Jr. living in New Jersey, deeds document that he purchased 93 acres in Woodbridge, on April 5, 1679, which he conveyed to his son Jonathan. In a deed dated 13 August 1694, Jonathan Clement and wife Elizabeth of Elizabethtown, New Jersey, sold a 12-acre house lot and other property in Woodbridge.

Robert Clements probably died in Haverhill, Massachusetts, in 1714. He left no will, having given his property to his children during his lifetime, and no administration is of record. His widow died in Haverhill 27 May 1715.

Robert Vivian #313

References:

Holman, Mary, Editor. *Ancestors and Descendants of Robert Clements of Leicestershire and Warwickshire, England, First Settler of Haverhill, Massachusetts, Volume I*, 1927.

Nelson, William, Editor. *Patents and Deeds and Other Early Records of New Jersey 1664-1703*, Clearfield Co., 1899.

SAMUEL CLIFT (abt. 1610-1683)

Samuel Clift, a clothier, was born about 1625. His first wife and mother of his seven children was Elizabeth Shortwood of the hamlet of Horsely, England. She was buried 11 September 1666. The Quaker Nailsworth England Meeting recorded a second marriage of Samuel to Joan Batterby of Hampton Roade on 4 February 1667.

English laws against Quakers were suspended in 1672, but they continued to endure many indignities and insults. In 1673, Lord John Carteret sold West Jersey to William Penn and eleven other Quakers. Penn and other Quaker leaders urged people of their faith to sail to America where they could settle and find religious freedom. Among those who answered the call was Samuel, his second wife Joane Betterby, two of his children, Joseph and Hannah, and his son-in-law Joseph English Jr. They sailed from England aboard the *Kent* in the summer of 1677, arriving in New Castle, Delaware, 16 August 1677. A large contingent of these passengers proceeded up the Delaware to the site of Burlington.

The Commissioners for William Penn and the rest of the Proprietors employed Richard Nobel to survey the spot of the settlement of Burlington and to divide the property among the group known as the "London Proprietors." Samuel Clift, his wife, and son accompanied one of the Proprietors to the site and were present when the ten land allotments were drawn in 1677. He presented the certificate from Nailsworth to the new Society of Friends at Burlington 16 August 1677.

Samuel Clift obtained from Sir Edmond Andros, Provincial Governor of New York, a grant of 262 acres for a plantation across the river from Burlington, the site of Bristol in Pennsylvania. Samuel established the ferry service between the Pennsylvania and New Jersey settlements and built an inn in Bristol to service the ferry business. In 1682, Samuel deeded his land and ferry to his son-in-law Joseph English Jr. Samuel died the following year in April 1683.

383 Margaret Louise Drody Thompson

References:

DeCou, George. *Burlington: a Provincial Capital, Historical Sketches*, Library Company, Burlington, NJ, 1973.

English, H. M. *A Genealogy of the English Family*, 1970

THOMAS CLIFTON (abt. 1606-1681)

Thomas Clifton was the son of Richard Clifton or Clyfton of Nottinghamshire, England. He appears to have been a relation of the Separatist minister of Scooby, the Rev. Richard Clifton. Thomas first married Ann Stokes at Granby, Nottingham, England.

The exact dates of his arrival in Massachusetts or when he became a widower are not known. The earliest mention of Thomas Clifton in the Massachusetts Bay Colony records was an entry on 18 January 1640, as follows: *Mr. James Parker is allowed to marry Thomas Clifton and Marie Butterworth (the widow of Henry Butterworth) within a month*. He was made a freeman of the Massachusetts Bay Colony, 2 June 1641. Rev. Parker sold Thomas a house and lands in Weymouth 26 November 1644; he also was granted eight additional acres.

Thomas Clifton was an original settler of Rehoboth, Massachusetts, where he became a Quaker at a town meeting held on 30 June 1644. Thomas drew lot 48, and in subsequent years added to his holdings by drawing two more lots. He and his daughter Hope were severely persecuted for their faith. The family moved to Rhode Island, where entries in the records of the Newport Friends meeting refer to the Clifton family and their daughters, Hope, Mary and Patience. Thomas apparently moved again, this time to the Plymouth Colony; where he was made freeman on 7 June 1648. He was a deputy in the Rhode Island colonial assembly in 1675.

In 1664, with the exodus of the Dutch, several men petitioned the new English Governor, for permission to negotiate with the Indians for lands surrounding the Navesink, west of the Hudson River. The Sachem Popomora agreed to terms and he and his brother went to New York to acknowledge the deed before Governor Nichols, 7 April 1665. Two other deeds followed and were recorded and on 8 April 1665. The Monmouth Patent required that the patentees and their associates, their heirs or assigns must within 3 years, settle there one hundred families at the least.

While living in Rhode Island Thomas bought a share of land in Monmouth, New Jersey. He was among a number of purchasers "who had been victims of persecution for their religious faith; some had felt the cruel lash, some had been imprisoned and others had been compelled to pay heavy fines, others had had near relations suffer thus. Among those who had suffered were Thomas Clifton and daughter Hope… (Edward Salter, 1890:11)."

On 14 April 1675, Clifton deeded his land in Shrewsbury, Monmouth, New Jersey to John Hance. It is not clear whether Thomas Clifton ever occupied his New Jersey land; however, on 9 July 1681 he was again at Newport, RI, where he drowned.

#366 David Lawrence Grinnell

References:

Arnold, James. *Vital Records of Rhode Island 1636-1850, v.* 4: VII: 64 (Internet archive).

Bliss, Leonard and George Tilton. *A History of Rehoboth, Massachusetts: It's History for 275 Years*, 1918

Torrey, Clarence. *New England Marriages Prior to 1700*, (Boston, NEHGS 2011) v:I:180, Baltimore, MD, USA: Genealogical Publishing Co., 2004.

FRANCIS COLLINS (1635 – 1720)

Francis Collins, a Quaker, son of Edward and Mary (-) Collins, was born 6 January 1635 in Wolvercote, Oxfordshire, England. His first wife was named Sarah Mayham, daughter of Richard and Margaret (Lane) Mayham of Ratcliffe. They were married on 2, January, 1663, at a Monthly Meeting. Sarah died at the family home, "Mountwell" in Haddonfield, West Jersey. Francis married his second wife Mary (Budd) Gosling on 4, February, 1687 at a Burlington Monthly Meeting. She was born 1665, daughter of Rev. Thomas Budd and Joanna (Knight) Budd, and was the widow of Dr. John Gosling, physician of Burlington. Francis Collins died just after his 85th birthday, his will of 20 April 1720 proved 6 February 1721.

Francis Collins spent his early youth in the parish of Wolvercote, where his father apprenticed him to a bricklayer. Francis later moved to Ratcliffecross where he first married. After suffering religious intolerance in England, he and his family moved to New Jersey. They arrived at Burlington, probably on the second voyage of the *Shield*. In 1682 he surveyed 500 acres in Newton Township, Gloucester County and 450 acres upon which the town of Haddonfield now stands. He built his home, named it "Mountwell", and joined the Friends' Newton Monthly Meeting.

Collins' career of public service began in 1682 with his appointment as a Justice of the County. He was named to Gov. Samuel Jennings' Council and returned as a Member of the Legislative Assembly representing the interest of Gloucester. At this session he was appointed one of the Commissioners for Dividing and Regulating Land and was one of the Committee to Adjust Difficulties between Proprietors and Edward Byllyng. At the 1684 Legislative Assembly he was made one of the Judges of the Several Courts of New Jersey, continuing as Justice until 1689. He was a signer of the *Concessions and Agreements* and served for many years as a member of the West Jersey Assembly.

His reputation as a builder and bricklayer well known, in 1682 Francis was engaged as a contractor of the First Meeting House in Burlington. He received Pounds 200 and 1,000 acres, part located "above the falls" (Trenton), as a gratuity from the Legislature for building a Market House and Court House at Burlington.

Mirabah L. LeJambre Combs #C24, Lucien A. LeJambre #C25, Susan E. LeJambre #C55

References:

Decou, George. *Moorestown and Her Neighbors*, 1973.

Clement, John. *First Emigrant Settlers in Newton Township*, Camden, NJ, 1877.

Hinshaw, William Wade. *Encyclopedia of American Quaker Genealogy, Vol.II*, VA, 1950.

New Jersey Archives, Abstract of Wills 1670-1720, Vol. 1, 23:103 (Internet archive).

New Jersey Historical Society, Proceedings Vol. 67

Prowell, George R. *The History of Camden County, New Jersey*, 1886 (Internet archive).

Woodward, Evan Morrison. History of Burlington County, New Jersey, 1883 (Internet archive).

JOHN CONGER (c 1645-1712)

The Conger (Belconger/ Koniger) family came from Alsace, a French province at the time of the massacre of St. Bartholomew in 1572, to Holland. The family then moved to England, where the name became anglicized into Conger. Later the family then emigrated to America.

John Conger participated in the first distribution of land at Woodbridge, in East Jersey. His patent to 170 acres of land was dated 18 November 1669. The land had access to the Rahway River, which at the time was navigable to any vessel then in use. In Woodbridge he held the office of constable and he was one of the commissioners appointed by the government to prosecute thieves who were cutting timber from the common ground.

John Conger's first wife Mary Kelly, by whom he had eight children, died about 1685. He then married Sarah Cawood, who was born about 1665 in Woodbridge, the daughter of Thomas Cawood and Rebecca Potter. John Conger and his second wife joined the Presbyterian Church at Woodbridge 12 May 1709. His will was dated 11 Jan.1710 and was probated 7 Oct.1712.

Annie Looper Alien #307

References:

Leonard, Maxine Crowell. *The Conger Family of America*, 1972

New Jersey Archives Series Calendar of Wills (Internet archive).

Nelson, William. *The Church Records of the Presbyterian Church of Woodbridge*, 1904.

The Essex Institute of Salem Massachusetts. *Vital Records of Newbury Massachusetts to the end of 1849, Salem*, 1911.

Footnote to History

Woodbridge was settled in the autumn of 1666 and was granted a charter on June 1, 1669 by King Charles of England. It is said that it was named in honor of the Reverend John Woodbridge of Newbury, Massachusetts.

HENRY COOK (c. 1671-1723)

Henry Cook was one of two children of Anthony and Jane (Crawford) Cook. His exact date and place of birth are not known, but he was baptized on 12 April 1671 in the Reformed Dutch Church in New York City. His father died in 1671 and his mother was remarried on 7 December 1672 in Kingston, NY, to William Fisher. Henry married Wyntje (Winifred) Franse Klauw sometime prior to 1695. Baptismal records for two of their children appear in the records of the Dutch Church in Kingston, NY, for the years 1695 and 1696.

The first record of Henry Cook in New Jersey is a deed dated 17 February 1701/2 for his purchase of 100 acres located in the Province of West Jersey from Francis Collins of the Town and County of Burlington, NJ.

Henry served on the grand jury at the Quarter Session Court of Burlington County in 1704, 1706, and 1709, and was chosen Constable for Mansfield Township in 1708. The Cook family settled in Maidenhead Township in the portion of Burlington County which became Hunterdon County in 1714. He was selected as surveyor of highways for Maidenhead in 1721.

Henry's will is dated 15 November 1723 and was proved 20 January 1724, indicating that he died shortly after the will was written. His will names wife Winifred, one adult and one minor son, three married daughters and three unmarried daughters. Winifred and his adult son, William, were appointed as executors and both of them signed only with a mark (X). The inventory of his estate was valued at £172 6s 6p.

#385 Lynn D. Constan

References:

Cook, Lewis D. "Anthony Cook of Ulster County, New York, and His Descendants in Mercer County, New Jersey," *The American Genealogist, Vol 47, No 4*, pp. 194-198, October 1971.

Footnote to History

Mansfield Township, established in 1688, was incorporated in 1798. The early pioneers were mostly Friends who had been land-owners and men of means and standing in England. They cleared the land for roads and houses and established businesses. Mansfield is in the northeast part of Burlington County and is bounded by Bordentown Township, Chesterfield Township, Springfield Township and Florence Township.

CORNELIS WILLEMSE COUWENHOVEN (1672-1736)

Cornelius Couwenhoven was born at Flatlands Brooklyn, Long Island, New York in 1672. He purchased 500 acres in Middletown, New Jersey in 1695. He was married to Margaretta Schenck. Cornelis died May 16, 1736 and was buried on his farm in Middletown. His will divided his many land purchases between his sons William and Rulif with bequests also made to his wife and eleven daughters.

Charlotte Van Horne Squarcy #357

Evelyn Hunt Ogden (Registrar)

References:

Bergen, Teunis G. Register in Alphabetical Order of Early Settlers of Kings County, Long Island, N.Y., 1881.

Nelson, William, Editor. *Documents Relating to the Colonial History of the State of New Jersey, Vol XXI*, 1899.

Riker, David M. *Genealogical and Biographical Directory to Persons in New Netherlands from 1613 to 1674, Vol. III.*, 1999.

Map of Raritan Bay

Footnote to History

Three villages, Shrewsbury, Portland Point and Middletown, were settled by English families from western Long Island and New England. The land was part of the grant signed by Governor Nichols in 1665, known as the Monmouth Patent.

THOMAS COX (1620 - 1681)

Thomas Cox was born c. 1620 in Herefordshire, England and died in 1681 in Middletown, New Jersey. He married Elizabeth Blashford at Mespath Kills (now Newtown) on 17 April 1665. She died after 1691 in Middletown, New Jersey.

Thomas was a first settler of Mespath Kills, Long Island, New York, in 1665. He took up land in Middletown, New Jersey on 30 December 1667 from the Indians to whom he paid in full for portions guaranteed him under the Nicolls Patent. He was a Monmouth Patentee and assigned lot #8 in Middletown and lot #21 in the Poplar Field, 31 December 1667.

Tho. Cocks his marke is the top of the right eare cutt off and a swallow taile and a hole in the left eare, recorded on 4 January 1668. With three others he was chosen that same year to make prudential laws for Middletown and in the next year he was appointed rate maker of the town.

Within a few years after his settlement at Middletown, Thomas had become an extensive land owner and a recognized man of affairs in Middletown, Monmouth County, serving as a juryman and overseer of fences and constable. The first record of his mark on documents is 8 November 1673.

Chosen deputy to meet the Governor and Council at Woodbridge on 1 January 1676, he was chosen a town overseer, and two years later was named to see that highways were mended and cleared. He received tobacco for surveying of "Towne bounds."

A man who stood well in the estimation of the people with whom he had cast his lot, Cox was believed to have taken an active part in all the movements of his day. He was a Baptist and was the father of four sons and probably two daughters.

Helen L. Schanck #C75

References:

Cox, Henry Miller. *The Cox Family in America*, 1912 (Internet archive)

Clemens, William Montgomery. *Marriage Records Before 1699, Pomton Lakes, 1926* (Internet archive).

Horner, William S. *This Old Monmouth of Ours*, Clearfield, 2009.

Monnette, Orra Eugene. *First Settlers of Ye Plantations of Piscataway and Woodbridge Olde East Jersey, 1664-1714*. Leroy Carman press, CA, 1930.

Stillwell, John D. *Historical and Genealogical Miscellany Early Settlers of New Jersey and Their Descendants*, New York, 1906.

Sitherwood, Francis G. *Throckmorton Family History, 1930*.

Taylor, Clarissa and Frank Bass. *Taylor Snow Genealogy*, Freeport, Illinois, 1935.

DR. DANIEL COXE (1640-1730)

Dr. Daniel Coxe was an eminent physician, writer on chemistry and medicine, staunch Church of England man and physician to Charles II and later to Queen Anne. Although he never came to the New World he acquired some 600,000 acres of the Propriety of West Jersey, together with the right to govern. He appointed Edward Hunloke his Deputy Governor of the largely Quaker West Jersey.

Dr. Coxe's eldest son, the third Daniel Coxe, was baptized in London in 1673. He traveled to America in 1702, probably with Lord Cornbury, who was appointed Daniel Commander of the forces of West Jersey. Colonel Daniel did not stay long in West Jersey. By 1704 he was back in London waging a defense against some of the New Jersey Proprietors.

In 1706, notwithstanding the hostility of the Quakers, Lord Cornbury appointed Colonel Coxe an associate Judge of the Supreme Court of the Province of West Jersey. Overlooking his contempt for Quakers, in 1707, Daniel married Sarah Eckley, the daughter of John Eckley, a Philadelphia Quaker. The couple were married by Lord Cornbury's chaplain, and two days later the bride was baptized by the same chaplain. Most of Daniel III's life in New Jersey was spent in Burlington; however, in his later years he lived at Trenton, where he died 25 April 1739.

Dr. Evelyn Ogden from documents submitted by #391 Barbara Ann McCormick Petrov

1719 Trent House, Trenton NJ. Source; Wikimedia

References:

New Jersey Historical Society. Collections of the New Jersey Historical Society, Vol. IX, 1916

JASPER CRANE (1605 - 1681)

Jasper Crane, born c. 1605 probably in Spoxton, Somersetshire, England, came with his wife Alice (-) to New England. He died in Newark, New Jersey, his will dated there 19 October 1681. His wife Alice was not mentioned in the will therefore presumed to have died earlier.

Jasper Crane was in the New Haven colony by 1642 when his son Delivered Crane was born there 12 July. He was one of many settlers at New Haven who attempted the settlement of lands on the Delaware and was repulsed by the Dutch, Swedes and Finns. Returning to Connecticut, his name is found heading the list of those in Branford who on 30 October 1666 signed the *Concessions and Agreements* to establish a Congregational Church-controlled settlement in Newark, New Jersey. He was about 65 years of age at this time, a close friend of Robert Treat and the others undertaking the new settlement in New Jersey.

Experienced as a merchant, surveyor, magistrate, selectman, he became the first President of the Newark Town Court and the first Deputy to the General Assembly of New Jersey at Elizabethtown.

In the 1667 drawing of home lots, Jasper and his sons Delivered and John Crane drew lots 49, 62 and 40. Jasper served the new colony at Newark in many capacities from 1666 until 1678. His will was dated 1 October 1678, the inventory of his estate was made on 28 October 1681, and letters of administration were granted on the estate 15 November 1681 to his son John and Thomas Huntington, a son-in-law.

Robert D. McPherson #C68

Property allotted to Jasper Crane, John Crane, Delivered Crane

Drawing prepared for the bicentennial of the Newark by Samuel Conger and William Whitehead for the New Jersey Historical Society.

References:

Atwater, Edward E. *History of the Colony of New Haven*, to its Absorption into Connecticut, 1902 (Internet archive).

Crane, Ellery Bicknell. *History of the Crane Family*, 1895 (Internet archive).

New Jersey Archives, Calendar of New Jersey Records 1664-1703, Vol. XXI (Internet archive).

The New Jersey Historical Society. *Records of the Town of Newark 1666-1836*, Newark, N.J. Published by the Society, 1864, reprint 1966.

JAMES DAVIS (1675 – 1769)

James Davis was born in Pilesgrove, New Jersey in 1675. His parents were Joris Christoffelse Davidse, born in 1653 in Beverwyck, NY, and Janetje Johanna Lopers, born about 1650 in Marbletown, NY. James married on 30 April 1702, Elizabeth Sandford who was born in North Carolina. He died after 23 May 1769, in Elizabethtown.

Dr. Evelyn Ogden summarized from documents submitted by

Mary Jamia Jasper Case Jacobsen # 377B

1762 Seven Stars Tavern; source: Wikipedia

References:

DeVos, Andres & Christopher Kit Davis. *My Families of Early Ulster County, NY*, 2008.

DAVID DEMAREST (1620 – 1693)

David Demarest, a Huguenot, was born about 1620 in Beauchamps, Picardy, France. David first shows up in the history when he married Marie Sohier on 24 July 1643 in the Walloon Church, Middleburg, Island of Walcheren, Zeeland.

After his marriage and start of a family, his life is divided into four eras of about a decade each; Middleburg 1643-1651; Mannheim, Germany 1651-1663; Staten Island and New Harlem, New Amsterdam/New York City 1663-1678; and finally, the "French Patent" along the Hackensack River in 1678 until his death in 1693.

The Demarest family came to the New World on the Bonte Koe (Spotted Cow). The Emigrant's Account book has David de Marie, wife and four children. Not much is known about his activities on Staten Island; in New Harlem he was a lot owner, magistrate and constable.

David and his surviving sons, Jean, Samuel and David and their families, moved to the Hackensack area in May 1678. He built a house and a mill near what is now the Old Bridge. The land had been purchased from the Tappan Indians for wampum and useful articles; the deed dated June 8, 1677. That and later purchases may have amounted to 5,000 acres.

Though there is no physical evidence of it now, there was a French Church built there that lasted for several years near the present French Burying Grounds. In his final will, written 26 August 1689, he refers to himself as a Yeoman and Miller. By the time of his death he had seen some twenty-six grandchildren born to his sons.

Lt. Col. James A. Shepherd USMC (Ret) #337

References:

Demarest, Voorhis. *The Demarest Family, Vol. I*, 1964

Koehler, Albert F. *The Huguenots or Early French of New Jersey*, 1995

Major, David C. and John S., *A Huguenot on the Hackensack, David Demarest and His Legacy*, 2007

ROBERT DENNIS (c. 1619 - 1683+)

Robert Dennis was probably born in County Essex, England. He was in Yarmouth, Massachusetts from 1643 to 1669. He married Mary (-), no marriage or death dates known.

There have been many conflicting statements published about Robert Dennis' life in New England, but there are many records to substantiate his activities there. He was a surveyor, farmer, carpenter, jurist and tax collector.

The family moved to New Jersey at the invitation of Governor Carteret. A patent for land in Woodbridge dated December 1667, named him as *Robert Dennis of Yarmouth*, with others.

Dennis was named a "Burgess" to represent Woodbridge in May 1668. In December 1674 he and his wife Mary conveyed land to four of their eight children. His land in Woodbridge was named as a boundary in several deeds, and the published archives of New Jersey contain many references to him and his sons. Robert died after April 1683.

James L. Dennis #C49

References:

Dally, Rev. Joseph W. *Vital Records of Woodbridge, New Jersey*, New Brunswick, 1873.

New Jersey State Archives, First Series, Vol. XXI (Internet archive).

Swift, Charles E. *History of Old Yarmouth*, 1884 (Internet archive).

Footnote to History

Measuring had its own folk origins: a knitted sock foot was gauged by measuring it around the fist of the wearer-to be. For a yard of cloth, the end was held to the point of the nose and pulled to the extent of the arm

DANIEL DOD (1649-1701/1714)

Daniel Dod was born in 1649 in Branford, Connecticut. He married Phebe Brown, daughter of John Brown who named his daughter Phebe Dod in his will dated 1689. It is family tradition that Daniel died from a fall from a load of hay, sometime between 1701 and 1714 in Newark, New Jersey. His wife's death date is unknown.

Although he was still a minor, Daniel appeared on the first Tax List of Newark in 1666. His estate was approved at 150£ with deductions of 100£. In 1668 he applied for, was later granted and paid for a one-and-a-half-acre lot in the Northwest Section, at present Orange and High Streets, in Newark. He was granted various other pieces of land, including acreage in the second and third purchases from the Indians, as they were completed. Eventually he and many of his descendants occupied those lands in what is now Bloomfield, New Jersey.

Daniel returned to Branford in 1671 to sell his father's property and described himself in the deed *as in his 22nd year, the lawful heir of Daniel Dod, deceased.*

In the Town Records of Newark, Dod was mentioned in 1677 and 1680 as being appointed one of the Warners of Town Meetings. He and Edward Ball were appointed in 1678 to run the Northern line of the Town. In 1686/87 he was named to an advisory committee concerning establishment with the Proprietors of the Town Bounds. With the other residents he signed an agreement in 1687/88 concerning support of the minister. He and Nathaniel Ward were assigned in 1701 to set the rate of payment for the minister.

When the third purchase of land from the Indians made it possible, Dod was named to the Committee in 1699 to extend the "Town Bounds" to the South Branch of the Passaic River. After 1701 there are no public records for this Daniel Dod. Later records seem to refer to his son and a nephew, both named Daniel Dod.

Janice Crowell Wheeler #C33

References:

Dodd, Allison & Rev. Joseph F. Folsom. Genealogy and History of the Daniel Dod Family in America 1646-1940,

Folsom, Joseph, Editor. *Bloomfield Old and New*, 1912 (Internet archive)

Pierson, David L. *Narratives of Newark*, Newark, 1917.

The New Jersey Historical Society. *Records of the Town of Newark 1666-1836*, Newark, N.J. Published by the Society, 1864, reprint 1966.

CORNELIS DOREMUS (c 1655-1715)

Cornelis Doremus was born in France, but moved with his family to Holland. On 12 May 1675, in Arnemuyden, Holland, he married Janneke Joris. After living in Middleburg, Holland for many years, the family emigrated to America sometime after the birth of their son Johannes who was baptized in Middleburg in 1684, but before son Thomas's baptism on 11 April 1687 in Bergen, New Jersey.

Cornelis was a planter and in 1708 he purchased an extensive farm of 150 acres at Wesel (now Paterson). In 1711 he purchased an additional, much larger farm of 350 acres on Wesel Mountain, where he settled his son Thomas. Janneke and Cornelis were the parents of nine children, six sons and three daughters. Cornelis died at Wesel c. 1715. There is no record of the date of death of his widow.

Dr. Evelyn Ogden summarized from documents submitted by Robert Giffin # 311

Paterson Great Falls, Passaic River

Reference:

Nelson, William. (Edith Whitcraft Eberhart- Revised, Edited and Supplemented 1990). *The Doremus Family in America 1687-1987*. 1897, Revision 1990.

Footnote to History

In 1660, Peter Stuyvesant, the Dutch Director General of New Netherlands, granted permission to settlers to establish a semi-autonomous colony of Bergen, between the Hackensack and Hudson Rivers.

SAMUEL DOTY (1643-1715)

Samuel Doty, born in 1643, was theof Edward Doty (Dotten, Doughty, Doughten) who came to Massachusettes on the Mayflower and Faith Clarke Doty, born in the Plymouth Colony, Massachusetts. Samuel move to the new settlement of Piscatawy, where he married Jane Harmon on 15 November 1678. He died between 18 September, the date of his will, and 8 November 1715 when the will was proved in Piscataway. His wife Jane survived him.

In July 1675 "Samuel "Doughty" was commissioned Lieutenant of the New Piscataway Company of militia. On 4 July 1681 Lt. Samuel Doty was a member of the Military Commission for New Piscataway. His extensive holdings are named as a boundary in several early Piscataway deeds. He received a patent for 100 acres of land at Sacunck on Bound Brook in 1691, then on 3 October 1693 he received a patent for another 100 acres of unsurveyed land in Middlesex County.

The Doty's had thirteen children, four of whom were baptized in Piscataway, their baptisms recorded in the Piscataway Town Book between 1679 and 1685.

Eva Lomerson Collins#C57

East Jersey Old Town Village, Piscataway, NJ

References:

Doty, Ethan Allen. *Doty-Doten Family in America*, NY, 1897 (Internet archive).

New Jersey Archives, New Jersey Wills, Abstracts, 1670-1730 (Internet archive).

Footnote to History

Piscataway was founded in 1666, on the banks of the Raritan River, part of the land known as the Elizabethtown Colony granted by Governor Nichols.

GAVINE DRUMMOND (1659-1724)

Gavine Drummond, son of Robert Drummond and Isabel Melvine, was born in 1659, Prestonpans, Scotland. A notary public in Edinburgh, and brother of John Drummond, merchant burgess in Edinbugth, Gavine purchased land from his kinsman, John Drummond of Lundine, an East Jersey Proprietor, and later, Earl and Duke of Melfort in Scotland.

Settling on his land in Shrewsbury, East New Jersey in 1684, Gavine married Mary Layton, daughter of William and Violet Layton. They had numerous children. Gavine was appointed Clerk of the Court of Sessions for Middlesex County in 1701. Like other hopeful settlers, he cultivated his land, built a thriving sawmill, and speculated in other properties.

Gavine died intestate in 1724. His land passed to his second son, Robert (Gavine junior, the eldest son, died intestate and without issue in 1748). Upon Robert's death the land was inherited by his son, Gavine, third of the name. Portions of the original tract of land remained within the family's possession until the early twentieth century.

#335 John Altobello

References:

New Jersey Archives, Liber A, p. 305 (Internet archive).

New Jersey Archives, Liber F-3, p, 355 (Internet archive).

New Jersey Archives, Liber E, p. 268 (Internet archive).

The National records of Scotland. "Old Parish Records dist. 718 / Vol. 10, Prestonpans births and marriages of Scotland (Internet archive).

SARAH DUBOIS (1664-1726)

Let's go back almost 900 years to the summer of 1137, to a grand castle outside of Bordeaux. She's beautiful- tall-elegant, with reddish blonde hair and beautiful blue eyes. She is the most sought after heiress in all of Christendom. She is head strong, fifteen years old, ambitious, high-spirited, well-traveled and literate. She is Duchess Eleanor of Aquitaine and Countess of Poitou. She marries Louis VII of France and Henry II of England. The mother of two kings - Richard the Lion Hearted and King John of Magna Charta fame - Eleanor counts Charlemagne and kings of Italy as her earlier grandparents. She is the many great grandmother of Sarah DuBois, baptized 14 September 1664, at New Paltz, New York.

Sarah DuBois's father Louis DuBois and his wife Catherine Blanchan arrived from England at Wiltwyck (Kingston), New York on the ship *St. Jean Baptist* on 6 August 1661. Her Father was known as Louis the Walloon, a wealthy man who founded New Paltz. Sarah grew up as part of the Huguenot society in America, French Protestants who immigrated to America.

Sarah DuBois married 12 December 1682, Joosten Jansen Van Meter (John), born ca. 1656. Their son John Jansen Van Meter settled in Somerset County New Jersey, where he married Sarah Bodine. She was also from a French Huguenot family, which had settled along the Raritan, in Somerset County, New Jersey. Sarah Bodine was born in 1687 and died ca. 1709 in Somerset.

Meanwhile, Sarah DuBois was now a widow living in Salem County in the Western Division of New Jersey. She purchased with John VanMeter, Issac VanMeter, and Jacob DuBois 3,000 acres of land on the branch of Prince Maurices River at the head of the main branch of the Cohansey, in the county of Salem (now Cumberland) from Daniel Coxe for 750£. Sarah DuBois died in 1726 in Salem County, New Jersey.

377 Mary Jamia Jasper Case Jacobsen, PhD, PsyD.

References:

DuBois Family Association Newsletter, 2002.

Heidgerd, William. *The American Descendants of Chertien DuBois of Wicres, France*. Part One 1968.

Weir, Alison. *Eleanor of Acquitaine*, 1999.

JONATHAN DUNHAM (1639/40 – 1702)

Jonathan Dunham was born 4 November 1639/40 in Salisbury, Massachusetts. He married in 1661 Mary Bloomfield, daughter of Thomas and Mary Bloomfield of Newbury, Massachusetts. He came to Woodbridge, New Jersey, in 1665 with his wife's family, where he died about 1702/3. His wife's date of death is unknown.

Under a contract with the Town of Woodbridge, dated 8 June 1670, he received 213 acres of land for erecting the first gristmill in this part of the country for the benefit of the inhabitants of the town. On 18 May 1670 he was a member of a jury sitting at Elizabethtown. In 1671 he was appointed overseer of the highways; the following year and in 1675 he officiated as Clerk of the Township Court.

In 1673 he was chosen Deputy to the General Assembly representing the Woodbridge district; in September 1673 he was a member of the militia when East Jersey was taken over by the Dutch. In 1674 and in 1694 he was an Assessor or Rate Maker for Woodbridge and in July 1674 he was appointed an Attorney to defend the interest of Woodbridge in settlement of a controversy with Piscataway over a claim for some upland and meadows. Later, in 1686, he was one of the citizens empowered by the people to prevent encroachment and trespass upon the rights of the Corporation, with full authority to prosecute and punish any such offender.

Dunham was one of the persons delegated to superintend laying out and appropriating the second division of land of the Woodbridge Freeholders. In 1701 he was one of a dozen citizens chosen to procure the services of a suitable town minister and was again chosen Deputy to the General Assembly of New Jersey at Elizabethtown and Perth Amboy, representing the Woodbridge district. The property owners trusted him, with other Associates, to attend to important provisions of 100 acres of land for educational purposes.

The Dunham Homestead built in 1670 is presently the Rectory of Trinity Church, Woodbridge, New Jersey. The mother of President Barack Obama, Stanley Ann Dunham, is the seventh great-granddaughter of Jonathan and Mary Dunham.

Lester Robert Dunham # C12

1671 Jonathan Dunham House, Woodbridge: Source: Wikimedia

References:

Dally, Joseph A. *Woodbridge and Vicinity: A Story of a New Jersey Township*, 1873 (Internet archive).

Holt, David W. *The Old Families of Salisbury and Amesbury, Massachusetts*, 1897 (Internet archive).

Monnette, Orra Eugene. First Settlers of Ye Plantations of Piscataway and Woodbridge Olde East Jersey, 1664-1714. Leroy Carman press, CA, 1930.

Town Records of Woodbridge, New Jersey Records at Court House,

Salem, Massachusetts Manuscripts of Oliver B. Leonard, at New Jersey Historical Society, Newark, New Jersey.

NICHOLAS DUPUI (1634-1691)

Nicholas DuPui, a member of the lesser or minor nobility of France and a merchant, a seller of camlet or cloth used to make cloaks and petticoats, was born in Paris c.1634. He fled Artois France and arrived in New Amsterdam 12 Oct. 1662 aboard the ship *Purmerland Church*, captained by Benjamin Barent. He was accompanied by his wife Catherine Renard (de Vos) born c.1634 and their three sons: John age 7, Moses 5 and Nicholas 2. Six additional children were born in the new world. Moses would later marry Maria Wynkoop and become one of the three trustees to receive a grant from Queen Ann of England to form Rochester, Ulster County New York in 1703.

Nicholas prospered in the new world. On 19 March 1663 he patented a 480-acre plantation on Staten Island, and in June of 1665 he was sworn in as Beer and Weigh House Porter. He was also engaged in the fish packing business and enrolled in the service of Capt. Cornelius Steenwyck's Company of Militia for service against the English in 1673.

The family moved to Bergen New Jersey in 1677 and was admitted to The Dutch Reformed Church for membership. There he purchased 480 acres and 210 acres of land, respectively on 16 April 1687.

Nicholas later returned to New York City where he died at his home on Beaver Street c. 1691. His wife died c.1705.

Ronald DePue # 333

References:

Schoonmaker, Marius. The History of Kinston, New York: From its Early Settlement to the Year 1820, Burr Printing House, NY 1888.

Nelson, William, Editor. *Documents Relating to the Colonial History of the State of New Jersey, Vol. XXI, Calendar of Records in the Office of the Secretary of State*. (Internet archive).

Colonial Conveyances East West New Jersey 1664-1794, p.148, New Jersey Archives (Internet archives).

Footnote to History

The oldest continuous congregation in New Jersey is the Old Bergen Church in Jersey City. In 1660, the settlers of Bergen began holding services in the log schoolhouse. In 1661, the First Dutch Reformed Church was built on about four acres reserved for that purpose as well as a burial ground.

JACOB DU TRIEUX (abt. 1645-1709)

Jacob du Trieux was baptized on 2 December 1645 in New Amsterdam, New Netherlands. His grandparents, Philippe du Trieux and Jacquemine Noiret, were French Huguenots who fled to the Netherlands from France to escape religious oppression; it was there that Jacob's father (Philippe, Jr.) was born in 1619. Philippe and Jacquemine du Trieux eventually risked their lives, crossing the Atlantic in the spring of 1624 to settle in the New World with Philippe Jr. and daughter Maria duTrieux.

Jacob du Trieux married Elizabeth Lysbeth Post on 26 September 1674 in New Orange, New York. While many immigrants of Dutch descent were moving on to settle in or near Albany, New York at the time, Jacob and Lysbeth moved to settle in New Jersey. A deed for the purchase of land in Monmouth County, New Jersey, dated 7 March 1675, can be found in Deed Book E, page 43, in Monmouth County. At least one son, Philip, was born in 1676 in Monmouth County, New Jersey. Jacob's son Philip remained in Monmouth County for the rest of his life, marrying Sarah LaRue there in 1703 and dying in Monmouth County on 24 November 1750. However, Jacob and Lysbeth moved on to New Castle County, Delaware in the latter part of the 17th century. It was in New Castle County, Delaware that Jacob du Trieux died on 27 December 1709. Lysbeth remained in new Castle County, Delaware until her death in 1733.

In the latter years of Jacob du Trieux's life, the surname evolved into Truax or Truex. Thousands of descendants of Jacob du Trieux have been and still are known by the surname Truax throughout the United States. Historians might suggest that it was the life-changing decision of Jacob's grandparents to uproot their lives to come to the shores of the New World that changed the course of history in many aspects. For example, both President Theodore Roosevelt and Eleanor Roosevelt descend from the du Trieux family. The number of descendants from this family has grown exponentially, residing throughout the United States and around the world.

James Paul Hess #374

References:

Hornor, William. *This Old Monmouth of Ours*, Moreau Brothers, Freehold, NJ, 1932. Reprint Clearfield, 2009.

Smith, Barbara Carver. "The Truax/Truex Families of Monmouth and Ocean Counties," *The New York Genealogical and Biographical Record, volume LVII, 1926*, 1991.

The Association of Descendants of Philippe du Trieux, First edition, 1991.

The New York Genealogical and Biographical Record, Vol LVII, 1926 (Internet archive)

JOHN ELLISON (abt. 1695–abt. 1775)

John Ellison was born about 1695 in Monmouth County, New Jersey. He married Susannah Boude. Their son James was born in 1730 in Shrewsbury, Monmouth County, New Jersey. John died in Mansfield Twp., New Jersey in 1761 and his wife died in January 1795.

Summarized by Dr. Evelyn Ogden from documents
submitted by Alice Elizabeth Lange Jacobs #297

Map of Shrewsberry (circled) in Monmouth County

References:

Knox County Kentucky Kinfolk, Vol. IX., No 1, January 1985

JOSHUA ELY (16xx– 1702)

Joshua Ely was born in England and came to Trenton, New Jersey from Dunham, Nottinghamshire. He married first Mary Senior, who died in 1698 at Trenton, New Jersey. He married second on 9 November 1699 Rachel Lee who survived him. He died in Burlington County between 6 November 1700 and 16 June 1702, the dates of his will.

In October 1678 the Ship *Shield* from the port of Hull, Yorkshire, England, dropped anchor in the Delaware River before the present site of the city of Burlington, New Jersey. It was the first trans-Atlantic ship to go so far upstream. Among the passengers were Mahlon Stacy and his wife Rebecca Ely Stacy, sister to Joshua Ely.

Joshua Ely with his family had joined the West Jersey Colony some time prior to 1685 when 400 acres of Balifield, Nottingham Township, Burlington County plantation were transferred to him. He was commissioned a Justice of Burlington County in 1699 and again in 1700. This office was one of high importance in colonial days and generally carried with it the title of Justice of the several courts: Common Pleas, Quarter Sessions and Orphans Court.

Of the many children of Joshua Ely, two had died and were buried at Skegly, Nottinghamshire, England. The surviving children and his wife Rachel were named in his will made 6 November 1700 at Burlington, New Jersey. Two were twins: Benjamin and Ruth. One child, Hannah, was not mentioned in her father's will, but "at age 14 years" on 13 October 1712, her uncle, Mahlon Stacy, was appointed her guardian.

Warren Richard Clayton #131

The Delaware River near Trenton

References:

Ely, Reuben Pownall et al. *An Historical Narrative of the Ely, Revell and Stacy Families, of Trenton and Burlington, West Jersey, 1678 – 1683*, New York, 1910.

New Jersey Archives, Wills - Abstracts. Vol. 1:154 (Internet archive).

JOSEPH ENGLISH II (16xx -1725)

It is not hyperbole to say that Joseph English had a part in the greatest migration of a people from one continent to another for reasons at least partly religious. Sailing over a thousand leagues of sea, Joseph arrived in Burlington, West Jersey, in 1677, with his wife Hannah and her family, the Clifts. Here they progressed from wigwam living upon their arrival, to occupying multiple large estates - an early example of the realization of the "American Dream."

Joseph's early years in America were dedicated to a cooperative effort with his aging father-in-law Samuel Clift to establish a ferry service between West Jersey and Pennsylvania. Upon Clift's death in 1683, he inherited 30 acres of land, a house, and the ferry. He continued to manage that venture until 8 May 1686, when he leased it to Abraham Cooks.

Joseph appears to have had a genius for making good property investments in both New Jersey and Pennsylvania along the Delaware River. On a small scale, he maintained, a land office of his own, buying and selling land to later immigrants. Deeds referred to him as *Yeoman* (landed gentry) of Burlington County. His prized purchase was the estate at Labour Point, after the death of its owner John Cripps, who had sailed with English on the *Kent* in 1677. The Cripps-English site was described as the most beautiful estate on the Delaware River. It was directly opposite Pennsbury Manor, the private residence of William Penn. It was where his family reached maturity, where he spent most of his life and realized the purpose and hopes of coming to America. Prior to purchasing this estate he acquired another in Great Egg Harbor, Mansfield Township, where the "English Creek" which enters the Delaware was named for him. He gave this property to his son John four years after he had purchased it.

The illness that would claim his life in 1725 occurred on a Pennsylvania purchase he made in 1714 in the forks of the Brandywine. His will was written 40 days before he died; it was recorded where his family lived in New Jersey. The will bears an armorial seal of the Scottish thistle and The English Rose under a Tudor Crown, symbolizing the coup of Queen Anne's reign of joining Scotland and England. The motto "same as always" was used by Queen Elizabeth.

Joseph English's will names children: Joseph, as oldest son; William; Elizabeth (the oldest daughter and probably deceased when his will was written since the will names her husband Peter), Rachel (Mrs. Thomas Greene); and Hannah English (Mrs. John Wells).

383A Margaret Louise Drody Thompson

Reference:

Hoppin, Charles Arthur. *The Washington Ancestry Vol. 2*, 1932.

DAVID FALCONER (1630-1713)

David Falconer was born c. 1630 in Montrose, Scotland; married 7 March 1672 Margaret Molleson, daughter of Gilbert Molleson in Aberdeen, Scotland; died 18 April 1713 at Kingswells and was buried at Urie, Scotland; as was his wife who died 22 July 1697.

David Falconer was imprisoned in Scotland several times for his activities as a Quaker. He was appointed business manager (factor) to Col. David Barclay of Urie and his son Robert Barclay, the main theologian of Quakerism. On 1 May 1671 he was admitted *Merchant and Guild-brother of the City of Aberdeen*. His marriage in 1672 was to Robert Barclay's sister-in-law. He was a successful merchant in Edinburgh from 1674 to 1689, and as their Treasurer he kept the books of the Edinburgh Monthly Meeting.

When the Duke of York (later James II) made William Penn the Proprietor of Pennsylvania and Robert Barclay, David's brother-in-law, Proprietor and Governor of East New Jersey, Falconer purchased several parcels of land there while he continued to administer Barclay's affairs, (including those involving the settlement of East New Jersey). Barclay sold Falconer 500 acres in New Jersey on 20 and 21 February 1682/83, and subsequent to this purchase David was characterized as a "Proprietor" in several archival documents.

George E. Spaulding, Jr. #178

References:

Barclay, Hubert F. *A History of the Barclay Family*, Part 111:108, London, 1935.

Brown, Hume P. The Register of the Privy Council of Scotland, Series, Vol. 1, 1877 (Internet archive).

Dictionary of Meeting Books Society of Friends, Edinburgh, manuscript, Friends House Library, London.

Digest of Friends Monthly Meeting Records, Scotland, the Genealogical Society of Pennsylvania, Fgn. S IF.

New Jersey Archives, Calendar of New Jersey Records, 1664-1703, First Series, Vol. XXI (Internet archive)

Scottish Records Office – "Testament of Sibella Ogilvie, recorded at Brechin", 18 August 1635.

EDWARD FITZ-RANDOLPH (c.1607 - 1675/6)

Edward Fitz-Randolph was baptized 5 July 1607 at Sutton-on-Ashfleld, Nottinghamshire, England; married on 10 May 1637 Elizabeth Blossom, daughter of Elder Thomas and Ann (Heilson) Blossom, born in Leyden in 1620. Edward died between 1675 and 1676 in Piscataway, New Jersey. Elizabeth married on 30 June 1685 Captain John Pike. She died in her 93rd year and is buried beside Edward Fitz-Randolph in the west corner of St. James Churchyard in Piscataway.

Edward Fitz-Randolph and his widowed mother came to America in 1630 on the *Winthrop Fleet*, settling first in Situate, Massachusetts. He was yeoman and does not appear to have held any public office. He moved his family to Barnstable in 1639 where he was a juryman in 1641 and his name appears on the list of those able to bear arms in 1641.

In 1669 Edward sold his Massachusetts property and moved most of his family to Piscataway, New Jersey because New England patriotism and religion were too restrictive. After his death and about four days after her second marriage, Elizabeth deeded 300 acres of their father's land to sons Joseph, John, Thomas and Benjamin.

Florence S. Whitehead #C76

Edward Fitz-Randolf; source: Karen Fitz-Randolph, www.ancestry.com

References:

Randolph, Woodford Clayton. "Edward Fitz-Randolph, Branch Lines," 2006.

Clayton, Woodward. *History of Union and Middlesex Counties, NJ*. 1882 (*Internet* archive).

Williams, George F. *Saints and Strangers: Being the Lives of the Pilgrim Fathers and their Families*, 1981.

JOSEPH FRAZEE (1635-1713)

Joseph Ephraim Frazee (Frasey) was born in Scotland 1635. He was a "One-Lot-Right" Associate in the Elizabethtown purchase, taking the Oath of Allegiance there on 19 February 1665. In the same year he married Mary Osborn, daughter of Steven Osborne, a "Two-Lot-Right" Elizabethtown associate, and Sarah Stanborough. The family came with many others from Eastern Long Island to Elizabethtown. It is not clear where Frazee lived prior to New Jersey; however, since he married the Osborne daughter shortly after coming to Elizabethtown although it may be that Frazee also came from Long Island.

As a One-Lot-Right man Joseph received a six-acre town lot and in May 1676, 120 acres beyond the town. In 1685 he was awarded an additional warrant for 50 acres as compensation for two "highways" passing through his land, one leading to Vincents and the other to Woodbridge.

The Frazees had twelve children. Joseph died 8 January 1713; his will was proved 10 February 1714. His wife and two of his sons were executors.

#296 Evelyn Hunt Ogden

The Frazee House is a Union County Landmark

Reference:

First Presbyterian Church of Elizabeth, *Church of the Founding Fathers of New Jersey, 1664-1964*, Carbrook Press, Maine, 1964.

THOMAS FRENCH (1639 – 1699)

Thomas French was baptized 3 November 1639 in the Protestant Episcopal Church of St. Peter and St. Paul, Nether Heyford, Northamptonshire, England. He first married Jane Atkins at the Parish Church of Whilton, England on 12 June 1660 and later married Elizabeth Stanton on 25 August 1696 at the Philadelphia Monthly Meeting. Thomas died in 1699 at Rancocas, New Jersey.

Thomas was the son of Thomas and Sara French, and although baptized in the established church in England, the family were Quakers and suffered for their faith numerous times. At one time Thomas was sentenced to forty-two months in prison for refusing to pay tithes. Being a man of intense commitment, he signed the *Concessions and Agreements* at London in 1676 which provided for the settlement of New Jersey. Thomas arrived at Burlington, New Jersey 23 July 1680 bringing his wife Jane and their four sons and five daughters, the oldest child being sixteen years.

Thomas was a cooper and settled his family on a tract of about 600 acres along the banks of the Rancocas, about four miles from Burlington. He held an influential place in the colony and was commissioner of highways 1684-85. In the Burlington Monthly Meeting of Quakers, he became an active and courageous member, standing up for principles he cared about. His wife Jane died 5 August 1692 at Rancocas after the birth of their 13th child, who also died a few days later. Thomas married about four years later Elizabeth Stanton and they had one daughter.

A copy of French's will dated 3 May 1699 states that he was about to sail for England, where he owned land in Nether Heyford, Northamptonshire. He left a large estate of lands to his children, for he had about 1200 acres of improved land, and as he was a Proprietor of West Jersey, he also held about 2,000 acres as his unsurveyed proprietary share. Thomas and his first wife were buried in a private burial plot on the homestead plantation, the exact location now unknown. Elizabeth, his second wife, survived him and was devised the house and 420 acres which would revert to his daughters named.

Edsall Riley Johnston, Jr. #175

References:

Genealogy of the Descendants of Thomas French, by Howard Barclay French, Vol. I, 1909

New Jersey Archives, New Jersey Wills, Abstracts, Vol. 1:174 (Internet archive).

HANNAH FULLER (1636 - aft.1686)

Hannah Fuller was born circa 1636 in Scituate, Massachusetts, the daughter of Samuel Fuller and Jane Lothrop. Samuel had arrived on the Mayflower as a child. His parents perished in that first awful year and Samuel was raised by his uncle Dr. Samuel Fuller, also a Mayflower survivor.

Hannah married Nicholas Bonham in Barnstable, Massachusetts, 1 Jan. 1658/9. They relocated to Piscataway, East Jersey, 6 May 1667. Nicholas signed the Oath of Allegiance in Piscataway in 1672. The Bonhams founded Bonhamtown to the east of Piscataway. They had eight children. Nicholas died 20 July 1684; Hannah died after 1686 at Piscataway. Their daughter Mary married the Rev. Edmund Dunham, and their son Edmund the second married Dinah Fitz-Randolph. Their son Edmund the third married Mary Dunn, who was the daughter of Hugh Dunn and Amy Sutton. Edmund Fuller the third and Mary had a daughter Elizabeth Dunham who married Capt. Jacob Martin who served with Washington at Valley Forge. He was also the great grandson of John Martin (one of the original founders of Piscataway).

Douglas W. McFarlane Marshall #318

The Raritan River

References:

Fuller, Edward, Editor. *Mayflower Families Through Five Generations, Vol IV, 2nd Edition,1997*.

Meuly, Walter C. *History of Piscataway Township 1666-1976*, 1976.

HANANIAH GAUNTT (1647 – 1721)

Hananiah Gauntt was said to be a tall and powerful man, well educated, plain, sincere and honest. With a mind capable of penetrating to the truth and right, the education of his children and the duty to his neighbors occupied his entire time. Addition of the final "T" to the family name was supposedly Hananiah's idea so that his descendants would know each other down through the generations to come. On 10 May 1679, he married Dorothy Butler at Barnstable County, MA.

On becoming a Quaker, Hananiah and others of the new faith came under great persecution. Looking for a more peaceful place in one of the other colonies, he left Yarmouth, Barnstable, Massachusetts and on 30 January 1668 bought land in Monmouth County, NJ from his brother, Zachariah Gauntt, who had gone there before him. In 1670 Hananiah *transferred to my brother Israel Gauntt my whole share of lands at a place called New Eason in NJ, with cattle and horses that I then had in said New Eason.* A thorough search of old maps of New Jersey failed to reveal a New Eason, but it is possibly Eatonton, New Jersey, about two miles south of Shrewsbury, Monmouth County. A deed of 4 March 1678 identifies Hananiah as "husbandman", whereas a deed of 6 Feb, 1677 identifies "Hanny" as a carpenter and Israel as a shoemaker.

About 1680 Hananiah moved to first to Rhode Island and then finally settled in Springfield, Burlington County., New Jersey, where he bought 500 acres of land there by the name of 'Hananicaon' (an Indian name). The deed states that Hananiah Gauntt of Rhode Island bought 500 acres at Oneanickon (another spelling) from George Hutchinson, a Burlington County distiller. The deed is dated 11 May, 1685. There is also a deed for 200 a. of land on Burlington Island in the Delaware River that Hananiah purchased from George Hutchinson in 1690. Hananiah served on the Burlington County Court in 1686, 1688, and 1706. He was the "Overseer of Highways" in the Birch Creek area from 1691-1693. In the early 1700's, he applied for permission to establish a Quaker Meeting at Little Egg Harbor, New Jersey. His grandson, Hananiah, was one of the originators of the Friends Meeting at Bordentown, NJ.

Dorothy Gauntt died 26 April 1714 and Hananiah died in 1721; they are buried on the Jobstown property. His will is dated 17 Jul 17, 1720; inventoried on 15 Nov, 1721; and was probated 23 Dec, 1721.

Martha Sullivan Smith, # 412

References:

Gauntt, David. "Peter Gaunt, 1610-1680 and Some of his Descendants: Patents and Deeds and Other", 1988.

Nelson, William, Editor. *Patents and Deeds and Other Early Records of New Jersey 1664-1703*, Clearfield Co., 1899.

WILLIAM GIFFORD (1615-1687)

William Gifford was born about 1615, England, died 9 Apr or 21 Dec 1687. He married first Patience Russell and second, in 1683 at Sandwich, Massachusetts, Mary Mills. Mary was a daughter of John and Sarah Mills of Blackpoint, MA. (now Scarborough, ME). Mary arrived in New England after 1643 and was living in 1734 per Friends records. William was a member of the Society of Friends, and his wife, Mary, was a traveling Quaker missionary.

William Gifford is found at Sandwich in 1650, and authorized as one of four men to call a town meeting in 1651. Although he repeatedly suffered the persecutions visited upon the Quakers, he prospered in material affairs and became a large land owner. William owned land in Massachusetts, Rhode Island, Connecticut and New Jersey. Some of William's Rhode Island lands were purchased in 1670 from "Mistress Sarah Warren of Plymouth, widow of Richard Warren," including one half her share in the land at Dartmouth. His Massachusetts possessions consisted of lands in Sandwich, Falmouth and Dartmouth.

Records of the Colony of New Plymouth in New England record various confrontations with authorities. William was before the court of that settlement in 1647 or before. The sentence of the court against him was that he be whipped at the court's discretion and banished. He continued to reside in Sandwich until his death, with the exception of five years between 1665-1670, when he with George Allen and the sons of Peter Gaunt, all of Sandwich, together with others, were first proprietors of and settled Monmouth County, New Jersey, having purchased the land of the Indians and to whom the Monmouth Patent was granted, 8 April 1665. In a deed by his son Christopher he was described as a tailor.

William Gifford was fined by the authorities for committing fornication before marriage or contract, fined *each five pounds to the use of the colonies and again for taking his wife without orderly marriage, forasmuch as there were many cercomstances in the action that did alleuiate the fault, is onely fined fifty shillings, the Court abateing the fine in the extent of it respecting the pmises*. William Gifford married his second wife, Mary Mills, on 16 July 1683 in the Quaker manner; unrecognized by the colonial authorities.

Michael Sayre Maiden, Jr. # 295

References:

Davis, Libby Noyes. *Genealogical Dictionary of Maine and New Hampshire*, NEHGR, Oct 1974, reprint 1983.

Horner, William S. *This Old Monmouth of Ours*, Clearfield, 2009.

Huntington, E.B History of Stamford Connecticut from Settlement in 1641, to Present Time, 1868 (Internet archive),

Lovell, R.A. *A Cape Cod Town*, 1984.

New Jersey Colonial Documents, Calendar of Wills, pg 130 (Internet archive).

Nelson, William, Editor. *Patents and Deeds and Other Early Records of New Jersey 1664-1703*, Clearfield Co., 1899.

New Jersey Colonial Documents, East Jersey Deeds, Etc., Liber F. pgs 111, 108, 133, 17 (Internet archive).

Sandwich, Harry E. *Gifford Genealogy 1626-1896*, 1896 (Internet archive).

Shurtleff, Nathaniel B., M. D, Editor. *Records of the Colony of New Plymouth in New England*, 1855.

Wilbour, Benjamin. *Little Compton Families*, 2003.

The Northern part of the Monmouth Patent

MATTHEW GRACEY (GRACIE) (16xx-1715)

The Grasset family was Huguenots, originating in Ancientia Poicton, France, immigrating via La Rochelle to London, then to New York, Staten Island and then New Jersey. The name Gracy is from the French word gris meaning grey. The name when pronounced in French sounds as Grah-cee. It soon took on many forms, such as Gracie, Greasie, Graycy and other variations.

The earliest record of Matthew Gracey is a deeding of land in Monmouth County, New Jersey on 13 November 1694 to John Cockburn. The name of his wife is unknown. They had at least one child who they named Matthew. Matthew Gracey Sr. died in New Jersey in 1715.

Matthew Gracey, Jr. is recorded in 1715 in the New York State Military Records, where *Math. Grace a farmer* is in the New Jersey militia regiment under the command of *Col. Tho; 1st Company, Col. Parker as Capt. and Nathaniel Moore as Lt.*

In 1727 Matthew Gracey, Jr. inventoried the estate of Eleazer Contrill of Middletown, Monmouth County. He married Rebecca Applegate, 20 June 1735, in Monmouth County, New Jersey. The only known child of Rebecca and Matthew Gracey was Parthenia Bethany Gracey, born about 1752.

David Lawrence Grinnell # 366

Map of Middletown (circled) in Monmouth county

References:

Colonial Conveyances, Vol. I, p. 200, Province E and W. Jersey (Internet archive).

Gracy, Alice Duggan. *The Gracy Family of New York and Texas*, 1986.

New York Genealogical and Biographical Society Record, "The Huguenots: French Genealogist, No. 1, 19, First Annual Issue 1977.

JOHN GREGORY (1612/15 – 1689)

John Gregory was likely born in Nottingham England c 1612/15. He was a man who was very active in civic affairs, holding offices such as selectman and deputy to the colonial legislature in Hartford, Connecticut. He sat in a special meeting that discussed the possibility of declaring war on Holland. He was also part of the settlement group in Norwalk, Connecticut.

John Gregory was a leader in the plan that led to the founding of Newark. In 1662, he met with Dutch authorities for permission to build a settlement in the area. In 1666, Gregory and Robert Treat conferred with Governor Carteret of New Jersey, concerning establishment of a new settlement. With Carteret approval, Treat and Gregory selected the site for Newark, which was subsequently purchased from the Indians. Gregory selected a town site in the new town; however, he never lived there, and in 1668 his lot was sold to Henry Lyon.

He and his wife Sarah had sons John, Jacim Gregory, Judah Gregory, Joseph and Thomas . Daughters, Phoebe and Sarah, married brothers John and James Benedict, respectively. His will was presented for probate on 9 October 1689. His estate was worth 215 Pounds 4s 6 p.

Steve Hollands #358

The Meadowlands between Elizabethtown and Newark

References:

Gregory, Grant. *Ancestors and Descendants of Henry Gregory*, Published, Provencetown, MA, 1938.

Vital Records of Norwalk, CT. (Internet archive)

JAMES GROVER (16xx - 1686)

James Grover was active in the settlement of East Jersey. He settled in1648 at Gravesend, Long Island. In 1655 he was sent by the English Colonists on a mission to Oliver Cromwell. He was one of the grantees of the Monmouth Patent, in New Jersey. He died in 1686.

Abigail Grover, daughter of James, was active in the settlement of East Jersey. She married Benjamin Borden on 1 Sept 1670. Benjamin settled some of his father's lands in Monmouth County, New Jersey; first at Shrewsbury and latter Middletown. In 1695 and 1698 he was elected to the assembly of Middletown. In 1713 the family moved to Evesham, Burlington County Abbigail died 8 Jan 1720. Benjamin left a large estate at his death about 1728.

Summarized by Dr. Evelyn Ogden from documents submitted by # 403 Jay Pernell Wells

Along the Coast of Monmouth County

References:

William and Mary Quarterly, Vol. 1, "Adams-Clopton.Genealogies of Virginia Families," 2010.

Moriarty, G. Andrews The Bordens of Headcorn, Co. Kent, HEHG Registrar, 1930.

SAMUEL HALE (1639/40-1709)

Samuel Hale was born the 9th of February 1639/40 at Newbury, Massachusetts, a son of Thomas and Thomasine Dowsett Hale. He married 1st Lydia Musgrave (although no official record has been found of this event), and 2nd Sarah Ilsley, a daughter of William and Barbara Stevens Ilsley. She was born at Newbury, Massachusetts on 8 of August 1655 and died at Woodbridge, New Jersey 16 January 1680/81. They had two daughters, Sarah born in the year 1675 (she died young) and Mary who married 1st a Higgens and 2nd, Moses Rolfe, with whom she had ten children.

According to sources, Samuel moved to Woodbridge, New Jersey about the year 1670, along with a large group of residents from Newbury, Massachusetts. Samuel was a prominent and active citizen of Woodbridge, holding many religious and civic offices. He was an Officer of the Militia, Justice of the Peace, Marshall of the Woodbridge Town Court, and served on various committees at Woodbridge during the years 1682, 1693, 1695, and 1697, a Constable in 1680, Associate Justice of the Woodbridge Town Court in 1683, 1687, 1689, Lieutenant of the Militia Company 1682-1697, Tax Collector (1684) and was a large landowner in the Woodbridge, New Jersey area. Samuel was active in the church at Woodbridge, New Jersey, and his name appears on the list of members.

Samuel Hale died at Woodbridge, New Jersey of small pox at the age of 69 years, 7 months and 3 days on 5 November 1709. His will, dated the 23rd of May, 1707 names his "well beloved son in law, Moses Rolfe" as his only legatee and executor.

#413A Byron D. Roff

Sketch of Woodbridge Church/Meetinghouse, 1675
image credit: www.fpwoodbridgenj.com

References:

Findagrave.com

Hale, Robert S. *Hale Family*, 1889.

Last Will and Testament of Samuel Hale 1707

JOHN HAMPTON (1640 – 1702)

Encouraged by the proprietors of East Jersey, John Hampton (Hamton) came to America from Scotland as part of the early Quaker migrations beginning in 1682. The proprietors of East Jersey desired to create a safe haven for Sottish Quakers and Presbyterians, both groups facing increasing persecution in Great Britain. Hampton was from Elphinstown (Ephingtown), East Lothian, Scotland. He and his family were among the first to arrive in this Quaker migration. Hampton and his eldest daughter Janett were listed as "redemptioners" in early records, indentured for four years. Hampton received a deed from the Proprietors for 10 acres at Amboy Point in his first year in East Jersey.

Skilled "gardeners," Hampton and fellow Scotsman John Reid were enlisted by the East Jersey proprietors as Overseers. As such, Hampton and Reid helped provide leadership to the Scottish colonists and were granted extensive lands in both Middlesex and Monmouth Counties for their services. As a portion of these lands, Hampton received a Patent for 164 acres on the Neversink River, in Monmouth County on 8 Jan 1685.

John Hampton was a well-respected Elder in the Friends meeting and was often appointed to participate in various quarterly and annual meetings held in the region. At one such meeting held in Burlington, Hampton is listed among the Elders present, and guests included William Penn.

A widower, John Hampton married Martha Brown of Shrewsbury in 1686. The marriage was recorded in the records of the public meeting house of Friends in Shrewsbury. Hampton resided for several years in Shrewsbury after this marriage. While residing there, his eldest daughter Janett married Robert Rhea (Ray).

In 1695, Hampton removed to Freehold where he is listed as paying quit rent on 544 acres there. Martha Brown Hampton died in 1697, and the next year John Hampton married once more, to Jane Curtis Osborne. A son, Joseph, was born to them in 1702. John Hampton died in Freehold that same year.

John Hampton had nine children by his various wives: Janett, John, David, Andrew, Jonathan, Noah, Elizabeth, Lydia, and Joseph.

William Hampton #397

References:

Hampton, V. B. *In the Footsteps of Joseph Hampton and the Pennsylvania Quakers*, 1940.

Dobson, D. *Scottish Emigration to Colonial America, 1607-1785,* Athens Georgia; University of Georgia Press, 2004.

Doylestown: Bucks County Historical Society.

Landsman, N. *Scotland and Its First American Colony, 1683-1765*. Princeton: Princeton University Press, 1985.

THOMAS HAND (c. 1646-1714)

In the middle of the 1690s, three brothers came to Cape May County from the eastern end of Long Island. Shamgar, Benjamin, and Thomas Hand were sons of John Hand and Alice Gransden. John Hand came to the "new country" from Stanstede, Kent, England, circa 1636 to Lynn Massachusetts. The Hands arrived in Southampton, Long Island, around 1644. Subsequently John was one of the founders of the adjacent community of East Hampton. He died in East Hampton shortly before 24 January 1660.

According to the old Cape May County land deeds, Thomas Hand purchased 400 acres of land on the Delaware Bay side of Cape May in 1695, while Benjamin purchased 373 acres in 1692 and Shamgar purchased 700 acres in 1695, both on the Atlantic Ocean side of Cape May. Shamgar was listed as a "gentleman", Benjamin as a "yeoman" (a colonial word for someone who owned the land on which he farmed), and Thomas, a "whaler".

Thomas is listed in several books as having been born in Southampton in 1646. However, in his will drawn on 21 October 1707, Thomas states that he is "aged fifty-nine years." This age would imply that he was born in 1647 or 1648. His will was proved on 3 November 1714 and his inventory was proved on 29 November 1714. At the top of the inventory is the date of 9 October 1714 which may be his actual date of death. Depending on his birth year, he would have been between 62 and 64 years old at the time of his death. When he wrote his will, he said that he was "in good health and strength and memory" but recognized "the frailty and mortality of all men".

We know little about Thomas Hand's life. He came to Cape May as a whaler, but in his will he lists his occupation as a "yooman" (sic). This would imply that he switched from whaling to farming late in his life.

From his will and land deeds we know that he had five sons, Jeremiah Hand, Thomas, Recompense, John, and George (in no particular order of age). He also had three daughters, Alice, Deborah, and Prudence. Recompense was given most of Thomas' land and improvements. His wife, Katherine, was given her choice of one room in their house along with two slaves, one male and one female, during *the time of her widowhood and no longer*. The inventory of his personal estate amounted to 502 pounds, 14 shillings.

David Hand Coward #361

Evelyn Hunt Ogden (Registrar)

References:

Documents Relating to the Colonial History of the State of New Jersey, Vol. XXI, Calendar of Wills, Vol. XXIII. William Nelson, Paterson, NJ 1901

Mayflower Pilgrim Descendants in Cape May County New Jersey. Rev Paul Sturtevant Howe. Genealogical Publishing Co. Inc. 1977

Early Architecture of Cape May County New Jersey by Joan Berkey (2008)

THOMAS HARDING (c 1635-1708)

Thomas Harding was born in Benningham, Glouchester, England circa 1635 and was baptized Feb. 21, 1636 at St. Nicholas, Anglican Church, Gloucester, England. His parents are believed to have been Thomas and Agnes North Harding, who were married April 29, 1629. Thomas Harding married Eleanor Bagwell at a Church of England church in the City of London, All Hallows-on-the-wall (London Wall) February 26, 1662. Eleanor died July 10, 1692 and Thomas married Elizabeth Nichols July 3, 1693, who preceded him in death in New Jersey. Thomas Harding's will acknowledges Mary, daughter with Eleanor, and two additional daughters Hope and Rebecca understood as daughters he had with Elizabeth.

Thomas Harding, a box maker in London, purchased 1/32nd share in William Penn's Colony of West Jersey from Daniel Wills of Northampton who had bought the shares directly from William Penn Jan 23, 1677.

On March 3, 1677 Thomas signed *The Concessions and Agreements of the Proprietors, Freeholders and Inhabitants of the Province of West Jersey in America* prior to departing England. Thomas and Eleanor sailed on the Kent with their daughter Mary Harding, betrothed to Henry Ballenger (who came to America on the return voyage of the Kent. Sailing with the Hardings on the Kent, were Master Gregory Harlow and approximately 230 other Quakers including William Penn.

Thomas Harding of Wollingborough in the County of Burlington and Province of New Jersey, passed away on Feb 8, 1707, and is buried at the Rancocas Quaker Burying Ground in Burlington County, New Jersey.

#409 Katheryn Marie Martin Beck

#414 Taylor Marie Beck

References:

Sheppard, *Walter Lee. Passengers and Ships Prior to 1684*, 2007.

DeCou, George. *The Historic Rancocas Sketches of the Towns and Pioneer Settlers in Rancocas Valle*, 1949.

Harvey, Lanson Bettis.*The Ballinger Family from 1660-1900 including Seven Generations*, 1929.

Reeves, Emma Barrett. *Three Centuries of Ballingers in America*, 1977.

RICHARD HARTSHORNE (1641 - 1722)

Richard Hartshorne was born in Hathern, Leicestershire, England, on 24 October, 1641, son of Hugh and Kathrine (-) Hartshorne. He married Margaret Carr, daughter of Monmouth patentee Robert Carr, in Newport, Rhode Island, on 27 April 1670, and died in Middletown, New Jersey in 1722.

Hartshorne immigrated September 1669, acquired land on the Navesink at Waycake, near The Highlands, and on The Hook. He built a home at Portland Point. Records show he owned other lands in Middletown, at Manasquan, at the head of Barnegat Bay, both sides of the Manasquan River, and both sides of the King's Highway in Middletown, over 2,000 acres in all.

A devout Quaker, Richard was a personal friend of George Fox and entertained him at Shrewsbury, as described later by Fox in his journals. He was asked by William Penn and others to survey for Quaker settlements along the Delaware in 1676.

A member of the Provincial Assembly for 20 years, Speaker 1686-93 and 1696-98, he served as Deputy 1688, 1692 and 1693. He was also Town Clerk, Sheriff, Commissioner of Highways, Judge of Court of Sessions, Member of Governors Council and Practitioner before the Courts, Constable of Middletown, Clerk of the Court of Small Causes, and one of the Judges of the Court of Common Right at Perth Amboy.

Said to have been "a man of good reputation and benevolent disposition", he was a steadying and conciliatory influence during the years of constant upheaval between the settlers and Proprietors, as an influential spokesman for the conservative wing of the Anti-Proprietary group, and later in disagreements with the Royal Governor, Lord Cornbury.

In 1722, in his eighty-first year, not owing 5 shillings to any man or woman, Richard Hartshorne was buried next to his wife in the Hartshorne Burying Ground, on the north side of the highway in Middletown Village.

Clarence Mott Pickard #C95

References:

Fund, Arthur Layton. "Richard Hartshorne of Middletown," *N.J. (1641-1722), in Proc. NJ Historical Society, April 1949*.

Hathern (Leicestershire) Parish Register 1600-1650. (Internet archive).

Hinshaw, W.W. *Encyclopedia of Quaker Genealogy*, "The Friends' Records of Shrewsbury, New Jersey," 1999.

Horner, William S. *This Old Monmouth of Ours*, Clearfield, 2009.

New Jersey Archives, Vol. 1, XIII (Internet archive).

Stillwell, John D. *Historical and Genealogical Miscellany Early Settlers of New Jersey and Their Descendants*, New York, 1906. (Internet archive)

MATTHIAS HATFIELD (16xx - 1687)

Matthias Hatfield probably came to this country from Holland in 1660 with Cornelius Melyn, formerly the Patroon of Staten Island, and settled in New Haven, CT. Matthias took the Oath of Fidelity in New Haven on May 1, 1660. He was a weaver by trade. He married Maria Melyn Paradys, the daughter of Cornelius Melyn, on August 25, 1664, in New Haven.

Matthias Hatfield and his wife Maria were among the first settlers of Elizabethtown, New Jersey. He took the Oath of Allegiance with sixty-four others on February 19th, 1665. Matthias was one of the original Associates of Elizabethtown. He was a boatman, as well as a weaver, and was a man of considerable means. He was allotted large acreage, and purchased 208 additional acres in Elizabethtown. He purchased a house from Abraham Lubberson on December 5, 1673, located on the lower part of Pearl Street, at its junction with Hatfield Street, and the house was extant into the 20th century.

The First Presbyterian Church of Elizabethtown was erected on a portion of Matthias Hatfield's land, as evidenced by a deed made in 1677. He gave the land to the town for a church and a burial place.

Matthias attended The Dutch Reformed Church, now St. John's Church, and was probably buried in the rear of that church when he died in December, 1687. His will was dated April 19, 1684, and was proved on December 13, 1687.

Patricia W. Blakely #181

Hatfield House, built 1667, Elizabethtown razed 1943

References:

Hatfield, Abraham. *The Descendants of Matthias Hatfield*, New York Genealogical and Biographical Society, 1954.

New Haven Colonial Records, 1638-1694, p. 141. (Internet archive).

Hatfield, Rev. Edwin. *History of Elizabeth*, 1868. (Internet archive).

Misc.in Archives of the New York Historical Society, (Internet Archive).

JOHN HAVENS (c. 1635 - c. 1687)

John Havens, son of William and Dionis (-) Havens, may have been born in Aberystwith, Cardinganshire, Wales before his parents were in Portsmouth, Rhode Island in 1639. John married first Ann (-), then married Hannah or Anna Stannard, who survived him. She is recorded in John's will of 14 March 1686/7, proved 22 November 1687 as Anna, and as Hannah Havens, widow, on the Inventory of his estate made 10 December 1687.

The Havens family originally may have been Antinomians in Rhode Island, followers of Ann Hutchinson. In New Jersey they lived among the 1665 settlers in Shrewsbury who came from Rhode Island.

On 27 February 1667/8 an Oath of Allegiance was administered to all the inhabitants of Navesink, New Jersey, of whom one was John Havens, son of William of Portsmouth, whose grant of land is set down as 120 acres. In John's will, he devised land in Sessoconneta, and Little Silver, New Jersey.

Deanna May Scherrer # 118

Along the Navesink River

References:

Havens, Henry C. *The Havens Family in New Jersey*, 2014.

Newell, John. *Early Havens History - Havens-Crombie Line*, 1963.

New Jersey Archives, New Jersey Wills, Abstracts 1670-1730, (Internet archive).

RICHARD HIGGINS (abt. 1609– aft. 1674)

Richard Higgins was among the original settlers of Piscataway and Woodbridge, New Jersey. His name is among 54 individuals in a Dutch document dated 28 July 1673, "sworn" names of "piscattoway" and "woodbridge." The original settlers of Piscataway and Woodbridge were recruited from three main lines of immigration, namely a) direct from England; b) Piscataqua Country, New Hampshire, Dover, Portsmouth, Hampshire or c) Massachusetts, Haverhill, Newbury, Ipswich, etc. and a few from the Plymouth Colony.

Richard Higgins married his first wife, Lydia Chandler, in Plymouth, 11 December 1634, they had two sons Jonathan and Benjamin. Lydia died in 1640, shortly after the birth of Benjamin. His second wife was Mary Yates, with whom he had a daughter Mary and a son Eliakim. Richard died in Piscataway, after 20 November 1674.

Summarized by Dr. Evelyn Ogden from documents submitted by #376 Mary Ellen Waterhouse Rogan

Map showing Piscataway and Woodbridge

References:

Anderson, Robert Charles. *The Pilgrim Migration: Immigrants to the Plymouth Colony 1620-1633*, NewEngland Historic Genealogical Society, Boston, 2004.

Monnette, Orra Eugene. First Settlers of Ye Plantations of Piscataway and Woodbridge Olde East Jersey, 1664-1714. Leroy Carman press, CA, 1930.

REV. OBADIAH HOLMES (1606/7 – 1682)

Obadiah Holmes was born near Manchester, England in 1606/7 and baptized at Didsbury 18 March 1609/10. He married Katharine Hyde at the Collegiate Church of Manchester, England, 20 November 1630. He died 15 October 1682 in Newport, Rhode Island, and is buried in the Holmes Burying Ground in Middletown, Rhode Island.

Obadiah Holmes with his wife Katharine and son Jonathan arrived in Boston in 1638 where tradition says they brought the first tall case clock ever brought to America. He soon went to Salem, Massachusetts where he and two others established a glass works, probably the first in this country. He removed to Rehoboth in 1646 and to Newport (now Middletown) Rhode Island in 1650 where he resided for the rest of his life. In 1651 he went to Lynn, Massachusetts, to visit former neighbors and because he held services which were not in accord with the established church there he was sentenced on 31 July 1651 to thirty lashes from a three cord whip. The sentence was carried out and the scars remained for the rest of his life. In Newport he was the second minister of the First Baptist Church in America, and he held this pastorate until his death.

In 1657 Obadiah Holmes became interested in the colonization of New Jersey, due in part to the marriage of his daughter to John Bowne, one of the prime movers in its settlement. He subscribed to the purchase of lands there and with eleven others was a Monmouth Patentee named in the original Nicolls patent for settling of lands in Monmouth and Middlesex counties, 8 April 1665. The town book of Old Middletown in its first entry dated 30 December 1667 shows that the house lots laid out in Middletown were 36 in number; Obadiah Holmes was assigned lot #20. In 1667 his name appears with that of his eldest son, Jonathan, among the organizers of the First Baptist Church at Middletown, New Jersey.

Although Rev. Obadiah did not move away from Middletown, Rhode Island, two of his sons, Obadiah, who became the High Sheriff of Monmouth County in 1699 and Jonathan did take up residence; Obadiah permanently, and Jonathan temporarily.

Lucy Hazen Barnes #163

References:

Bruce, Eileen Digges, *Our Holmes Ancestors*, 1949.

Elmer, Lucius, *Early Settlement and Progress of Cumberland County*, 1869.

Ellis, Franklin, *History of Monmouth County, New Jersey*, 1885. (Internet archive).

Rutherford, Anna, et.al. *The American Family of Rev. Obadiah Holmes*, 1915. (Internet archive).

Stillwell, John D. *Historical and Genealogical Miscellany Early Settlers of New Jersey and Their Descendants*, New York, 1906. (Internet archive)

THOMAS HOWELL (abt. 1659–1687)

Thomas Howell was born about 1635 in Harleston, Stafford, England and died October 1687 in Cooper's Creek, Waterford Twp., Gloucester, New Jersey. He married Katherine, last name unknown, in 1659 in Harleston, Stafford, England. She was born in 1640 in Farnsworth, Warwick, England.

Thomas Howell was one of the pioneers in the settlement of West Jersey. On 31 August and 1 September 1677, Benjamin Bartlett conveyed to Howell by deeds a one-eighth of one-hundredth part or share of West New Jersey. In 1682 he came with his sons Daniel and Mordecai to settle on 650 acres on the north side of Cooper's Creek, Gloucester, New Jersey. He died in October 1687 in Gloucester, NJ. His will indicated that he did not know if his wife was "alive or dead", but if she comes, she is to have the use of the household goods during her life. Katherine did come after his death and settled in Philadelphia PA; she died there 4 October 1695.

Summarized by Dr. Evelyn Ogden from documents
submitted by #387 Arthur Howell Johnson, Jr.

The Delaware River, near Cooper's Creek

References:

Clement, John. *Sketches of the First Emigrant Settlers in Newton Township, Old Gloucester County, West Jersey.* Camden, NJ, 1877, (Internet archives).

Jordan, John. W. *Colonial Families of Philadelphia, Vol. II.* Lewis Publishing, NY, 1911.

Will of Thomas Howell. Office of the Secretary of State, Trenton, New Jersey.

HENRY JACQUES (c. 1618-1687)

Henry Jacques (Jaques) was born in England, possibly in Wiltshire, about 1618. He came to New England in 1640, settling in Newbury, Massachusetts. He married in Newbury on 8 October 1648 to Ann Knight, who was baptized in Romsey, Hampshire, England on 5 May 1631, and was the daughter of Richard Knight and Agnes (-). The family of Richard Knight emigrated in 1635 on the *James*, which sailed from Southampton for New York. They settled in Newbury, Massachusetts.

Richard Knight prepared his will on 17 August 1681. He wrote, c*oncerning my son-in-law Henry Jacques and Ann his wife, when they were married, I gave them thirty acres of upland and meadow and now I give unto him three pounds to be paid within three years after my decease and likewise, I give unto Ann his wife, five pounds to be paid within five years after my decease or before if my executors can well do it.* Richard Knight died on 4 August 1683.

Henry Jacques was a carpenter employed in 1661 to build the new meetinghouse in Newbury, Massachusetts. On 16 May 1669, he was listed as a Freeman of the Colony of Massachusetts.

In 1667, Jacques was an associate of Daniel Pierce in the grant of Woodbridge, New Jersey. He is listed in the records of Woodbridge with his son Henry Jr. as the owner of 368 acres.

He died in Newbury, Massachusetts, on 24 February 1687, aged 69. His wife Ann died 22 February 1704. In his will, Henry gave his wife one half of his dwelling house, one half the great cellar, and one third part of his orchard with ten rods of suitable ground for a garden to be kept sufficiently fenced. He also provided firewood for her and two cows out of his stock, which she was to have until her demise. He also gave her a horse and man to carry her to meetings or otherwise as she should have occasion, along with six pounds annually, with one half of all his household goods for her natural life and ten pounds to be disposed among her children as she saw cause. He named his son Daniel Jacques, and his daughters: Mary the wife of Richard Brown; daughter Hannah, the wife of Ephraim Plummer; daughter Sarah, the wife of John Hale; daughter Elizabeth; daughter Abigail. Also named was his grandson Henry, the son of his son Henry Jacques, deceased. Henry Jacques referred to his estate lying in Woodbridge Town in the Province of East New Jersey, and that it was his *will that it should be divided among the three sons of his son Henry Jacques, late of Woodbridge Town.* He also named his grandson Richard, a son of his son Richard Jacques (deceased); and appointed his son Stephen Jacques to be his true and lawful heir and bequeathed unto him the greater portion of his estate. Henry Jacques also stated that it was his *will that whereas Jasper his Indian hath been a good servant to him that it was his will that he serve well and faithfully six years after his decease and then he should have his freedom being by his executor set at liberty and he did hereby will and appoint him to do so.*

The children of Henry and Ann (Knight) Jacques, all born in Newbury are as follows:

Henry, born 30 Jul 1649, moved to Woodbridge, New Jersey and died there before his father, leaving three sons. Henry Jr. married Hannah, (probably the daughter of John Freeman.) and settled in Woodbridge in 1665, where he and his father received a patent of 368 acres from the proprietors. He died in 1679. His children were:

1. Henry Jacques who died in 1750,
2. John Jacques was born in 1674,
3. Hannah Jacques, born in 1675,
4. Jonathan Jacques, born in 1679.
5. Mary Jacques, b. 12 Nov 1651, d. 13 Oct 1653,

6. Mary Jacques, b 28 Oct 1653; m 7 May 1674, Richard Brown of Newbury; he died 12 Oct 1716,
7. Hannah Jacques, b ___, m. 15 Jan 1680 Ephraim Plummer of Newbury; he died 1715,
8. Richard Jacques, b. in 1658; m. 18 Jan 1682, Ruth Plummer, daughter of Samuel Plummer of Newbury, by whom he had a posthumous son Richard, d. 28 May 1683
9. Stephen Jacques, b. 9 Sep 1661, m. 13 May 1648, Deborah Plummer, daughter of Samuel Plummer of Newbury, by whom he had several children,
10. Sarah Jacques, b. 20 Mar 1664; m. 10 Oct 1683, John Hale, who d. 4 Mar 1726,
11. Daniel Jacques, b. 20 Feb 1667, m. 20 Mar 1693, Mary Williams of Newbury, by whom he had children; she died, and he then married Susanna _____,
12. Elizabeth Jacques; m. Richard Knight of Newbury,
13. Ruth Jacques, b. 14 Apr 1672; m. 29 Nov 1692, Stephen Emery of Newbury; Ruth d. 9 Jan 1764; Stephen d. 1 Feb 1747,
14. Abigail Jacques, b. 11 Mar 1674; m. Benjamin Knight of Newbury; he died in 1737.

Heather Elizabeth Welty Speas # 329

References:

Anderson. Robert Charles. *The Great Migration – Immigrants to New England, 1634-1635, Volume IV*. Great Migration Project. New England Historical Society, pages 212-214, Boston 2005.

Appleton, William S. *Early Wills Illustrating the Ancestry of Harriot Coffin, with General and Biographical Notes by her Grandson.*: Appleton, David Clapp & Son, Boston 1893.

Dally, Rev. Joseph. *Woodbridge and Vicinity: The Story of a New Jersey Township*, A.E. Gordon: New Brunswick, NJ: 1873. (Internet archive).

Koehler, Albert F. *The Huguenots or Early French in New Jersey*, pgs 15-16, Bloomfield, NJ 1955.

Whitehead William. D. *Contributions to the Early History of Perth Amboy and Adjoining Country*, Appleton & Co. New York: 1856. (Internet archive).

JEFFERY JONES (c.1643 - 1717)

Jeffery Jones' birth date, place and parentage are unknown, as is also true of his wife who survived him. Jones died at Elizabethtown, Essex County, New Jersey, his will dated 2 December, proved 31 December 1717.

Jeffery Jones is first recorded at Southold, L.I. in 1664. He sold his house and lot there and became one of the 80 Associates of the Elizabethtown Patent of 1666 and received a lot of 180 acres on the west side of the Rahway River south of Crane's Brook. His land is mentioned as a boundary in many deeds of the period.

On 15 February 1668, Jones was one of 25 who were granted a "charter for the Whale fishery" for three years. He was one of the agents who established the boundary line with Newark on 20 May 1668.

On 14 May 1695 an action of Trespass and Ejectment was brought against Jones by the Proprietors in the name of James Fullerton, because of Jones' refusal to take out a Patent from the Proprietors and to pay them quit rents. He appealed to the King in Council where it was lost on a plea of possession for twenty years. This case set a precedent for all future cases of this nature and was referred to as late as 1749.

Barbara Carver Smith #C3

Whaling extended down the coast of New Jersey to Barnegat Inlet

References:

Documents Relating to the Colonial History of the State of New Jersey, Various volumes Internet archive).

Hatfield, Rev. Edwin F. *The History of Elizabeth, New Jersey*, 1868. (Internet archive).

Miller, George. Minutes of Board of Proprietors of the Eastern Division of New Jersey, 1685 to 1705, Board of Proprietors, 1949.

Thayer, Theodore. *As We Were: The Story of Old Elizabethtown*, 1964.

The Newark Museum Quarterly "Whaling Days in New Jersey," Spring-Summer 1975

ISAAC KINGSLAND (1648 – 1698)

Isaac Kingsland, born at London, England in 1648, came to America in 1673. He married Elizabeth (-) about 1678, and died in New Barbadoes in 1698.

Isaac was appointed High Sheriff of Bergen County at a meeting of the New Jersey Governor's Council on 14 March 1682/3 and eight days later, he was appointed to the same office for Essex County. On 26 November 1684 New Jersey Governor Gawen Lawrie made him a member of his council and he continued to serve in this office under Governors Campbell and Hamilton.

At a meeting of the Board of Proprietors held on 14 May 1686, Isaac petitioned for headland for himself, his wife, one child, four white servants and eight negro slaves. The Board did not grant head land, but did award him 500 acres of land on the Passaic River. By a deed dated 26 March 1671, William Sanford purchased 15,300 acres of land in trust for Nathaniel Kingsland of Barbadoes, located between the Hackensack and Passaic Rivers, which ran from a line opposite Newark to present day Rutherford. Nathaniel transferred one third of this land to William Sanford on 1 June 1671 and retained the remainder. By his will proved 1 April 1687, Nathaniel gave his nephew, Isaac Kingsland, one third of the remainder, about 3,400 acres.

On 11 December 1686, Isaac was commissioned captain for a company of foot soldiers made up of citizens from Acquackanock and New Barbadoes, and on 27 May 1687, he was appointed a justice in the Court of Common Right. By his will dated 1 January 1697/8, proved 4 March 1697/8, Isaac left one third of his real estate to his eldest son, Edmund, the remainder to his other children. When each daughter married, she received a lot and the materials to build a house; his wife received the income from the estate during her life. His personal estate, valued at £220, 9 sh. *included negro slaves, farm animals, farm equipment, clothing and household goods.*

Arthur D. Quackenbush, Jr. #115

References:

New Jersey Archives, Documents Relating to the Colonial History of the State of New Jersey, Vol. 13, Journal of the Governor and Council, Vol. I 1682-1714, New Jersey Dept. Of State. (Microfilm).

New Jersey Archives, New Jersey Wills, Abstracts, 1670 - 1730, p. 275 (Internet archive).

Footnote to History

As whales were abundant along the coast, a whaling company was organized at Elizabethtown, which obtained a charter from the government Feb 15, 1669, granting to John Ogden, Sr., Caleb Carwithe, Jacob Moleing, Wm. Johnson, and Jeffrey Jones, all of Elizabeth Town and their company consisting of 21 persons, the exclusive right for three years of taking whales along the coast from Barnegat to the eastern part of the province, one twentieth part of the oil in casts to be given to the Lord Proprietors.

JOHN LIMING (16xx-aft. 1697)

John Liming (Limming, Lyming, Lemon) is believed to have been born in Dover, England, date unknown, and he died sometime after 1697 in New Jersey. He appears on the list of immigrants on the ship Nevis Merchant in 1665 that was bound to Nevis, Leeward Island as John Lyming; along with some other associates who later settled in Monmouth County, New Jersey.

He married Patience Wainwright about 1680 in New Jersey and they had three sons: John Liming Jr., William and Thomas. Tradition is that the family was Baptist, among the many Baptists who first colonized Monmouth County.

In 1681 his hog mark was registered in the Middletown book as John Lemon, but this mark was confused with Obadiah Holmes' and was corrected in 1689 by Jonathan Holmes. John's hog mark was identified as a "crop one the right Eare and a square cut of the inside of the neare Eare and a cut in the fore side of the neare eare." John appears in a court proceeding in 1683. In 1701, he signed a petition to the King as John Leming. In 1717, he was sued by Mordeaci Lincoln as "John Limming."

#410 Dallas John Riedesel

References:

Leming, Sam K. *Leming Family History and Genealogy*, 1881.

Slater, Edwin. *A History of Monmouth and Ocean Counties*, 1890. *(Internet archive)*.

Stillwell, John E. *Historical and Genealogical Miscellany*, *Vol. II, 1906*. *(Internet archive)*.

Footnote to History

No significant settlement occurred in the Manasquan area until after 1685, when sale of the Squan lots began. About the year 1703, a Quaker Meeting settled at Squan, it was held in private houses, till about the year 1730 when their Meeting House built. The current Meeting House on the original site on route 35, was built in 1884.

FRANCIS LINLE (LINDSLEY/LINDLEY) (16xx – 1704)

Francis Linle (Linsley/Lindley) was born in England, date and location unknown. He and his brother John emigrated from England and settled in the New Haven Colony about 1640. The names of John and Francis Linle appear in the New Haven records in 1645. In 1646, Francis Linle was appointed to keep the herds of cows and heifers in Branford.

Francis Linle married Susanna Cullpeper in 1655, in Branford, and their children Deborah, Ruth, Ebenezer and John were born there. Sons Benjamin, Joseph and Jonathan were born in Newark, New Jersey, after 1666.

Francis Linle moved with the first Puritan settlers to Newark, which was settled in 1666. His name appears among the forty additional settlers who signed the Fundamental Agreements in 1667. The Agreement stated provide for the maintenance of the purity of Religion professed in the Congregational Churches. At a town meeting in 1667, Francis Linle drew home lot number 44 on Market Street (opposite where the court house stood in 1924).

The original patent received by Francis Linle from the Proprietors of the Province of East New Jersey for his land in 1697, is in the possession of the New Jersey Historical Society's Lindsley collection. This is the oldest document of its kind pertaining to this family known to be in existence in America and it is the first time the surname is spelled "Lindsley."

Before his death in Newark in 1704, he gave land to his sons Benjamin, Ebenezer, Joseph and Jonathan. The deed to his son Ebenezer, in the possession of the New Jersey Historical Society, is probably the only extant document signed by Francis.

Margaret A. Brann # 353

References:

Biographical and Genealogical History of Newark, New Jersey. (Internet archive).

Lindly, John M. *The History of the Lindley-Lindsley-Linsley Families in America, 1639-1930.* 1924.

Municipalities of Essex County, 1666-1924, Vol. 1. 1925. (Internet).

New Jersey Genesis, Vol. 1-7, 1953.

Pierson, David L. *Narratives of Newark.* 1895. (Internet archive).

Records of the Town of Newark, New Jersey, from its Settlement in 1666, 2009. (Internet archive).

HENRY LYON (16xx - 1703)

Henry Lyon and his two brothers, Thomas and Richard Lyon of Perthshire, Scotland were in Oliver Cromwell's army, a part of the guard who witnessed the execution of King Charles I. Fleeing to America immediately thereafter, in 1648, Henry Lyon settled in the New Haven Colony, at Milford, Connecticut.

He married Elizabeth Bateman, daughter of William Bateman of Fairfield, Connecticut, in 1652. They resided with her parents in Fairfield until 1654, when William Bateman sold Henry Lyon the house and lot. Henry was executor of his father-in-law's will dated 24, 1656 and received half of his estate.

Henry, Elizabeth and children moved to Newark, New Jersey in 1666, where Henry was a founder with the Milford colonists. They re-located to Elizabethtown, New Jersey, in 1673 where they became large land owners. The Lyons had eight children, Thomas Lyon, Mary Lyon, Samuel Lyon, Joseph Lyon, Nathaniel Lyon, John Lyon, Benjamin Lyon and Ebenezer Lyon.

Henry held various posts during his life in New Jersey, among them were the first Treasurer and first Keeper of the Ordinary of Newark, a member of the General Assembly of New Jersey at Elizabethtown in 1675, Justice of the Peace in 1681, Judge of the Small Causes in 1681, member of the Governor's Council in 1681, Commissioner in 1682, and many other positions until the end of his life.

Elizabeth died before 1689, after which Henry married Mary (-). He returned to Newark in 1696 and remained there until his death in 1703.

David Richard Finch # 332

Properties allotted to Thomas Lyon, Samuel Lyon, Henry Lyon

Drawing prepared for the bicentennial of the Newark by Samuel Conger and William Whitehead for the New Jersey Historical Society.

References:

Lyon Memorial, Vol. II, by Sidney Elizabeth Lyon, 1907.

Ridge, Bradley B. *The Bateman Connection*, 1978.

SAMUEL MARSH (c.1620 - 1683)

Samuel Marsh was born in England c. 1620; died in Rahway, New Jersey between 1683 when he made his will, and 27 May 1685 when his "wife Mary of Elizabethtown" was granted letters of administration on the estate. He married c. 1647 Mary (-), her parentage, birth and death dates unknown.

Samuel Marsh was in New Haven Colony by 1646, where in April he was a member of the New Haven Militia and was made a Freeman on 2 May 1647. With his wife and seven children Samuel removed to Elizabethtown, New Jersey and his son Samuel, Jr., became one of the original 80 Associates in that venture, or is so recorded. On 16 February 1665, Samuel, Sr. took the Oath of Allegiance to King Charles II, and acquired several pieces of land for various uses.

Marsh became active in the disturbances in Elizabethtown during the long controversy with Governor Carteret over land boundaries and titles. In 1671 Samuel was indicted with several others for the destruction of Richard Mitchell's fence which impinged on someone else's land. The trial was a mockery and the defendants although technically fined, paid no fines.

A re-recording of the official inhabitants in Elizabeth Town was done and both Samuel Marsh, Sr. and Jr. appeared on that list dated 11 September 1673. On 14 May 1675/6, a general survey of lands was completed and Samuel Marsh, Sr. received his patent for 180 acres, and his son Samuel, Jr. also received his patent for 180 acres.

Marjorie Barber Schuster #C29

References:

Hatfield Rev. Edwin. *History of Elizabeth, New Jersey*, 1868. (Internet archive).

Hoadly, Charles J. *Records of the Colony of New Haven*, 2008.

Marsh, Warren L. *Marsh Family Bulletin, by, Vol. 1*, 1955

New Jersey Archives, New Jersey Wills, Abstracts 1670-1739, Vol. 1. (Internet archive).

New Jersey Archives, Calendar of New Jersey Records, Vol. XXI. (Internet archive).

WILLIAM MATLACK (1648-1738)

William Matlack was born in Cropwell Village, near Nottinghamshire in 1648. He came to America aboard the ship *Kent* under an agreement with Daniel Willis to serve as a carpenter for four years, settling in the area that is now Burlington, New Jersey. As a carpenter, he worked on the first houses built in Burlington as well as the first corn mill in West Jersey. His leisure time was spent among the natives, watching their peculiarities and striving to win their good will.

In 1682 he married Mary Hancock who had emigrated from Warwickshire, England with her brother the previous year. They settled on a 100-acre tract of land in Chester Township, Burlington County. Known as headlands, this was the quantity of land that each male person coming as a servant was entitled under the conditions established by the proprietors. John Roberts and Timothy Hancock also obtained property in the area. When the three located the land along a creek they called it Penisaukin (now Pennsauken), giving the stream the same name as that by which the Indians called their adjoining village.

Many of the young men who came as servants and received their 100 acres were persons of education and became prominent citizens in the colony, as was the case with William Matlack. In 1701 he purchased about 1000 acres situated in Waterford and Gloucester townships on both sides of Cooper's Creek. He continued to purchase land throughout his life, transferring much of it to his sons.

Alan Russell Matlack # 300
Nancy Elise Matlack #315
Amy Adele Matlack #316

Along the Delaware River

Reference:

Clement, John, *Sketches of the First Emigrant Settlers Newton Township, Old Gloucester County, West Jersey*, Sinnickson Chew, Camden, N.J. 1877. (Ancestry.com).

WILLIAM MEEKER (16xx - 1690)

The progenitor of the New Jersey branch of the Meeker family was William Meeker, who came from Leamington, Warwickshire, England about 1635 to the Massachusetts Bay, and thence removed to New Haven colony, of which he was one of the founders. While residing there he married Sarah Preston, a native of Yorkshire, England.

In the spring of 1665, with his family and others of New Haven colony (whom tradition says he brought in his own sloop), he landed on the site that became known as Elizabethtown Point, New Jersey. He was enrolled with his eldest son, Joseph Meeker, among the original "Elizabethtown Associates," who had acquired title by purchase of the Indians, and by grant from Governor Nichols, for the ground, a portion of which now comprises the entire county of Union.

Sir Philip Carteret was appointed governor of New Jersey by the Duke of York, who had been granted the entire territory by the King. The Duke of York and subsequently Carteret at first did not recognize the Elizabethtown grant from Governor Nichols. The Associates believed this to be invasions of their New Jersey purchase rights, which culminated in dissatisfaction, a revolt on their part, and eventually the flight of Governor Carteret.

Chosen by the Associates, and holding a commission from Governor Carteret as constable of the town, William Meeker became an active adherent of Captain James Carteret, who succeeded the absent governor. Later this was considered an offence and in 1675 he was adjudged to lose his estate. The people of Elizabethtown and Newark, appreciating his fidelity to their interests, presented him with a tract of land at Lyons Farm, where the family homestead was built by his son. William Meeker died in 1690. The children of William and Sarah (Preston) Meeker were: Joseph , Benjamin , Sarah , Mary and John .

375 Sara Frasier Sellgren

References:

Biography and Genealogy of the City of Newark and Essex County, New Jersey p. 117, 1889. (Internet archive).

Meedker, Leroy. *The Meeker Family of Early New Jersey as revealed in the Correspondence of Charles H. Meek.* 1973.

JEAN PIERRE MELLOT (1658–1704)

Jean Pierre Mellot (Marlatt, Melot, Merlet, Marlet) was the son of Gideon Merlet, a French Huguenot, and Margaret Martin. He emigrated to New Netherlands on the ship Purmerland Church, with his parents and three minor siblings, in October 1662. The family first settled on Staten Island and later moved to Perth Amboy, New Jersey. On 12 April 1693, John Peterson Melot, listed as a blacksmith from Perth Amboy, purchased 180 acres in Piscataway. On 27 October of 1693, he leased a farm on the Bound Brook to Henry Pontony (alias Lafortune).

Summarized by Dr. Evelyn Ogden from documents
submitted by # 380 Sharon Lee Morrison Spry

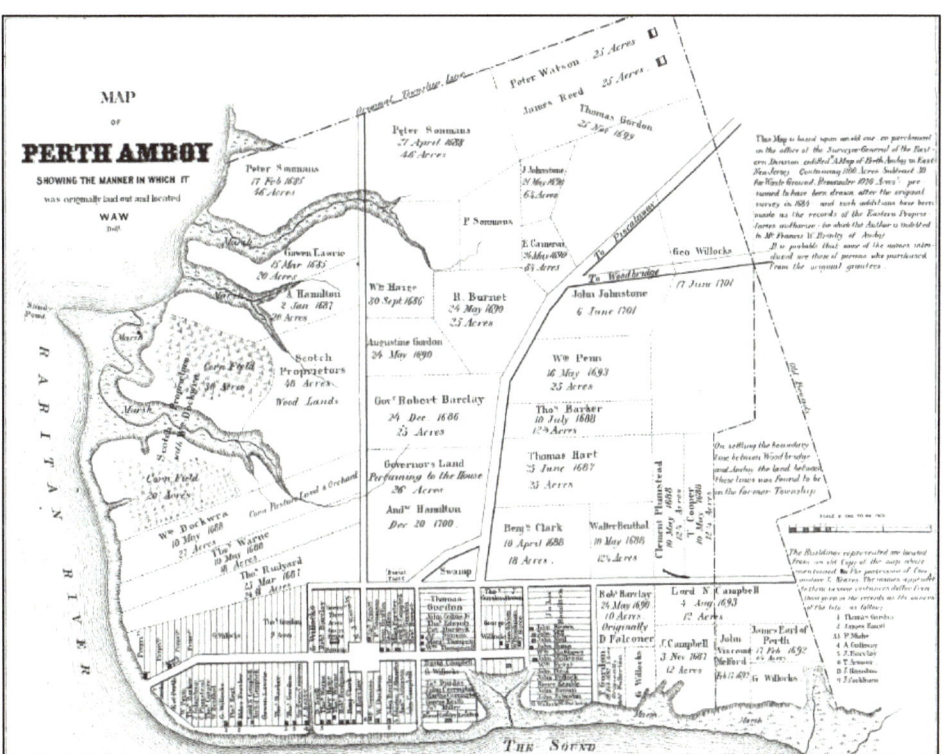

Map of Perth Amboy

References:

Nelson, William, Editor. *Patents and Deeds and Other Early Records of New Jersey 1664-1703*, 1899. (Reprint).

Records of the Church of Leide, Holland. (Internet archive).

Will of Jean Pierre Mello

SAMUEL MOORE (c.1630 - 1688)

Samuel Moore was born c. 1630 at Malden, County Essex, England; died at Woodbridge, New Jersey on 27 May 1688. He married first, 3 May 1653 at Newbury, Massachusetts, Hannah Plummer, daughter of Francis Plummer. She died 8 December 1654. He married second, 12 December 1656 at Newbury, Mary Ilsley, daughter of William and Barbara (Stevens) Ilsley of Newbury who died after 3 June 1678 at Woodbridge. He married third, 23 December 1678 Anne Jacques, widow of Henry Jacques, Jr., of Woodbridge.

Samuel Moore was a resident of Newbury, Massachusetts, before 1653. About 1666 he removed to Woodbridge, New Jersey, where he filed in Piscataway Township surveys for a number of tracts of land. He was assigned a patent for 70 acres on 27 December 1667 and about 1670 received a patent for 356 acres.

Moore served as Town Clerk for 19 years, was sent as Deputy to the General Assembly and returned to that office five times. In 1668, he was chosen a delegate to the first Legislature held in the Province of New Jersey at Elizabeth Town; in 1669 was an aide to the Surveyor General and was also appointed Constable. Between 1670 and 1687 Moore was overseer of the highways, rate-maker and gatherer and assistant justice of the Township Court; President of the Township Court in 1672 and 1674; Marshall of the Province of East Jersey under Governor Carteret 1672-3 and was also Treasurer of the Province. In 1683, he was appointed the first High Sheriff of Middlesex County, at that time a position of great dignity and responsibility.

The inventory of 7 June 1688 gave Samuel Moore's personal estate as *£132.16.11 and included 1 negro boy of 15 and two negro girls*. Thomas Gordon, administrator, leased to Richard Dole and Samuel Moore, Jr., on 22 April 1690, one grist mill, mill house and bakery in Woodbridge belonging to Samuel Moore, deceased.

Barbara Carver Smith #C3

References:

Americana, Vol. XXXIII, 1939

Dally, Rev. Joseph W. *Woodbridge and Vicinity*, 1873. (Internet archive).

Hatfield, Rev. Edwin F. *History of Elizabeth, NJ*, 1868. (Internet archive).

Kreger, John M. *Township of Woodbridge, N.J. 1669-1781*, 197?, (Internet archive).

Monette, Orra Eugene. *Settlers of ye Plantations of Piscataway and Woodbridge*, 1930.

New Jersey Archives, Documents Relating to the Colonial History of the State of New Jersey, Vol. XXI (Internet archive)

New England Historical and Genealogical Register, Vol. CXXII, 1906. (Internet archive).

LEWIS MORRIS (c.1660-1696)

On 25 October 1676, 3840 acres were conveyed to Col. Lewis Morris of Barbados and his associates in the Iron Works at Navesink, between the Swimming River and Falls River, the whole to be called Tinton Manor. Additional property was conveyed in 1681, to Col. Morris of Tinton Manor, for Ramsant's Point, originally owned by Christopher Almy. Col Morris conveyed to Lewis, son of Thomas Morris, on 15 April 1698, 330 acres called Passage Point or Navamson Neck. Col Morris was member of the Meetings of Shrewsbury and New York Province.

In his will dated Feb 12, 1690, Col. named his wife Mary as executrix and his vice nephew Lewis, son of his deceased brother Richard Morris, as his principal heir. In a document dated Dec 10, 1702, other tracts of land in Monmouth County were conveyed to Richard Morris, heir at law of Col. Lewis Morris, in consideration of his services with the Ministers of State in England.

Lewis Morris died in 1696. A letter of administration was granted on April 1, 1696, on the estate to his wife Elizabeth Almy Morris.

Summarized by Dr. Evelyn Ogden from documents
submitted by #363 Jennifer Kim Sallee Chang

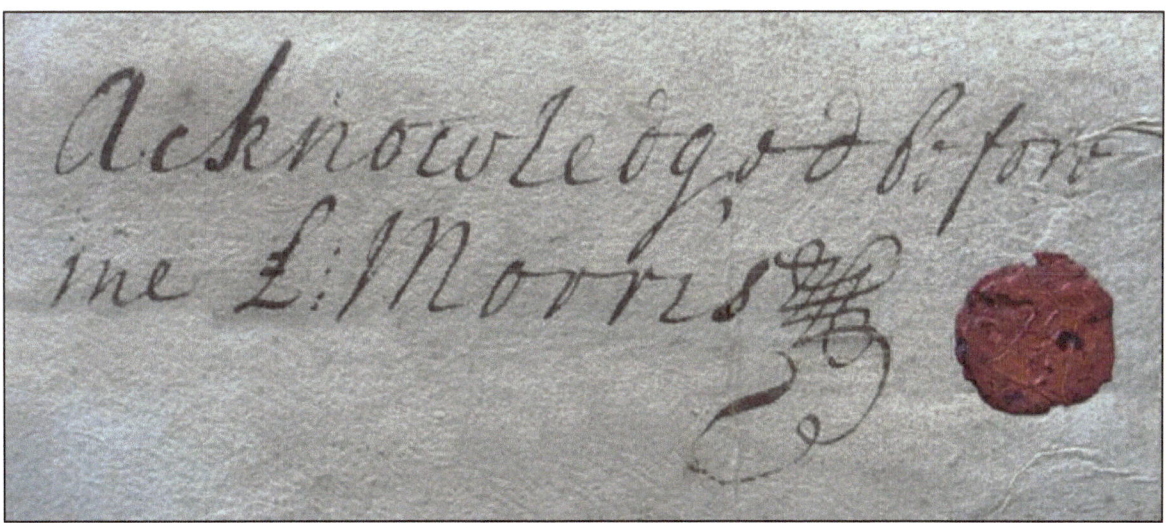

Signature and seal of Gov. Lewis Morris, nephew and heir of Col. Lewis Morris

References:

Nelson, William, Editor. *Patents and Deeds and Other Early Records of New Jersey 1664-1703*, 1899. (Reprint).

Smith, Samuel. *Lewis Morris Anglo-American Stateman, 1613-1691*, Amazon Books, 1983.

THOMAS MORRIS (16xx -1673)

Thomas Morris, a Puritan, was born in England, time and place still undiscovered. He married Elizabeth (-), but time and place are not known, however, it probably was in Massachusetts about 1639. He died at Morris Cove in New Haven, Connecticut, 21 July 1673 and his wife died there in 1681.

Thomas Morris is believed to have arrived in Boston 26 June 1637, and then by 1640 settled in New Haven, Connecticut. A Puritan, he was deeply religious, a friend of Robert Treat and the other men who decided to build their ideal Puritan settlement in New Jersey. He was a shipwright, wheelwright and carpenter, and it is tradition that the group sailed to New Jersey in a ship built and owned by Thomas Morris.

In 1667, Morris subscribed to the Fundamental Agreements entered into by the group planning Newark. In the first division of land there, he received Lot #31 for which he was assessed £ 385. This lot lay between Broad and Washington Streets in Newark, now bisected by New Street, lying on the upland area of the city. There is no evidence that Morris ever improved this land or built on it. He had been a pioneer in at least two other areas in New England and developed a fine and profitable shipbuilding business in New Haven. His family was grown up and setting up for themselves.

Thomas Morris' name is found in 1670/71 among those who were to receive a lot in the second division of salt meadow in Newark. This is the last time his name appeared in the town records. Thomas was too old to want to live once more through the rigors of pioneering; he had a comfortable home and a good business in Connecticut. He had sons who could inherit the Newark land, so when he made his will 1 July 1672 in New Haven, he gave his estate to his daughters and his one living son, John. John removed to Newark where he died in 1675, but John's son, John, lived on in Newark and died there in 1749 at the age of 83.

Harriet Stryker-Rodda #C1

References:

Carhart, Lucy Ann Morris. The *Morris Family* ,1911. (Internet archive).

Catalogue of First Church Members of New Haven, 1914. (Internet archive)

New Haven Vital Records. (Internet archive).

New Jersey Historical Society. *Records of the Town of Newark, 1666-1836*, 1864, reprint 1966.

Pope, Charles H. *Pioneers of Massachusetts, 1900.* (Internet archive).

SAMUEL NICHOLSON [1634 – 1685]

Samuel Nicholson was born in Wiseton [alt sp, Wyston, Weston], Nottinghamshire, England about 1634. He married Ann[e] Abel in England around 1658; they had six children all born in England; Parabol Rachel [1659], Moses [1661], Elizabeth [1664], Samuel [1666], Joseph [1669], and Abel [1672].

Samuel was a yeoman farmer and prominent member of the community. He and his family were members of The Religious Society of Friends, otherwise known as Quakers. On August 7, 1675 [Julian calendar June 28, 1675] Samuel, along with 31 others, joined John Fenwick's scheme to establish a colony in West Jersey, North America and signed an agreement entitled, The Fundamental Articles for the Government of the Colony (known as Fenwick's Colony or Salem Colony).

Soon afterwards Samuel, Ann, and their 5 children [Moses had died in 1663], along with 42 other settlers sailed from England on board the ship, Griffin, under ship's master Captain Robert Griffith. Arriving along the Delaware River shore in West Jersey on September 23, 1675, the following day the colonists sailed up the Assamhocking [now Salem] Creek and named their landing spot, New Salem.

Samuel Nicholson had previously purchased the rights to 2,000 acres of land in the new settlement, suggesting he was a prominent person among the group. After arriving in New Salem "...he proceeded to survey outside the town limits of Salem, and south of it, his tract of 2,000 acres, obtaining full title and possession in the tenth month of 1675…." According to chronicler, John Clement, "...next after the patroon [John Fenwick], Samuel Nicholson was, perhaps the wealthiest man in the colony at that time, as he appears to have made several large surveys of land in the county, and also several purchases of real estate."

In June 1676, Samuel Nicholson signed the Agreement of Settlement and Division of Lands with the chief purchasers of the Fenwick's Colony, which, in part, laid out the Town of New Salem into 16 acre lots. Samuel purchased a 16-acre town lot on Wharf St. [now Broadway] and built a house of hewn logs. The first Monthly Meeting of the Society of Friends was held in this house and subsequent meetings were held there periodically up to 1681. When the need for a dedicated Meeting House became apparent, Samuel and Ann Nicholson deeded the house and a 16-acre lot to the 'Salem Monthly Meeting" for a Meeting House and burial ground [this is the land around the Salem Oak]. As a result, the first in-town house of Samuel and Ann Nicholson became the first Meeting House of the Society of Friends in West Jersey.

Samuel and his family resided on their large tract of land in an area that became known as Elsinborough [Elsinboro]. Samuel also served as the first Justice of the Peace in the colony. Before his death in1685, he divided his estate among his wife, Ann, eldest son, Samuel, and youngest son, Abel. Upon her death in 1693, Ann left her estate to her three granddaughters, Rachel, Mary, and Elizabeth Abbott and her sons, Samuel, Joseph and Abel. (September 2015 was the 340th Anniversary of the Samuel Nicholson family arrival in New Jersey.)

404 Lynda G. & James M. Condon

References:

Clement, John, Sketches of the First Immigrant Settlers, Newton Township, Old *Encyclopedia of American Quaker Genealogy: Philadelphia, Salem County*, New Jersey. 1877. (Internet archive).

Flegel, Mary Parsons. "Nicholson Research Report," August 4, 2014

Gloucester County West New Jersey, Genealogical Publishing, pgs. 216 – 222, 1877. (Internet archive).

Haines, Richard. *Genealogy of the Stokes Family*, 1903. (Internet archive).

Koedel, Craig R. *South Jersey Heritage: A Social, Economic and Cultural History*, Chapter 4. (Internet archive).

Salem County Office of Archives & Records Management Timeline 1

Shourds, Thomas & G.F. Nixon, *History and Genealogy of Fenwick's Colony*, 1876.

West Jersey History Project NJA Vol. 21 [Salem Surveys]. (Internet archive).

1722 Nicholson House, Elsinboro, Salem County, NJ   Source: Wikimedia

Footnote to History

Salem was founded when John Fenwick and Edward Byllinge purchased from Lord Berkley land on the east side of the Delaware River in 1674, to establish a colony of English Quakers. The portion that Fenwick was allotted became known as the Salem Tenth or one tenth of West Jersey. On 25 June 1676 the division of lands was signed:

Agreement of settlement and division of lands by the chief purchasers of Fenwick's Colony and others now residing there, to wit: every purchaser to have half of his land in the liberties of Chohansick, the other half in the liberty of Allowwayes; a neck of two to be laid out for a town at Chohansick half for the Chief proprietor, the other half in town lots for purchasers; the lots to be 16 acres; the Town of New Salem to be divided by street, the land S.E. of that street to be laid out in 16 acre lots for purchasers, the other side to be disposed of by the Chief proprietor for the encouragement of trade. SIGNED: J. FENWICK, JOHN ADAMS his mark, HIPOLITE LEFEURE, EDWARD CHAMPNEYS, RICHARD WITACAR, WILLIAM MALSTER, ROBERT WADE.

JOHN OGDEN (1609 – 1682)

The Ogdens were from the corner of central England where West Riding Yorkshire and Lancashershire meet, an area dominated by the moors of Bronte fame, structures of cut stone and quarries (including one that still bears the Ogden name). John Ogden was born 19 September 1609. On 8 May 1637, he married Jane Bond. The family, with three young sons, along with John's younger brother Richard and his family, sailed to New England in 1640. By 1641, they were settled in the English colony of Stamford, Connecticut, with a cousin, another John Ogden.

Undoubtedly John and Richard Ogden were skilled stone masons, since in 1642, Willem Kieft, the governor of New Amsterdam, contracted with the brothers to *build a large stone Dutch style church within the fort, for the fee of 2500 guilders in cash, beaver or other merchandise, with a bonus of 100 guilders if the work was done in a workmanlike manner.* Dutch trouble with the Indians delayed completion until 1645, however, the brothers were awarded the bonus for their work.

In 1644, John Ogden and associates secured from the Dutch a patent for the "Great Plains of Hempstead" on Long Island, with the promise to settle 100 families within five years. Unhappy with the Dutch treatment of the Indians, in 1647 John received permission from the English authorities at Southampton, Long Island, to plant a colony of six families at Northampton and in 1649 the family moved to the Eastern End of Long Island. The family stayed in the area for 24 years, with John expanding his land holdings, building mills, and organizing a whaling company and *granted the "privilege of taking whales along the coast."* With a reputation for leadership, he soon became a magistrate, a town treasurer and a commissioner for treating with the Indians, and representative from Southampton to the Assembly at Hartford.

In 1664, the English drove the Dutch from New Amsterdam and the territory they claimed. Within weeks John Ogden and associates successfully petitioned the new English Governor Nicolls and were granted permission to settle the first plantation and purchase from the Indians 500,000 acres, between the Raritan River and Passaic River, west of the Staten Island, in what became known as New Jersey. The Elizabethtown Associates paid the Indians *twenty fathom of trading cloth, two made coats, two guns, two kettles, ten bars of lead, twenty handfuls of powder, and after one year four hundred fathom of white wampum.* John Ogden, John Bailey (his share subsequently sold to Governor Carteret), Nathaniel Denton (his share was subsequently sold to John Ogden), Thomas Benedick, John Foster, John Baker and Luke Watson were the principles in the Association, with fifty-six year old John Ogden their acknowledged leader.

Lord Berkeley and Sir George Carteret were given the province of New Jersey; and in July 1665 they appointed Philip Carteret the first governor. Landing in August 1665 at Acher Kol, Carteret read his commission naming him governor of Nova Caesarea or New Jersey and explained to those gathered that New Jersey had been granted to Berkeley and Carteret. He was also granted the inhabitants of New Jersey the liberal *Concessions and Agreements* charter, guaranteeing them among other provisions the all the rights of English freeman. He went on to explain the Proprietary role in the new colony. However, John Ogden stepped forward, representing the interests of the Associates, and explained to Carteret how the land had been purchased from the Indians and the deed confirmed by Governor Nicolls.

Governor Carteret acknowledged the rights and land deeds of the Associates. He changed the name of the town, from Achter Kol to Elizabethtown, in honor of the wife of a Sir George Carteret. Favorably impressed with the developing settlement he wrote that he *determined to locate himself with the Ogden Company and make their plantation the seat of his government* and thus Elizabethtown became the first capital of New Jersey. The Governor appointed John Ogden Justice of the Peace: *Whereas, I have conceived a good Opinion of the ability, prudence and integrity, of you John Ogden Gentleman, in the management of public affairs…appoint John Ogden Justice of the Peace…with full power and authority to execute all such laws…*

John Ogden and his three adult sons, John Jr., David, and Jonathan, took the oath of allegiance to King Charles II on Feb 19, 1665, in Elizabethtown and were individual among the eighty original land-owning Associates of Elizabethtown. A meetinghouse (church) was required under the land patent and John Ogden and his sons built what was the first English speaking church in New Jersey. In 1668, Carteret called for the freeholders in each of the several towns of the province to make choice of two of their number to meet in first General Assembly of New Jersey, at Elizabethtown. John Ogden was elected by the settlers and attended this first New Jersey legislature, in the meetinghouse his family had built.

John Ogden had interests in addition to farming. Soon after his arrival, he built a dam across the creek and a corn mill, a tanyard, and a brickyard. He also extended his whaling rights from Rhode Island down to Barnegat Inlet.

In 1673, the Dutch reclaimed New Amsterdam and New Jersey. The independent and practical settlers of Elizabethtown, led by John Ogden successfully led deputies from Elizabethtown, Newark, Woodbridge, Piscataway, Middletown, and Shrewsbury, to petition the Dutch to grant them all their former privileges. On 1 Sept. 1673, the Dutch made John Ogden *schout* or sheriff of the six towns. On 13 September 1673 the men of the towns took the oath of allegiance to the Dutch. However, peace between England and Holland was restored in 1674, and England regained the Dutch territories.

John Ogden died in 1682, at the age of 73. His will left all of his estate to *my dear and beloved wife and so hath been for above forty years.* Jane Bond Ogden died circa 1691. The Ogdens were buried in the churchyard of the First Presbyterian Church of Elizabeth

The Ogdens had six children (also founders of New Jersey):

1. John Jr., b. England, 3 Mar 1638; d. 24 Nov 1702; m. Elizabeth Plum
2. David, b. England, 11 Jan 1639; d. c Feb 1692; m. Elizabeth (Swaine) Ward
3. Jonathan , b. England, 11 Jan. 1639; d. 3 Jan 1732; m. Rebecca (Wood)
4. Joseph, b. America, 9 Nov 1642 d. before 15 Jan 1690; m. Sarah Whitehead
5. Benjamin, b. America, c.1654; d. 20 Nov 1722; m. Hannah Woodruff
6. Mary Ogden, b. America, ___; d. __; m. John Woodruff

The Belcher-Ogden House

1046 East Jersey Street, Elizabeth, NJ

The Ogden Belcher House stands on the town lot of John Ogden Jr a founder of Elizabethtown. The orange brick section of the house may date from 1680; In the year 1680, it is known, a large brick mansion, called Second Government House, was built for Governor Carteret. The Royal Governor Jonathan Belcher lived in the house from 1751-1757. Lafayette and Alexander Hamilton attended the wedding of Catherine Peartree-Smith to Elisha Boudinot at the house in 1778, when it was owned by William Peartree Smith. In 1797 Colonel Aaron Ogden, a descendant of the original owner, purchased what was then the old brick mansion. Col. Ogden was a distinguished officer in the War for Independence and the 1812 wartime governor of New Jersey.

Lester Robert Dunham # C12

Evelyn Hunt Ogden #296

References:

Ellison, H.C. *Church of the Founding Fathers of New Jersey: A History: First Presbyterian Church, Elizabeth, New Jersey 1664-1964* Carbrook Press, Maine, 1964.

New Jersey Archives, Documents Relating to Colonial History of the State of New Jersey 1664 – 1703, Vol. XXI. (Internet archive).

Savage, James, *Genealogical Dictionary of New England*, Vol. 3., Boston, 1862. (Internet archive).

Thayer, Theodore, *As We Were: The Story of Old Elizabethtown*, Grassman Publishing, Elizabeth, NJ, 1964.

Wheeler, William Ogden, *The Ogden Family in America: The Elizabethtown Branch and their English Ancestry*, (Private printing) Lippincott, Philadelphia, 1907. (Internet archive).

Footnote to History

As whales were abundant along the coast, a whaling company was organized at Elizabethtown, which obtained a charter from the government Feb 15, 1669, granting to John Ogden, Sr., Caleb Carwithy, Jacob Moleing, Wm. Johnson, and Jeffrey Jones, all of Elizabethtown and their compomy consisting of 21 persons, the exclusive right for three years, of taking whales washed ashore along the coast from Barnegat to the eastern part of the province, one twentieth part of the oil in casts to be given to the Lord Proprietors.

GEORGE PACK (c. 1634-1704)

George Pack, born in England, emigrated to America in the 1650's, probably with his parents. It is likely that he settled first in the Milford area of Connecticut. In 1665, he was among the eighty Associates, who with a patent granted by the new English Governor of New York, Governor Richard Nicolls, purchased a large track of land west of the Hudson River from the Indian Sachems of Staten Island, and then settled the first English town in eastern New Jersey. With the coming of Sir George Carteret as Proprietary Governor, the settlement was names Elizabethtown, after the governor's wife. George took the Oath of Allegiance and Fidelity in the town on 19 February 1665.

George and his wife Anna had six children; among them, Samuel, Hannah, Elizabeth, Abigail and Jeziah. Anna died around 1681, after her death, George moved to Rahway where he married Elizabeth Moore, the daughter of Samuel and Hannah Moore, in March 1683. They had four children: Bethiah, Thomas, Job and Benjamin. George died in Rahway on 2 October 1704. His will, the original of which is in the State House in Trenton, New Jersey, mentions his wife Elizabeth and his children.

Timothy Christopher Finton #310

Evelyn Hunt Ogden (Registrar)

The Rahway River

References:

Ellison, Harry C. *Church of the Founding Fathers of New Jersey: A History of the First Presbyterian Church Elizabeth, New Jersey 1664-1964*. Carbrook Press, Cornish Maine. 1964.

Original Associates (1664) – Town Book B 1729

Will of George Pack. State House Trenton, New Jersey

JOHN PANCOAST (PANCKHURST) (c. 1630 – 1694)

On the 13th day of May in the year 1680, the record of the Quaker Men's Monthly Meeting at Ugbrook, Northampton, England provided the following document to:

ye ffrds. And Brethren in New Jersey, in America, greetings. Whereas this friend John Panckhurst of Ashton having laid his intentions of transporting himself into New Jersey and desired a Certificate from this meeting. These many therefore let you understand that ye sd John Panckhurst hath lived soberly as becometh ye truth and yt he is clear from all women as to relative in marriage soe far as we understand. And that friends here have not anything against his transporting himself by reason yt we do not understand but that he hath left all things clear as to his debts: all we thought meet to signifie etc., in testimony thereunto we whose names are here written have set our hand by the direction of ye sd meeting I shall rest you ffrds and brethren.

Signed by Thomas Poole and eight others.

Shortly after securing this Certificate of Removal, John Pancoast left his home at Ashton, five miles from Northampton in Northamptonshire, England, and with his family of eight children (two sons and six daughters), came into America on the ship Paradise, William Evelyn, Master, landing at Burlington on the fourth of October, 1680.

John Pancoast, as he came to be known in America, was the son of Joseph Panckhurst and the grandson of the Reverend Samuel Panckhurst of Ashton. It is believed that the Reverend Samuel Panckhurst, born in 1580, was a clergyman of the Church of England.

Within three weeks of his landing, John's first survey was recorded for *100 acres of land in Burlington County on the north side of Assiscunk Creek against Mattacopenny Branch*. Four days later, 18 October 1680, John Pancoast recorded a deed for *1/32 of a 10-90th share of the province of West Jersey*.

Among the early Jersey Records, the name of John Pancoast is found in several places. As different surveys are made to him; as he signs as a Proprietor, business papers; and in the court of ear-marks for cattle made 8 August 1685, as follows: *John Pancoast. Left ear slit, ye Right cur out.*

John also took an active part in civil affairs of the province. He served as regulator of weights and measures in 1681 and was a Constable of Yorkshire Tenth in 1692. He served as member of the General Assembly of the Province of West New Jersey in 1685.

John Pancoast and his first wife, Elizabeth, had nine children who came to America, three sons and six daughters. However, Elizabeth died in England and John was a widower when he and eight children came over in 1680. One son, James, had preceded them, unknown to them at that time. It seems that James, who was a bound apprentice to a watchmaker in London, was kidnapped and brought to Maryland and sold by the Captain to some gentleman there. However, James worked out his time, bought a tract of land on the Potomac in 1687, acquired a nice estate, and became a leading citizen of Prince Georges County.

John Pancoast married as his second wife, Ann Snowden, the fall of 1682. Seven year later, in 1689, again a widower, he married his third wife, Jane Chapman. Jane, as the widow of Thomas Curtis, had married John Chapman, who died within a few months. When she married John Pancoast, less than five months later, they were reproved for their haste by the Burlington Meeting of Friends. John Pancoast died in December of 1694 and his widow later married her fourth husband, Thomas Crosse.

Shortly after arriving in New Jersey, John's daughter Ann Pancoast married Thomas Smith. Their marriage was recorded as having taken place the 14th of May 1681 and that Thomas Smith was of Cohansey in the Fenwick Colony. Thomas had bought 1000 acres from John Fenwick and located it in Shrewesburie Neck, south of the Cohansey. Of a later transaction is found this record of the land patent. Jan. 26, 1678/80 John Fenwick to Thomas Smith, late of Moseley, Parish of Chadleton, Co., of Stafford, now Shrowesburie Neck, Fenwick Colony, gentlemen, and William Johnson, for 500 acres at Shrowesburie Neck, here after to be called Moseleys Shield and Johnsons Cottage.

By 1684 Thomas Smith was a member of the General Assembly and one of the first to settle on a 16 acre town lot on Main Street, Greenwich, when it was laid out in 1681. Thomas and Ann Pancoast Smith were the progenitors of the Smith family who were early settlers of Frederick County, Virginia. It is through this line that the author of this article descends.

Michael Harrison Charles #299

The Burlington Monthly Meeting was established in 1678. The first meeting house, hexagonal in design and constructed of brick, was finished in 1687. The present one was built in front of the site of the hexagonal house in 1783.

References:

Pancoast, Bennett S. *The Pancoast Family in American*, (Internet online).

Garner, Grace Kelso. *Earliest Settlers Western Frederick Eastern Hampshire Counties in Virginia*, 1978.

REV. ABRAHAM PIERSON (1611-1678)

Abraham Pierson was born in Yorkshire, England (christened in Guiseley Chapel, 22 September 1611), the son of Thomas and Grace Marshall Pierson. He graduated Trinity College, Cambridge in 1632 and came to America in 1639. He was in Boston and Lynn, MA in1640; Southampton, Long Island to 1647; Branford, CT to 1666; then he removed with the group led by Robert Treat to Newark, NJ where he died 9 August 1678. Around 1642, he married either Abigail Mitchell or Abigail Wheelwright (the record is not clear).

After he was ordained in Boston as a Congregational minister, he was pastor of the Southampton church, and led a group of dissidents to Branford, CT in 1647. There he learned the language of the Native Americans and prepared a catechism for them. He also united with John Davenport, founder of the New Haven colony, in opposing the union of the CT (Hartford) and New Haven colonies in 1665. He was said to be quite rigid and inflexible in his theology, and this led to the removal of the Branford congregation to Newark NJ in 1666. He was the pastor of the First Church of Newark, where he preached for the remaining twelve years of his life.

He and Abigail had ten children. Daughter Abigail Pierson married John Davenport Jr., son of the founder of New Haven. Son Abraham Pierson also became a minister (Harvard 1668), succeeded his father as rector of the Newark church to 1692, and then returned to CT where he became the first President of Yale College. Daughter Rebecca Pieson (1654-1732) married Joseph Johnson (1651-1733) of Newark.

Ross Gamble Perry #359

Property allotted to Abraham Pierson

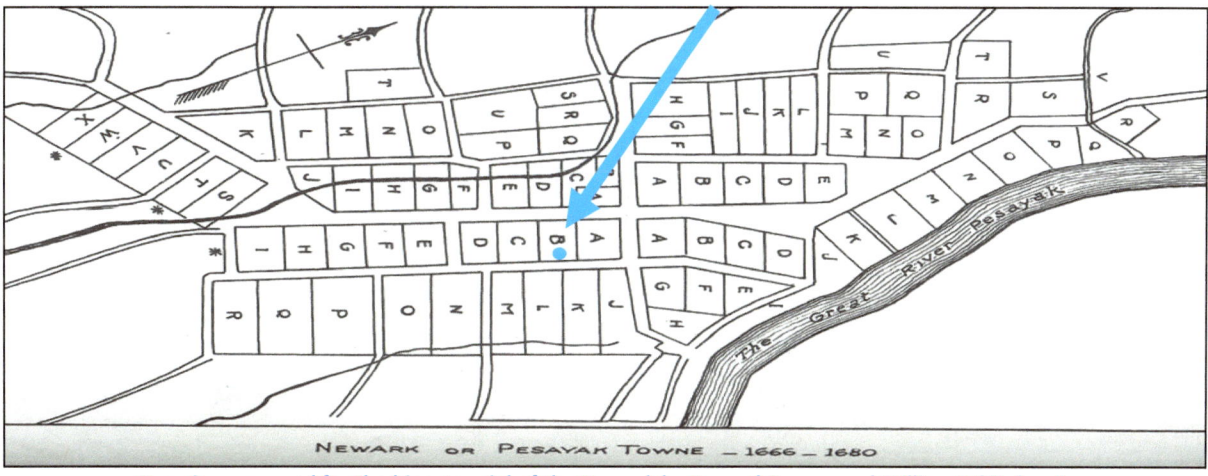

Drawing prepared for the bicentennial of the Newark by Samuel Conger and William Whitehead for the New Jersey Historical Society.

References:

Pierson Millennium. Richard E. Pierson and Jennifer Pierson, p. 89-90, 2007.

Proceedings Commemorative of the Settlement of Newark, 1866. p. 128 (Internet archive).

The Ancestry of Rev. Nathan Grier Parke. Parke and Jacobus, p. 80-83, 1959.

JOHN PIKE (1613 - 1689/90)

John Pike son of John and Dorothy (Day) Pike was baptized 8 November 1613 at Whiteparish, Wiltshire, England. His first wife was Mary, perhaps Turrill or Tarville. He married second, in Woodbridge, New Jersey 30 June 1685 Elizabeth Blossom, widow of Edward Fitz-Randolph. His will was dated 24 January 1688/9 and proved 20 January 1689/90.

John Pike probably came from England in the ship "James" to Newbury, Massachusetts in 1635 with his father. All of his children were born in Newbury to his first wife, and all of his living children, except Joseph, moved with him to New Jersey about 1665. Before moving, John Pike lived for over 30 years in or near Newbury, where he was a town officer a number of times and was representative in 1657 and 1658.

Mr. John Pike was the first name on the list of those who took the "Oath of Alegeance and Fidelitie" in Woodbridge beginning 27 February 1667-68. In 1668 the Governor granted him 380 acres of land in New Jersey. At Woodbridge, he was its first "President" in 1671, "the prominent man of the town" and for some years a magistrate. In 1675, he was appointed captain of the militia. His will mentions *late wife Mary*, children John Pike, Thomas, Ruth wife of Abr. Toppin, Joseph and Hana.

Don Charles Nearpass #C44

Grave of John Pike, First Presbyterian Church of Woodbridge, Founded 1669

References:

Colonial and Revolutionary Lineages of America, Vol. 2, pp. 250-251 (Online Books).

Hoyt, David W. *The Old Families of Salisbury and Amesbury, Massachusetts*, pp. 285-286, Reprint 1982.

Monnette, Orra E. *First Settlers of Ye Plantations of Piscataway and Woodbridge, Part 5*, p. 754, 1930,

New England Historical and Genealogical Register, 1912, Vol. 66 p.260. (Internet archive).

Records of the Pike Family Association of America, pp. 38-40, 1906.

New Jersey Archives, Documents Relating to the Colonial History of the State of New Jersey, Vol. 1, p. 50. (Internet archive).

RICHARD PITTENGER (PEWTINGER) (abt 1645 - 17xx)

Richard Pewtinger (Piewtinger, Pettinger, Pittinger) came to New Jersey in 1666 on the ship *Philip* with Philip Carteret as one of eighteen young men who were servants to Philip and his brother Sir George. The History of Elizabeth, New Jersey, states Carteret's immigrants were a distinct class, in an inferior station, with whom the original planters had little congeniality and familiarity. However, Pittenger was given land next to Philip Carteret in 1665. According to historical records, Richard was a witness to the marriage of Mrs. Margarita Stuyvesant and Hendrick Droogestradt in 1678. Margarite was the half-sister of Pieter Stuyvesant, who had been the Director-General of New Amsterdam, New Netherland, under the Dutch.

In 1700, according to the Reformed Dutch Church of New Amsterdam Church records, Richard married Annetje Anthony. The Pittengers had two sons, Richard II and Johnnes/John. It is probable that there were other children.

Marriages within the Dutch community abounded for at least four generations and their histories are recorded in New Jersey and New Harlem records. Richard Pittenger would have been proud of his descendants, which have included educators, theologians, patriots and one Congressional Medal of Honor recipient.

Sharon Pratt Patton #351

Governor Philip Carteret landed at the new English settlement at 1665;
Painting in the Hall of Records, Newark, NJ

References:

Calendar of Wills, New Jersey. Pg 368, 16 October 1715. (Internet archive).

Church Members List, 1700. Reformed Dutch Church of New Amsterdam (New York City)

Hatfield, Edwin F. *History of Elizabeth, New Jersey*. New York, 1868. (Internet archive).

Pittenger Jr, Tress E. *Pittenger Families of New Jersey – 1665 to 1800*, 1999. (Internet archive)

Toler, Henry Pennington. *New Harlem Register*, 1902. (Internet archive).

ELIZABETH POWELL (1677 – 1714)

Robert Powell was a chandler who emigrated from Martin-le-Grand, London, England, to West Jersey in 1677 on the Kent, disembarking with his wife at the mouth of Raccoon Creek. Most of Kent passengers remained for the winter in the Swedish settlement there. It is probable that Elizabeth was born at New Stockholm, the first English child born in Burlington County, New Jersey. She became known as Virginia Dare of Burlington.

Elizabeth's parents settled on a farm of 150 acres, on the north side of Assiscunck (Mill) Creek, West of Rancocas Village. Robert Powell was one of the Quakers who signed the *Concessions and Agreements* of the Proprietors, Freeholders and Inhabitants of the Province of West Jersey in America.

Elizabeth Powell, daughter of Robert and Prudence Powell, was born 7 August 1677 in Burlington County, New Jersey. She married first, at age 18, on 16 November 1695, James Newbold, who was baptized 20 January 1669/70 at St. Peter's Church, Sheffield, England. Elizabeth and James Newbold had one daughter, Ann, before he died in 1697, in Mansfield Township, Burlington County, West Jersey. Elizabeth married second, on 21 October 1699, at Daniel Wills' house in Northampton Township, Jacob DeCou, who was born 7 Feb 1668 in Yorkshire, England. The DeCous had a pair of twin girls, four sons and two daughters. Elizabeth died in June 1714, at age 37. Jacob DeCou died in December 1735/36, in Burlington County, New Jersey.

Mary McCall Middleton #C 54

References:

Boyd, Julian P. *Fundamental Laws and Constitutions of New Jersey, 1664-1964, in New Jersey Historical Series, by*, *Vol.17*:103

DeCou, S. Ellen and John Allen DeCou. *Genealogy of the DeCou Family, New Brunswick, New Jersey*, 1910.

"DeCou Family" in the *John P. Dorman Collection*, Rutgers University Library

Encyclopedia of American Quaker Genealogy, Vol. 2:181 (Internet archive)

Newbold and Stockton. *Newbold Family and Connections*, 1928.

Platt Jr., Charles.*Newbold Genealogy in America*, 1964.

BENJAMIN PRICE (1621-1712)

Benjamin Price was born 1621 in England, probably at Olney, Buckinghamshire. He married Mary Sayre, daughter of Thomas Sayre of Southampton, Long Island, New York; died at Elizabethtown, New Jersey between 30 August 1705 and 7 October 1712, the dates of his will.

The first record of Benjamin Price in this country appears to be 10 March 1639, when he was a witness to a deed for an island off the eastern end of Long Island by the agent of Lord Sterling to Lion Gardner now known as Gardiner's Island. Benjamin was employed as an overseer, or head farmer, on the island.

The Prices removed to East Hampton where in 1650 Benjamin was Town Recorder. He held that position alternately for many years, evidently having had a good education. His land allotment totaled about 40 acres, including a town lot. In 1665 Benjamin and six other residents purchased the eastern tip of Long Island, now known as Montauk, from the Indians. This area was rented by other townsmen as a pasture for their cattle.

In 1665 Benjamin joined with many other "East Enders", including his son Benjamin, Jr., in the Elizabethtown purchase where he took the oath of allegiance 19 February 1665, having agreed to the sale of his property in East Hampton. There were 80 Associates in this purchase: Benjamin received 270 acres.

Many problems arose in East New Jersey between the proprietors and the inhabitants over land and quitrent arrears. On 13 May 1699, Justice Benjamin Price, along with many other townsmen, attacked the Woodbridge jail with clubs and staves, to free two prisoners who had been jailed for stirring up opposition in the towns against the revenue act of March 1699. Benjamin had seven children, and outlived his wife, and most of the Elizabethtown founders.

Elaine Elliot Johnston #174

References:

Banta, Theodore M. Sayre Family, 1901. (Internet archive).

Gardiner, Curtiss C. *The Papers and Biography of Lion Gardner*, 1883. (Internet archive).

Gardiner, David. *Chronicles of Easthampton, New York*, 1871. (Internet archive).

Hatfield, Rev. Edwin F. *History of Elizabeth, New Jersey*, 1868, (Internet archive).

New Jersey Archives Vol. XXIII: 374 (Internet archive)

Pelletreau, William S. *History of Long Island, Vol. II*, 1908. (Internet archive).

Price, Frederick L. *The Trace of a Price Family*, 1981.

Pomfret, John E. *The Province of East New Jersey 1609-1702*, 1962.

JOHN PRIDMORE (PREDMORE) (1661-1702)

John Pridmore (Predmore) was born at Dorsetshire, England in 1661. When he immigrated to the New World is not known; however, he is recorded as among the first settlers of Piscataway and Woodbridge, New Jersey.

John Pridmore married Anne Higgins in 1682, at Piscataway, New Jersey. Anne Higgins was born in 1663 in Eastham, Massachusetts. She was the daughter of Richard Higgins and his second wife, Mary Yates of Plymouth. Richard Higgins was a resident and pioneer settler of Plymouth and Eastham, Massachusetts, as well as a settler of Piscataway, New Jersey.

Not much is known of the Higgins–Pridmore family, except that they were land owners, operated their own farms and performed services for the community. Among their holdings was land along the Raritan River (Predmore Swamp) reported to have become the site of Rutgers College.

South of Piscataway, in the center of the colony of New Jersey, by Cranbury Creek, a mill town began to be developed along an old Indian trail much used by colonial travelers. In 1697 Cranbury Towne received its charter from the King. Responding to the needs of travelers for a place to eat and drink, get fresh horses and spend the night, John Predmore Jr. operated a post house as early as 1730, on the site of the present Cranbury Inn. He also ran a stage from Philadelphia to New York in the 1750's. His house was replaced in 1780 by the Perrine House.

Daniel Byram Bush #345

References:

New Jersey Historical Society. *Manuscript Collection, NJ Genealogy Vol. VII*, No 4913-5541, Dec 19, 1914 & Dec 16, 1916.

First Settlers of Piscataway and Woodbridge, New Jersey, New Jersey Genealogy Vol. No 5115, (Internet archive).

Stryker Men of New Jersey in the Revolutionary War, New Jersey Historical Society. (Internet archive).

JOHN READING (1657-1717)

John Reading was born 14 September 1657 in Pipe Hill, Staffordshire England, the son of John Reading and his wife Mary. He was evidently an educated wealthy Quaker and in 1677 he purchased a 1/6 share of proprietary from Edward Byllynge, who held the patent to the West Jersey territory. He married Elizabeth in England on 22 February 1682 and emigrated from London prior to 1684. The family established a homestead in the area that would become Gloucester County. John was a surveyor and became active in civil administration; he was elected a member of the Burlington County Assembly in 1685. When Gloucester County was formed in 1688, was chosen Clerk and Recorder of Gloucester County in 1688, an office he held until 1702.

On 6 Sep. 1688 the resident proprietors organized a Council of West Jersey Proprietors to record proprietor *rights to the soil, supervise the distribution of dividends, issue warrants of survey, and have charge of un-appropriated lands*. John Reading was appointed one of the five commissioners from Gloucester County and was elected Secretary, a position he held for virtually the next 28 years. John Reading was a Captain of Militia in 1695, 1702, 1713, 1714, and Lieutenant Colonel in the Hunterdon County New Jersey Militia in 1715.

In 1703, the Council of Proprietors appointed John Reading, William Biddle and John Mills to survey and purchase from the Lenape-Delaware Indians the great tract of 150,000 acres between the Raritan and Delaware Rivers. In 1709, Col. Reading relocated from Gloucester County to the part of Burlington County that later became Amwell Township, Hunterdon County. His first purchase of land there was in 1704; in a deed dated 12 Nov. 1709 he calls his home Mount Amwell in the county of Burlington. The estate was located on the Delaware River near present day Stockton.

In 1711, Governor Hunter commissioned John Reading as one of the judges of the Supreme Court of the colony. In 1713, Queen Anne confirmed Governor Hunter's nomination of John Reading and he was sworn in as a member of the Royal Council of New Jersey on 5 Dec. 1713. Shortly after he became a member of the Royal Council a bill was presented for the organization of Hunterdon County. The minutes from the council for February 1713/14 indicate that it was *John Reading, Esq. who reported the bill out of committee*. It is believed that it was the work of Colonel Reading, and that he is entitled to be called the father of Hunterdon County.

John and Elizabeth had at least two children. Their son John Reading Jr.. became the first native born governor of the New Jersey colony. John Reading Sr. died 30 Oct. 1717 in Amwell Township, Hunterdon County, New Jersey at the age of 60.

David R. Reading #321

References:

Leach, J, G. *Genealogical and Biographical Memorials of the Reading, Howell, Watts, Latham, and Elkins Families.* 1898. (Internet archive).

Pomfret, John E. *The Province of West New Jersey 1609-1702.*, Princeton University Press, 1956.

Pomfret, John E *The West Jersey Proprietors and Their Lands*, D. Van Nostrand Inc., 1964.

First Settlers, Colonists and Biographies by Descendants

WALTER REEVE (1650/57 - 1698)

Walter Reeve was probably born between 1650 and 1657, either in England or Wales. He married first, Susanna Alger (-) about 1670 and after her death he married Ann Howell on 11 November (December), 1682. He died between 16 May 1698 and 18 June 1698, the dates of his will.

Although records show that several Reeves migrated from Long Island and settled in West Jersey, it is believed that Walter Reeve came to Burlington County either from England or from the West Indies, some time prior to 1673. He settled on 70 acres of land on the south side of the north branch of Rancocas Creek, midway between the present town of Rancocas and Mount Holly. He later acquired 350 acres by survey and 160 acres by purchase, plus the 70 acres to which he never took title. From his Rancocas property he engaged in export trade with foreign ports.

Walter Reeve followed the Church of England while most of his neighbors were Friends (Quakers). This difference in religion may have contributed to some of the difficulties with his neighbors, mainly over property boundaries. In 1685 he cut logs on land that was in dispute. In 1693 he secured an attachment for a haystack, placed by others on a "peece of marrish" which he claimed.

The inventory of Reeve's estate amounted to £ 242.19 of which £ 98 was for real property, which was listed as consisting *of a house and plantation of 160 acres, a dwelling house by the creek side and 200 acres.*

George L. Reeves #C 61

References:

New Jersey Archives, Marriage Records, Vol. XXII. (Internet archive).

New Jersey Archives, Liber B, Part 1. (Internet archive).

Reeves, H. F. *The Reeves Family*, 1951

Stevens and Birch. *The Reeves Family*, 1930

Footnote to History

On 21 November 1681 the West Jersey Assembly first met in Burlington, with Governor Samuel Jennings.

Biographies of Founders of New Jersey

EDWARD RIGGS (c. 1614 - 1668)

Edward Riggs, son of Edward Riggs, may have been born in Yorkshire, England c. 1614; married 5 April 1635 Elizabeth Roosa of Boston, Massachusetts; died in Newark, New Jersey 1668.

Edward Riggs was 19 or 20 years old when he came to New England with his parents and siblings and settled with them at Roxbury, Massachusetts in 1633. He was a Sergeant in the Pequot War of 1637 then settled in Milford, Connecticut, where he remained until 1666.

Riggs was on the committee to select the site for the new settlement to be made in New Jersey. His name is included among those who signed the *Fundamental Agreements* of the settlers on 24 June 1667 and the first Tax Board in 1667 gave him a valuation of £3,200. When the move was made to the site at Newark, New Jersey, his wife Elizabeth Roosa Riggs was the only woman on the site during the first summer; some of their children came with them. After Edward died in 1668, his widow married Caleb Carwithe prior to 1671.

Marian L. LoPresti #C48

Property allotted to Edward Riggs

Drawing prepared for the bicentennial of the Newark by Samuel Conger and William Whitehead for the New Jersey Historical Society.

References:

Sharpe, Campbell. *Seymour Past & Present*, Bassett, 1902.

Orcutt, S. *History of Derby, Connecticut*, 1880. (Internet archive).

Urquart, Frank John. *History of the City of Newark*, 1913. (Internet archive).

JOSEPH ROBINS (1670/71- 1709)

Joseph Robins was born in 1670/71; he married Anna Pack from Elizabethtown in 1692. Robins owned land conveyed to him by his grandfather Daniel Robins in 1696, in Crosswicks, Upper Freehold in what was then Monmouth County and which is now Burlington County. Joseph's will is dated 8 June 1709.

Summarized by Dr. Evelyn Ogden from documents

submitted by #371 Margaret Jo Thornton Dill

Crosswicks Friends Meetinghouse

References:

Vital Records of Woodbridge New Jersey: Calendar of New Jersey Wills, Vol. I (Internet archive).

Footnote to History

The Crosswicks Friends Meeting is the successor of the Chesterfield Monthly Meeting founded in 1684. By 1692, a small wooden meeting house had been built on the Quaker property at Crosswicks. In 1706 the building was replaced on the north side of the property. The current Crosswicks Meeting House was built in 1773.

MOSES ROLFE (1681-1746)

Moses Rolfe was born in the Arlington section of Cambridge, Massachusetts on the 14th day of October, 1681, a son of John and Mary Scullard. Moses married Mary Hale, a Woodbridge, New Jersey native, born November 28, 1678, daughter of Samuel and Sarah Isley Hale, on 4 June, 1702 at Woodbridge. Eleven children were born to them in Woodbridge, namely: Samuel, Elizabeth, Easter, Appiah, Richard, Nathaniel, Jonathan, Richard, Robert, and Henry .

According to sources, the Rolfe family (brothers and sisters of Moses, with the exception of sister, Rebecca Rolfe Whittemore, who stayed in Massachusetts), went to New Jersey in the year, 1685. Moses' brother, John, died intestate on 11 June 1696 and his estate papers show Moses as an heir and resident of Woodbridge, in 1696/97.

Moses was a member of the New Jersey Assembly from (1721-1727); Town Clerk of Woodbridge (1712-1731); Freeholders Clerk, Woodbridge (1712-1731); Justice of the Peace, Woodbridge (1718); Tax Collector of the County of Middlesex (1727); and lastly, Justice of the Peace of Middlesex and Somerset Counties (1713-1721).

In 1711, in the building of the Meeting House in Woodbridge, Moses contributed to the building of this place of worship whereby he paid for some supplies and let his slave help by drawing water for the builders.

Moses Rolfe died on 1 March 1746, at the age of 64, having left a sizable estate. He owned property in New York, as well as in New Jersey.

#413 Byron David Rolfe

References:

Nelson, William. Documents Relating to the Colonial History of the State of New Jersey, Vol XXIII, Calendar of Wills Vol. I 1670-1730. (Internet archive).

Rolfe, Frederick G. The Early Rolfe Settlers of New England, Vol. I, Books I and II, Gateway Press,1995.

Footnote to History

On 25 May 1668, the first representative Assembly in New Jersey met at Elizabethtown.

RICHARD ROUNSAVELL (1658-1703)

Richard Rounsavell was born on 12 Mar 1658 and christened on 22 Mar 1658, in the village of Padstow in Cornwall, England. He emigrated from England about 1680 to Stratford, in the Colony of Connecticut, where he had a half-acre home-lot and other lands. He married Hannah (last name unknown) between 1688 and 1690. About 1690 the family moved to Wickapogue, Southampton, Long Island.

About 1700 the family moved from Long Island, and became among the first settlers of Hopewell Township, Burlington County (now Hunterdon County) New Jersey. The couple had three children: Martha and Richard born before 1698, probably on Long Island, and Benjamin born in 1700 in Hopewell, New Jersey. It was in New Jersey that he signed his will on 5 Feb 1703 and probated 28 April 1704.

Summarized by Dr. Evelyn Ogden from documents

submitted by #298 Frank Lee Perryman

New Jersey Wildlife

References:

Rounsavell, Mark and Brian Rounsavell. *Richard Rounsavell and His Descendants*, Vol. II, 2002.

THOMAS SCATTERGOOD (16xx – 1697)

Thomas Scattergood was born in England, date unknown, where he married Elizabeth Jarvis, probably at Stepney Parish, London. He died between 8 and 11 November 1697, the dates of his will, at Burlington, New Jersey.

Thomas Scattergood probably arrived at Burlington, New Jersey, about 1677 with his wife and seven children. Tradition has it that the family lived for a number of years in a cave located on Craft's Creek, about one mile west of Columbus, New Jersey. This area was later included in the family plantation. This may be truth, which is stranger than fiction, or a myth which has arisen from the fact that the first mention of Thomas in the New Jersey Archives is dated 9th mo. 1685 (November), where he is cited as a neighbor bordering on land received in another man's deed. There has been speculation that some early pages of the original records have been lost and they could have mentioned a purchase by Thomas that took place much earlier.

A carpenter, Thomas and his wife Elizabeth came from the Parish of Stepney, London and were Quakers, raising their children in that faith also. He signed the testimony against George Keith which was issued by the Quakers in 1692. Little else is known concerning the Scattergood family. Sons Thomas, Joseph and Benjamin outlived their father, as did daughters Sarah, Hannah and Tomsin, but daughter Elizabeth predeceased her father, as did Thomas' wife Elizabeth, who died before his will was written. The inventory of his personal estate amounted to £125 5s 6p.

Edsall Riley Johnston, Jr. #175

References:

DeCou, George. *Burlington: A Provincial Capitol*, 1983.

New Jersey Archives, Vol. XXIII (Internet archive)

French, Howard Barclay. *Genealogy of Thomas French, Vol. I*, 1909. (Internet archive).

Schooley, James. *Trails of Our Fathers*, 1917. (Internet archive).

JOHN SCHENCK (1670-1753)

Roelof Schenck was born in 1619 at Amersfoort, Utrecht, Holland. He emigrated to New Amsterdam with his brother, Jan, and sister, Annetje, in 1650. John Schenck, the son of Roelof Schenck and Neeltje Van Couwenhoven, was born on March 1, 1670 at Flatlands, Kings County, New York.

He married his cousin, Sarah Willemse Van Kouwenhoven on October 1, 1692. She was born on December 20/27, 1674 at Kings County, New York, She was the daughter of William VanKouwenhoven and Jannetije Monfoort. John and Sarah shared the same great grandfather, Gerret Wolphertse Van Kouwenhoven, who emigrated from Holland to New Amsterdam around 1625 and was one of the head farmers for the Dutch West Indies Company.

Land deeds demonstrate that John Schenck settled in Monmouth County, New Jersey as early as March 30, 1697. On this date, he purchased land in Monmouth County from Peter Wickof. John and his wife, Sarah, had eleven children: Roelof, Sarah, Altje, Rachel, Maria, Leah, William, Jannetje, John, Antje, and Peter.

John Schenck died on January 30, 1753 and Sarah died on January 31, 1761, in Pleasant Valley, Monmouth County, New Jersey. Both John and his wife are buried at the Holmdel Cemetery in Holmdel, Monmouth County, New Jersey.

Theodore Matthew Duay, III #301

References:

Beekman, George C., *Early Dutch Settlers of Monmouth County, New Jersey*. Freehold: Moreau Brothers, Publishers, 1901, Second Edition reprint.

The Township of Neptune Historical Society. Pages 1, 4, & 6. 1974. (Internet archive).

Cocheu, Lincoln C., "The Van Kouwenhoven – Conover Family," *The New York Genealogical and Biographical Record*, Reprinted in *Genealogies of Long Island Families, Volume II*. (Baltimore: Genealogical Publishing Company, Inc., pgs. 506 – 510, 524. 1987.

Article reproduced on "Broderbund Software's Family Archive CD # 173," (*Genealogies of Long Island Families, 1600's – 1800's*).

Will of John Schenck, dated 11 Sept 1746, proved 03 June 1755, #2099-2102M, New Jersey State Archives. (Internet archive).

THOMAS SCHOOLEY (1650 – 1724)

Thomas Schooley, son of John Schooley and his first wife Elizabeth Fletcher, was born at Aston cum Aughton, Yorkshire, England in 1650. Elizabeth Fletcher was a daughter of Richard and Alice (-) Fletcher. Thomas married Sarah Parker, daughter of George and Sarah Parker of Northampton Township, Burlington County, New Jersey, on 8 October 1686 at Burlington, New Jersey. Thomas died at Chesterfield, Burlington County, between 6 February and 21 April 1724, the dates of his will.

The family name was originally spelled "Scholey," but the local pronunciation was "Schooley", so the modem spelling is now "Schooley". Thomas was a signer of the *Concessions and Agreements* in London in 1676 which provided for the settlement of parts of New Jersey. As a result of religious convictions, Thomas was the first of his family to depart for America. He was one of the second group of Quakers who came as heads of families on the File-Boat "Martha" from Hull, to settle at Burlington County in West Jersey in November 1677. He was 27 years old. His brother, Robert Scholey, was next of the family to arrive, followed by their father, John, whose first wife had died. John had married his second wife, Isabel Hancock, in England, and brought her along, with their son John, Jr. and perhaps daughters. There was much confusion concerning these various branches of the Scholey family in some early records.

Thomas lived most of his life at Onea Nickon in Chesterfield Township, Burlington County with his wife Sarah, who outlived him. Their six children were baptized at the Burlington Monthly Meeting of Quakers: Samuel, John, Elizabeth, Sarah, Mary and Alice.

Edsall Riley Johnston, Jr. #175

The Burlington Monthly Meeting was established in 1678. The first meeting house, hexagonal in design and constructed of brick, was finished in 1687. The present one was built in front of the site of the hexagonal house in 1783.

References:

Woodward, Major E. M. *History of Burlington County*, New Jersey, 1883.

Harrington, Jean Wolfe. *The Schooley Family of Clermont County, Ohio and Some of the Descendants Scattered Over the United States*, 1983.

New Jersey Archives, Vol. XXIII: 406. (Internet archive).

ANDERS SINNICKSON (c. 1651 -1699)

Anders Sinnickson was born in Sweden c. 1651, and was among 92 Finns aboard the Mercurius, bound for the colony of New Sweden. He arrived as part of a group of five which included his father Sinnick Broer, his mother, a sister and a brother, Broer Sinnickson.

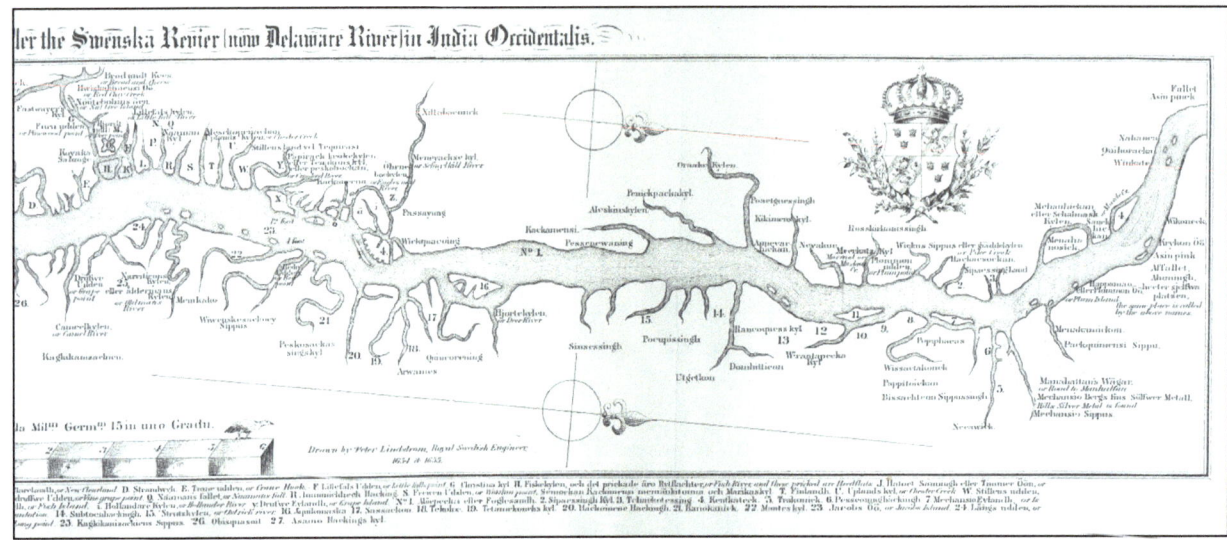

1655 New Swedish Chart of Delaware River; Source: Wikimedia

When the ship arrived in the Delaware, in March 1656, New Sweden did not exist anymore. The colony had been surrendered to the Dutch the preceding September. Even worse, the Dutch commander at Fort Casimir (New Castle) forbid the ship to dock and unload its cargoes and passengers. Under directions from Governor Peter Stuyvesant, the Mercurius was ordered back to Sweden.

The potentially deadly impasse was broken by local Swedish leaders and their Indian friends. Secretly during the night, Indians "in great numbers" boarded the Mercurius and defiantly ordered the ship's lieutenant to take the ship past the fort to Tinicum Island, where both passengers and cargo were unloaded. The Dutch did not dare to fire upon the ship with so many Indians aboard.

In 1677 Anders was residing at Feren Hook on the south side of Christina River, and by 1678 he had married Margaret Poulson. On 7 January 1678/9 he was sued for medicines supplied to his wife and child. Later in the same year he moved to Chestnut Neck in Salem County, where he was granted 260 acres north of Parting Creek. This would remain his home for the rest of his life.

After giving birth to two children (Ingrid and John), Anders' wife Margaret died. His second wife, Sarah, was the mother of his other five children. Anders Sinnickson wrote his will on 17 June 1696, but it was not proved until 4 April 1700. He had given two and one-half pounds for Holy Trinity Church but had probably died before 24 June 1699, when only his wife was assigned a pew in the new church. His widow, Sarah Sinnickson, was buried at the Penn's Neck church on 27 February 1719. All seven of his children married:

1. Ingrid Sinnickson, born c. 1678, married by 1696 Peter Bilderback and, after his death, John Hendrickson, Jr.
2. John Sinnickson, born c. 1682, married Ann Philpot Gilljohnson, 28 January 1725, and had three children: John, Sarah and Sinnick.

3. Andrew Sinnickson, born c. 1691, married Maria Weinam c. 1712.
4. Sinnick Sinnickson, born c. 1693, married Maria Philpot, 31 October 1717. He died in Penns Neck in 1750, survived by a son Andrew Sinnickson, who was later described by Pastor Nicholas Colin as the wealthiest Finn in West New Jersey.
5. Margaret Sinnickson, born c. 1695, married [1] Thomas Vickery, [2] Albert Bilderback, and [3] William Mecum.
6. Catharina Sinnickson, born c. 1697, married Christiern Peterson on 10 May 1716.
7. Dorothea Sinnickson, born c. 1699, married Oney Stanley, 27 November 1718.

Michael Sayre Maiden, Jr. # 295

References:

Craig, Peter Stebbins. 1693 Census of the Swedes on the Delaware, pp 22-3, 98-99, 146-7, 1993.

Craig, Peter Stebbins. *1671 Census of the Swedes on the Delaware*, pp 8, 39, 42, 71, 73, 1999.

Craig, Dr. Peter S. "Sinnick Broer the Finn and his Sinex, Sinnickson & Falkenberg Descendants", in *Swedish Colonial News*, Vol. 2, Number 7, 2002.

Dunn, Richard, Editor. *Papers of William Penn 1680-1684*, Vol. 2, p. 622, 1982.

Salem County Tercentenary Committee. *Fenwick's Colony*, 1964.

New Jersey Archives, First Series, Vol. XXI, pp 544, 568, 576. (Internet archive).

Footnote to History

In the 17th century, Sweden was a major European power and sought to extend its influence to the New World. In 1637, the New Sweden Company was formed to trade furs and tobacco. Under the command of Peter Minuit, who had been Governor of the Dutch Colony New Netherlands from 1626 to 1631, two ships sailed from Sweden in 1637, reaching Delaware Bay in March 1638. Over the next seventeen years, eleven vessels and 600 Swedes and Finns came to New Sweden, where they built settlements and established farms on both sides of the Delaware. The Dutch Governor Stuyvesant put an end to Swedish sovereignty in 1655. However, he permitted the colonists to continue as a Swedish Nation; governing by a court of their choosing, practicing their religion, organizing a militia, retaining their lands and trading with the native people. This agreement continued until William Penn received his charter for Pennsylvania and the three lower counties of Delaware.

GILES SLOCUM (c. 1623 – 1681)

Giles Slocum was baptized 28 Sep. 1623 at Somerset, England, and came to America prior to 1638. He married Joan Cook around 1640. The couple had nine children, probably all born in Portsmouth, RI: Joanna (m. Jacob Mott), John, Giles (m. Anne Lawton), Ebenezer (m. Mary Thurston), Nathaniel, Peleg (m. Mary Holder), Samuel, Mary (m. Abraham Tucker), Eliezer (m. Elephel Fitzgerald).

Giles Slocum was allotted thirty acres of land in Portsmouth, RI in 1648. In the same year he purchased from William Benton his homestead farm, which adjoined his brother-in-law John Cook's land. In 1655 Giles was on the roll of freeman. In 1668 his "ear mark" was recorded as a *crop in the right eare, with a slitt in the left eare and a hapeny under, of thirty years standing*. He acquired considerable land in Rhode Island and Massachusetts. He also purchased land near the northern part of what is now Long Branch, Monmouth County, New Jersey in 1697 and again in 1670. He gave his sons large tracts of land in Rhode Island, New Plymouth and New Jersey.

Giles Slocum and his wife were early members of the Society of Friends, and Giles remembered them with a bequest in his will. Giles died in Portsmouth, RI in 1681.

Donna Lee Wilkinson Malek   # 336

Monmouth County

References:

Crapo, Henry Howland. "Certain Comeovers", New Bedford, MA (Online).

RI Genealogical Register, Vol. 3, No. 1, pg 24, July 1980

Roberts, Gary Boyd. *Genealogies of RI Families, Vol. 1*, pg 220, Abe Books, 1989.

Cutter, William Richard. *New England Families: History of the Slocums and Slocombs of America, Vol. II* pg 700. 859. (Internet archive).

JOHN SMALLEY (1613–1692)

John Smalley, a tailor by trade, sailed with Edward Winslow and others on the William and Francis in 1632; departing London, March 9 and arriving in the Massachusetts Bay Colony, June 5. By 1637/38, John is recorded through land grants as having settled in the Plymouth Colony, where he continued to acquire and trade small parcels. In 1638, he married Ann Walden; they had four children who grew to adulthood: Hannah, John Jr., and twins Isaac and Mary. John was admitted as a freeman to the Plymouth Colony in 1641.

In 1644, John joined with seven other Plymouth families in negotiating a land purchase from the Native Americans on Cape Cod; where they founded the town of Nauset (later Eastham). He served in various public capacities, including as Constable in 1647, Surveyor of Highways in 1649, and Juror of the "Grand Inquest" several times between 1654 and 1667. Yet John chafed under the Plymouth authorities, whether due to his ownership of a tavern or their disapproval of his newly-discovered Baptist faith. Around 1669, John joined with neighbor Richard Higgins and others in moving to the Saconnet settlement (now Little Compton, Rhode Island); and then to Piscataway, New Jersey, approximately four years after its first settlers had arrived. He was accompanied by wife Ann and sons John Jr. and Isaac (Hannah and Mary remained in Eastham.)

Several years after obtaining his first land grant in Piscataway, John had it surveyed in 1677. In 1685, he took up another land grant—by 1690, owning 118-1/2 acres. John Jr. owned an additional 215 acres adjacent; Isaac would accumulate sizable holdings nearby. Their land was proximate to the Raritan Landing inland port, site of present-day Johnson Park. John was appointed Magistrate by the Dutch in 1673-74; commissioned Justice of the Peace in 1675; and appointed Justice of the Court of Sessions, serving for several years. John died in Piscataway in 1692; Ann's death followed in 1693/94. In 1689, John Jr. had helped to found the First Baptist Church of Piscataway, the second-oldest Baptist church in New Jersey and the 10th-oldest Baptist church in America. Ann is buried in its cemetery; John's gravesite is unknown.

#388 James Reed Campbell Jr.

References:

Underhill, Lora Altine. *Descendants of Edward Small of New England*, 1844. (Internet archive).

Anderson, Robert Charles. *The Great Migration Begins: Immigrants to New England, 1620-1633, Volume III*, (Internet archive).

Lee, Francis Bazeley, Editor. Genealogical *and Memorial History of the State of New Jersey, Volume II*, 1910. (internet archive).

JOHN SOMERS (1623/24-1723)

John Somers was born 1623/24 in Worchester, England. He left the birthplace of his forefathers for conscience sake as he was fully persuaded of the principles of George Fox. Much has been written about John's ancestors, among which were several knights with fascinating stores surrounding their lives. One such tale is about Sir George Somers, born 1554, whose ship the "Sea Venture" bound for Jamestown, Virginia, with supplies for the famishing Colony, sprang a leak, forcing them to land on the "Isles of Devils." Shakespeare's "Tempest" is believed to have been about this adventure of the Somer's family.

John Somers emigrated from England, with his first wife (who died on the voyage), in 1681/82 and settled in Upper Dublin, now Somerton, Pennsylvania. He married for a second time, Hannah Hodgkin. The marriage is recorded in the Abington Friends Meeting records "ye 2nd of 1st mo. 1684." Hannah was born in Worchester, England in 1667. John and Hannah were both ministers, so their house was used as a Meeting House for the Friends. In 1691/93 the family moved to Greater Egg Harbor, New Jersey. Records indicate that John purchased 3000 acres in New Jersey, in what became known as Somers Point, on 11 Mar 1695. As shown by the Journal and Votes of the House of Representatives of New Jersey he was appointed supervisor of roads at the first court held in Cape May County, Justice of the Peace 1698, assessor for Egg Harbor 1708, and a member of the fourth Assembly of the Province Assembly of 1709.

John and Hannah Somers had eight children, all of whom led productive lives in Somers Point. John died October 1723, and Hannah died in October 1738 at the Somers Plantation, Somers Point, New Jersey; both were buried in the family cemetery on the estate.

Reba Bradway Fidler Baglio   #348

References:

Somers, Hubert. "Somers Family in England and America".

Atlantic County Historical Society "A History of the Somers Mansion", Somers Point, N.J. 1942 (Ancestry.com).

JAMES STEELMAN (JONS MANSSON) (1660/70 - 1734/35)

James Mansson (Steelman) was the son of Hans Mansson, a Swedish cavalryman from Skara, Sweden. In 1641, Hans Mansson was arrested for damaging several apple and cherry trees in the Royal Garden in Varnhem, and was given the option of being sentenced to death or emigrating to New Sweden. Upon arrival to the New Sweden colony in November 1641, Hans served as an indentured laborer cultivating tobacco at the "Plantation at Upland" till 1648. Finally, he was able to settle on the west side of the Schuykill at Aronameck, now West Philadelphia, PA. In 1654 he married Ella Stille, affectionately known as "Mrs. Ella" within the Swedish community. In 1667 Hans Mansson settled his family in present day Cinnaminson Twp., Burlington County, New Jersey, on 100 acres on the east side of Pennsauken Creek, where he was buried in 1691. Captain Hans Mansson is listed in the Burlington County Records of freeholders and inhabitants in the "ye Cort of Burlington" on 3 August 1680. Upon the death of Captain Hans Mansson, his children and "Mrs. Ella" took the last name Steelman (Stilleman), anglicizing their name while establishing their family lineage from Hans Mansson and Ella Stille.

James Mansson Steelman (a.k.a. Jons Hansson), the son of Captain Hans and "Ella" Mansson was born in Aronameck PA, between 1660-1670. He married Susannah Toy in 1690 in Gloucester, New Jersey and was recorded living in Sinamensing (Cinnaminson Twp.), Burlington County, New Jersey in 1693. On 12 June 1700, James Steelmen and his wife, with several other church members, represented the Sinammensing District (Pennsauken Creek area that included the Great & Little Egg Harbor) at the consecration of the Gloria Day Church at Wicaco (present day Philadelphia. On 10 November 1695, James purchased several land parcels totaling 500 acres near Great Egg Harbor from Thomas Budd and moved his wife and family, along with his brother Peter and his wife Gertrude Keen, to this area. During James Steelman's lifetime in what is now the present day Absecon Beach, Somers Point area, he and his wife had six sons and two daughters. James became a prominent citizen and held various positions within the County of Gloucester. On 1 June 1696 he was elected "Overseer" of highway from Egg Harbor towards Gloucester, and again on 2 September 1700 "Overseer" of the road from Township Weymouth to a place called Penny Post." In 1718, James was appointed as one of the Trustees of Egg Harbor. From 1694 to 1734, James purchased and traded many large parcels of property around the Somers Point area, and upon his death he held over 600 acres and had an inventoried wealth of approximately 328£ listed in his will.

Earl Gordon Stannard III #317 and William Gammons White #320

References:

Craig, Peter Stebbins "The Stile Family in America 1641-1772 in *Swedish American Geneologist Vol VI No. 4* (Dec 1986)

Cook, Ross E. *Hans Hansson and the Steelman Family*, 1936. New Jersey State Archives. Book 3 of Deeds, pg 196, Clerk's Office of Gloucester County. (Internet archive). Swedish Colonial News, Vol2, No. 1, Winter 2000.

ROBERT STILES (1655-1728)

Robert Stiles was born about 1655, in Staffordshire, England and came to Philadelphia in 1680 with his sister Lucy Stiles. He married Priscilla Howell, daughter of Thomas and Catherine Howell, also of Staffordshire, England and another early settler of New Jersey. Robert Stiles soon moved from Philadelphia to Gloucester, New Jersey where he practiced the trade of rosin maker. Gabriel Thomas one of the first historians of New Jersey, said of Stiles, "The trade of Gloucester County consists chiefly of Pitch, Tar and Rosin, the latter of which is made by Robert Styles, an excellent Artisan in that sort of work, for he delivers it as clear as any Gum Arabick."

In 1695 Robert Stiles bought 425 acres on Pennsauken Creek near Moorestown, Burlington County. His son Robert Stiles Jr. later lived on this land. Other children included Johns, who died young, and Martha, who married Thomas Cole. Robert Stiles' sister Lucy married John Rudderow, Crown Surveyor who helped William Penn plan early Philadelphia and who later served as Judge of the Court of Commons Pleas Quarterly of Burlington County, New Jersey.

Matthew Stiles Bowdish #362

Pennsauken Creek

References:

Stiles, Henry R. *The Stiles Family in America*, 1895.

Stevenson, John R. *John Rudderow and His Descendants 1660-1733 in the New York*, 1898.

Genealogical and Biographical Record, April 1898.

RICHARD STOUT (c. 1615 - c. 1705)

Richard Stout came to New Netherlands from Nottinghamshire England, after seven years in the British Navy, which he joined reputedly after friction with his father over love affairs.

Richard married Penelope VanPrincis in 1644, who had been shipwrecked on Sandy Hook, New Jersey with her first husband who was killed. Her life has been written about many times because of her "constitution" and will to live after being mutilated and left for dead by local Indians. Eventually she was rescued, nursed to health by other local Indians and ultimately returned to the Dutch, in New Netherlands, where she met and married Richard Stout. They became the parents of a very large family which included at least ten children: John, Richard, James, Mary, Alice, Peter, Sarah, Jonathan, David, Benjamin.

Richard Stout became one of the first settlers of Gravesend, (New York) New Netherlands in 1643 and was allotted plantation-lot No. 18, in 1646. In 1661 he bought the adjoining farm, plantation-lot No.26. After spending almost 20 years in Gravesend, he and his family, with a number of his neighbors, left Gravesend and settled Middletown, Monmouth County, New Jersey as one of the original Monmouth Patentees. In 1667 he held lot No.6 in Middletown. In 1675, he deeded 1800 acres to his heirs, and in 1677 received 745 additional acres by patent.

Richard Stout's public life shows him as a member of the first General Assembly of New Jersey at Elizabethtown composed of deputies and patentees in 1671, as an overseer in 1669 and 1675, and as Indian Commissioner.

The Stout's were Baptists and in 1668, Richard and others met to organize the first Baptist Church in New Jersey. Richard and his son John were among the eighteen male charter members and for twenty years they met at the homes of the members until a log church could be built.

Richard Stout's will was written on 9 June 1703 and proved before Lord Cornsburg, Governor, Captain General & Etc., on 23 October 1705 at Perth Amboy. In it he left his orchard, all the land he owned and home to his wife and left one shilling each to his sons and daughters. He also left one shilling each to his daughter-in-law, Mary Stout and her son John.

#347 Judy Jackson Scovronsky

References:

Stillwell, John E. *Historical and Genealogical Miscellany, Vol. IV*. 1906. (Internet archive)

"History of American Women: Penelope Van Princis Stout"
http://womenhistory.blogspot.com/2007/11/penelope-van-princis-stout.html

Will of Richard Stout New Jersey, recorded in Liber 1, pg 120 of Wills at Trenton, New Jersey. (Internet archive).

Van Dyke, Mabel. National *Genealogical Society Quarterly, Vol. 52, Pt 1, No.2,* June 1964.

CAPTAIN SAMUEL SWAINE (SWAYNE) (c. 1620 - 1685)

The manifest of the ship *Elizabeth and Anne*, bound for Boston in May 1635, lists William Swayne (Swaine) as a gentleman from London, age fifty years. His son Samuel was about 16 at the time of sailing. The family first settled in Watertown where William had a grant of 60 acres. In 1637 he moved his family (including sons Samuel and Daniel and daughter Mary) to the new colony of Wethersfield, where he had acquired adventure lands. It was from here that Mary was kidnapped by Indians. She was rescued by a Dutch ship, and Lyon Gardner paid for her return. Preferring the theocratic constitution of New Haven, William Swaine purchased a plantation of 435 acres in Branford in 1644 and the family moved again, joining with the congregation of Rev. Abraham Pierson, who had moved there from Southampton Long Island.

Samuel Swaine married Joannah Ward c. 1645. Samuel, like all land owning settlers, was a farmer. He also constructed mills; was active in the militia, being appointed chief military officer in Branford; was a deputy to the New Haven legislature; and served as a judge. When New Haven was united with the Connecticut Colony in 1662, the leaders of Branford, Milford and Guilford were dismayed that their pure government by the church would be corrupted.

When in 1664, the Lord Proprietors of New Jersey offered inducements to settle New Jersey, Robert Treat and John Gregory were sent to explore the area and confer with Phillip Carteret in Elizabeth Town. They were favorably impressed with an area on the south side of the Passaic River, with wide expanses of salt hay marshes, a high plateau with few trees, crisscrossed with streams and backed by the Watchung Mountains covered with hardwoods. An agreement was quickly reached with Carteret to plant a colony.

Joanna and Samuel Swaine, with their seven daughters (an eighth daughter died in 1655) were among the first thirty families that arrived in Newark on 18 May, 1666. It is said that Elizabeth, the Swaines' seventeen-year-old eldest daughter, was the first to land on the shore, having been merrily handed up the bank by her gallant fiancé, Josiah Ward, in his ambition to secure for her the mark of priority.

Local Lenni Lenape, who were on their annual trip from the Delaware to fish, met the settlers, and claimed that Carteret did not have title to the land (the original Elizabeth Town purchase from the Indians on Staten Island included the Newark area). Samuel Swaine was left in charge while Robert Treat went up the river to the headquarters of the Hackensacks. It was agreed that the land would be purchased for gunpowder, lead, axes, coats, guns, swords, kettles, blankets, knives, hoes, breeches, and trooper coats (value $750). While Treat was gone, Samuel Swaine, with others, drew up a compact to ensure that the new colony would be a strict theocracy settled by families from Branford, Guilford, and Milford. The principles of the church were to govern the spiritual and civil life of the citizens. Only church members could become freeman of the town and participate in any vote.

Samuel Swaine was active in community affairs of the new colony. He represented Newark at the settlement of the boundary with Elizabeth Town; was a member of the first General Assembly of the Province Elizabethtown called by Governor Carteret in 1668 and again in 1672; was a member of judiciary; and was contracted to build a mill in the town. In his will dated 17 Mar. 1682, he left all of his estate to his beloved wife Joanna. He died prior to 1685. Joanna's will dated 1692 left her estate of the home lot in Newark, land at the Mountain beyond the great swamp, and a silver teabox, to five of her daughters (Elizabeth, Abigail, Joanna, Christiana, and Sarah) and son-in-laws (Phoebe and Mary (2) may have predeceased her). The Settler's Monument in Fairmount Cemetery marks the final resting place of the founders of Newark. A brass plaque depicts the landing of the settlers with Elizabeth Swaine stepping ashore. The children of Samuel Swaine and Joanna Ward were:

1. Elizabeth Swaine b. 1 May 1649 - d. 1706 Newark m. Josiah Ward b. c. 1645 m. 1666 d. bef. 1676 (Newark). m. David Ogden (from Elizabeth Town) b. 11 Jan 1639; m. c. 1676 d. will proved 27 Feb. 1692 (Newark)

2. Mary Swaine b. 1 May, 1649 d. 10 Nov.1655 (Branford)

3. Joanna Swaine b. 1651 d. 16 Sept., 1729 (Newark) m. Jasper Crane Jr. b. 2 Apr, 1651 d. 6 Mar., 1711/12

4. Phoebe Swaine b. 7 May 1654 –

5. Mary Swaine (2) b. 12 June, 1656 -

6. Christiana Swaine b. 25 April 1659 – d. Jan 1731/32 m. Nathaniel Ward b. 2 Nov. 1656

7. Sarah Swaine b. 7 Oct 1661 d.___ m. Thomas Johnson

8. Abigail Swaine d. ___ m. Eleazer Lampson

Evelyn Hunt Ogden # C 296

Property allotted to Samuel Swaine

Drawing prepared for the bicentennial of Newark by Samuel Conger and William Whitehead for the New Jersey Historical Society

The Founders Monument – The Landing at Newark in Fairmount Cemetary in Newark, New Jersey

References:

Atwater, E.E. *History of the Colony of New Haven to its Absorption into Connecticut*, 1881. (Internet archive).

Board of Commissioners of the City of Newark. *Municipal Yearbook 1947-48, Newark: City of Opportunity*. 2010.

Collections of the New Jersey Historical Society, Vol. II, *Records Town of Newark 1666-1836*, Abe Books, 1864.

Cunningham, John T. *Newark*, 2002.

Pierson, David Lawrence. *Narratives of Newark (in New Jersey) from the Days of Founding*, 1917. (Internet archive).

Pierson, David Lawrence. *Narratives of Newark (in New Jersey) from the Days of Founding*, 1917.

Stearns, Jonathan F. *Historical Discourse Relating to the First Church of Newark*, 1853. (Internet archive).

Tepper, M. "Passengers of the Elizabeth & Ann: Voyage of 1635". Transcription of records found in London, the Public Rolls Office.

JOHN THROCKMORTON (1601 – 1684)

John Throckmorton of Providence, Rhode Island, traditionally son of Bassingboume and Mary Hill Throckmorton, of Norwick, England, was baptized 8 May 1601 at Herts, England. He married, place and date unknown, Rebecca Covill, and died between 17 March 1683/4 and 25 April 1684 at Middletown, New Jersey while visiting his sons Job and John and was interred in a plot set aside thereby, and mentioned in the 1690 will of his son John Throckmorton.

John Throckmorton was one of the original proprietors of Providence Plantation, Rhode Island, a Deputy there 1664 - 1674. During the visitation of John Fox he was converted to The Society of Friends at Newport, Rhode Island. He had been one of the syndicators of the Mayflower voyage to Plymouth and came to Massachusetts to determine why there had been no financial return on their investment in ten years. He became active in the development of coastwise shipping among the colonies which probably was not what the Crown wanted. He founded in 1643 in Eastchester, New York, a colony on land which bore his name Throgmorton Neck, eventually shortened to Throg's Neck.

He was an unusually outspoken immigrant and left a trail of paper, much of it against various religious sects or people. By 1664 he was restless again and he became one of the Monmouth County, New Jersey Patentees. He remained a resident of Rhode Island and his trading ships plied the eastern waters. He deeded land in Middletown to his sons and "died an octogenarian while visiting" them there.

Rebecca Covill (possibly Comell), Mrs. Throckmorton, was cited in Providence as being a midwife. She is said to have predeceased her husband, but her place of interment is not known.

Clifton Rowland Brooks, M.D. #C41

References:

Moriarty Notebook, XIV: 17-18 at NEHGS (Internet archive).

Weis, Line. Anc. Roots of 60 Colonists, Vth ED. L. 208-42

The Gen. Reg. of the Soc. of Col. Wars, 1899-02: 783. (Internet archive).

Rhode Island Land Evidences, Vol. 1:163, 209. (Internet archive).

Austin. Genealogical Dictionary of RI, 1887, p. 200 (Internet archive)

Stillwell, John E. M. D. Historical & Genealogical Miscellany, Vol.5:75., 1906. (Internet archive).

Sitharwood, Francis. *Throckmorton Family History*, 1929

MARTIN TICHENOR (c.1615 – 1681)

Martin Tichenor was probably born in Sussex County, England, where the Tichenor surname flourished. He married at New Haven, Connecticut, on 16 May 1651, Mary Charles, daughter of John and Mary (Moss?) Charles. Mary died at Newark, New Jersey before 1673. Martin Tichenor died there in October 1681 and was buried with his wife in the churchyard of the First Church.

Martin Tichenor was a Puritan and first appears of record at the New Haven colony, taking the oath of allegiance on 5 August 1655. He married Mary Charles in 1651 and they were listed as members of the Congregational Church in 1655/6 and 1661/2. They moved about 1665 to Branford, where he purchased land from his father-in-law.

Tichenor was in the group of Milford settlers who removed to Newark in 1666. He and his son Daniel signed the Fundamental Agreements on 24 June 1667. Martin received home lot #20 between William Camp, Ephraim Pennington and Seth Tomkins. The location of this lot is marked by the present intersection of Tichenor Street and Broad Street in Newark, New Jersey. The southwest corner of the land lay at the extreme end of the town, along the road leading to the salt meadow, known as "Tichenor's Gate", and evidently a position of some vulnerability in the early days. We read that Martin received among several other grants of land a special one of one and a half acres "for his Staying so much on his place when the Town was first Settled", that is, "the first Summer."

He and his sons were active in the community. He was chosen a Heyward, and in 1673 was the Warner of Town Meetings. His eldest daughter, Hannah, married Ensign John Treat, son of Governor Robert Treat.

Martin's will was written 19 October 1681 and letters of administration issued to his son John, on an inventory of 27 October showing an estate of realty and personalty of Pounds 230.11. Martin and Mary had six children who survived infancy: John, Hannah, Daniel, Abigail, Samuel and Jonathan.

James L. Tichenor, Esq. # 155

References:

Hoadly, Charles J. *Records of the Colony and Plantation of New Haven*, 1857. (Internet archive.)

Savage, James. *Genealogical Dictionary of New England*, 1860. (Internet archive).

Atwater, Edward E. *History of the Colony of New Haven*, 1902. (Internet archive).

Jacobus, Donald L. *Families of Ancient New Haven, 1939.*

Waterman, Edgar F. and D.L. Jacobus. *The Granberry Family*, 1875.

New Jersey Historical Society. *Records of the Town of Newark 1666-1836*, published by the Proceedings of the New Jersey Historical Society, 10:434, 11:204, 1864. (Internet archive).

JOHN TILTON (1613 - 1688)

John Tilton was born in Wolston, Warwickshire, England on 4 March, 1613. He emigrated to Lynn, Massachusetts prior to 1640 and then moved to Scituate in Plymouth Colony in 1643. Sometime later, the Tiltons moved to Gravesend in Dutch New Netherlands, likely with the followers of Lady Deborah Moody; probably as a result of religious unrest against Quakers in English Massachusetts.

On 10 January 1661, John Tilton and his wife Mary (also known as Goody) were arrested and imprisoned *for being at the Quaker meeting 9 January, and at a Quaker meeting at Gravesend January 10.* John was sentenced to banishment from the Province, but through the influence of Lady Moody, he was pardoned. The Tilton's problems were not over. On 19 September 1662, the Director and Council notified the magistrates of all English towns on Long Island to assist Resolved Waldon in arresting *all persons who attend unlawful or prohibited meetings.* At the same time complaint was made against John Tilton for attending meetings of Quakers and harboring persons of that persuasion, and against Mary, his wife, for "attending meetings of that abominable sect called Quakers." They were both imprisoned, and on 6 Oct, were banished from the Province. The sentence was postponed until 7 May 1663, due to *the rigors of approaching winter.* Anthony Wright and others Friends offered them a home at Oyster Bay, which was outside the Dutch jurisdiction.

New Netherlands fell to the English in 1664; and on 1 January 1664, John Tilton Sr. and his son John Jr. were among those to whom land was deeded by the Indians at Shrewsbury, New Jersey (the Monmouth Purchase). It is not clear whether John Tilton Sr. actually resided in Shrewsbury; after his banishment from Gravesend for attending Quaker meetings, he had found refuge at Oyster Bay. In 1667, John and his wife moved back to Gravesend, and in 1668, he was again made Town Clerk. Mary "Goody" Tilton died 23 May, 1683 in Gravesend. John Tilton died in 1688, also at Gravesend; his will recorded on 3 April of that year divided his land among his children:

1. John Tilton born 1640, married Mary Coates and secondly, Rebecca Terry
2. Peter Tilton born 1641, married Rebecca Brazier
3. Sarah Tilton born 1644, married John Painter
4. Ester Tilton born 1647, married Samuel Spleer
5. Abigail Tilton born 1650, married Ralph Warner and secondly, William Scot
6. Thomas Tilton born 1652
7. Mary Tilton born 1654, married Henry Bowman

The Tilton's son Peter and his wife Rebecca Brazier lived and died in New Jersey. On 1 June 1697, Peter conveyed one hundred acres of land to this daughter Rebecca, wife of Daniel Applegate, between Hop and Swimming Rivers, in Middletown, New Jersey. Peter Tilton died in Middletown, 6 October 1700.

366F David Lawrence Grinnell

References:

Colket, Meredith B. Jr. *Founders of Early American Families: Immigrants from Europe 1607-1757* 2nd ed. (Cleveland, The Ohio Society with the authority of The General Court of the Order of the Founders and Patriots of America, p. 325. 2002.

Stillwell, John E., M.D. *Historical and Genealogical Miscellany: Early Settlers of New Jersey and their Descendants* Vol. V pp. 131, 133, 1906. (Internet archive).

ROBERT TREAT (1622/24 – 1710)

Robert Treat was born 1622/24 at Pitminster Parish, near Taunton, Somersetshire, England. He was the son of Richard Treat and Alice, daughter of Hugh Gaylord (Gaillard), also of Pitminster. He came first to Massachusetts in 1635 and removed shortly to Weathersfield, Connecticut where his father was a town founder. He married at Milford, Connecticut, 1647 Jane Tapp, daughter of Edmond and Anna (-) Tapp. He died at Milford 12 July 1710.

Treat interested himself in military affairs, joined the local Train Band at Milford and later became its Captain. On 24 May 1666 he, with ten others from Milford, Guilford and Branford entered into an agreement to take up lots on the Passaic River in the Province of East Jersey, which they named New Ark or Newark. Newark Town Records record that "Only Capt. Treat was allowed to have Eight Acres in his Town lot." *Fundamental Agreements* were signed in June 1667 at Newark with Treat as Recorder. He was deputy from Newark to the General Assembly of East Jersey 1667-1672. Now about fifty years of age, he returned to Milford, Connecticut.

On 18 September 1675, it was said that his arrival at Bloody Brook, in command of Connecticut troops turned the tide in the Indian battle. On 19 December 1675 with Treat as Major and Commanding Officer of Connecticut forces, King Philip was defeated at the Great Swamp Fight in what is now southern Rhode Island. Treat was chosen Deputy Governor of Connecticut 1676-1682, when he succeeded to the office of Governor, which he held until 1698, with an interim during the regime of Sir Edmond Andros, Governor of New England. He was appointed Colonel of Connecticut forces in 1687. It is said that while being forced to entertain Sir Edmond Andros that Robert Treat's associates hid the Connecticut Charter in the famous Charter Oak.

William Young Pryor #C2

References:

Collections of the New Jersey Historical Society, Vol. II, *Records Town of Newark 1666-1836*, Abe Books, 1864.

New England Marriages Prior to 1700, p. 753 (Internet archive).

Treat, J.H. *Treat Genealogy*, 1893.

Who Was Who, Marquis, p.536

CORNELIUS (TEUNISSEN) TUNISON (1694 - 1775)

Cornelius (Theunissen) Tunison, Sr. was born 10 Jan 1694 in Brooklyn, New York, one of eight children of Teunis Nyssen (Denyse) and Phebe (Femmetje) Seals. He married Neeltje Bogaet, the daughter of Tunis Gysbert Tunisons, Aug 28 1687. A deed dated 20 Jan 1687-8 conveyed to Cornelius Tinnisonne and his brother Jan (and others) a farm at Roysefield, Middlesex County., New Jersey, from John Royse. Cornelius Teunissen's name also appears on a deed dated Oct 14, 1689, from John and Elizabeth White for a tract of land, in what is now the center of the village of Somerville.

In 1717, he married Rebecca Folkerson from Brushwick, New York. Their son Cornelius Tunison Jr., was baptized on 8 Mar 1699, one of the first entered in Dutch, in the records of the newly established First Reformed Church of Raritan.

The couple had ten children. Cornelius died in Raritan 25 Aug 1775, and Rebecca died the same year.

Summarized by Dr. Evelyn Ogden from records
Submitted by James A. Tunison # 343

References:

Nelson, William, Editor. *Patents and Deeds and other Early Records of New Jersey 1664-1703*, 1899. Reprint 2000.

Snell, James P. *History of Hunterdon and Somerset Counties*, 1881. (Internet archive).

Footnote to History

The Earliest known ecclesiastical organization in Somerset County was that of the First Reformed Church of Raritan (now Somerville), originally known as the Reformed Dutch Church of Raritan, was organized March 9, 1699.

JAN TUNISEN (1654 - 1723)

Jan Tunisen (Tunison, Teunise, Tinnisonne, Tuynesen, Van Middleswart) was born c. 1654, baptized 12 Apr 1654, in the Reformed Dutch Church of New Amsterdam, the son of Teunis Nyssen and Phebe Sales (also known as Femmetje Jans). Jan married on 16 Nov 1679 at Brooklyn, Kings County, Long Island, New York, Catlyntje Tunisen Bogart, born c. 1657, baptized 16 Dec 1657 in the Reformed Dutch Church of New Amsterdam, the daughter of Tunis Gysbertse Bogaert and Sarah Joris Rapalje. Jan resided in the Wallabout in Long Island where he took the Oath of Allegiance to Britain in 1687.

On 20 Jan 1686/7, John Robinsone and his wife, Margarete of New York conveyed a deed to Jeromus Ripley, John (Jan) Tinnisone and Cornelius Tinnissone (brother of Jan), all of Kings Co., New York, for a farm at Roysefield, Middlesex Co., New Jersey. The farm had been conveyed to him by John Royse, 07 Dec 1685. Jeromus Ripley (also known as Jeremias Rapalje), an uncle of Catylntje Bogart, married a sister of Jan Tunison.

On 17 Aug 1699, Cornelius Tunisson of Somerset County., New Jersey, and wife Neiltie conveyed to John Tunisson Midle Swaert of the same county, his third of the above described property. In total, Corneilus conveyed 3 parcels: 300 acres at Roysfield, said Co., on the Raritan River; an unsurveyed lot on the said river; and a 60 acre island in Raritan River., opposite the preceding tract; in all 660 acres.

Beginning in 1699, Jan and his wife appear as witnesses for numerous baptisms at the First Dutch Reformed Church, Raritan (Somerville), Somerset County, New Jersey. Also in 1699, Jan Tuynesen was chosen as elder for the same church. In 1704, he was a member of the Assembly of New Jersey.

The Tunisen's children included: Femmetje, bap 05 Aug 1680 at Flatbush; Teunis, bap 16 Jul 1682 at Flatbush, married Adriaentje (-); Sarah, bap 01 Feb 1685 at Brooklyn, married c 1704 Jan Brokaw, son of Bourgon Broucard and Catherine LeFevre; and Abraham, bap 19 Sep 1699 in New Jersey. On 22 May 1723, Cornelius Ewetse and his wife Mary, of Kings Co., New York, conveyed to Jan Tunise Van Middleswart (Tunisen) of New Jersey, a house and lot at the Brooklyn ferry. Jan Tunisen died in 1723.

Jeffrey A. Myers, #402

References:

Teunis G. Bergen. Early Settlers of Kings County, Long Island, N.Y. pp. 93, 94. 1881.

The Editor, "Notes on Various Old Somerset Families, Tunison Families – Line of Dr. Garrett of Somerville", Somerset County Historical Quarterly Vol. 7, pp. 225-228. 1918.

"Records of the Reformed Dutch Church in New York", NYGBR, Vol. 5:151 & 5:181. 1874.

John Albert Bogart. The Bogart Family: Tunis Gysbert Bogaert and His Descendants (Scranton, Penn.: Printed by the Haddon Craftsman, p. 35. 1959.

David William Voorhees, editor, Records of The Reformed Protestant Dutch Church of Flatbush, Kings County, New York, Vol. 1, 1677-1720 (New York: Holland Society of New York,), p. 223, 1998.

"First Reformed Church of Raritan (Somerville) Baptisms", Somerset County Historical Quarterly, Vol. 2.,1915. (Internet archive).

JOHANNES UPDIKE (OPDYKE) (1651 - 1729)

Johannes Updike (Opdyke) was born in 1651, probably in Beverwyck/Albany, New York, where his parents, Laurens Janszen Updike and Stijntje (Christina) Pieters, first settled after their immigration to New Netherlands in about 1650. On 23 Dec. 1653, Laurens Janszen testified at the Court of Fort Orange and Beverwyck that he was 48 years old and was born at Hoesem (Holland). On January 14, 1650, Stijntje Pieters, his wife, gave her age as about 40 years. While he was at Beverwyck, Laurens Janszen was engaged in the fur trade. By 1653 Laurens had purchased land and moved his family to Gravesend, Long Island, where he died in 1659. On March 16, 1660, prior to her second marriage to Norwegian Laurens Petersen, Stijntje had guardians appointed for her children, Peter, Otto and Johannes (Opdyke).

Johannes grew up on Long Island, where about 1674 he married Catherine whose surname is unknown. Besides farming, Johannes actively bought and sold land in New York. However, in April 1697 he bought 250 acres in West Jersey above the falls of the Delaware River (near Trenton). The entire extended family moved from Dutch Kills to West Jersey, with their household goods and farm animals. There is a well preserved tradition among descendants that the carts of the Updike settlers were turned up at night to shelter the women and children, until a few days' work with axes and stout arms had prepared the first log homes.

By 1714, Johannes had moved to Hopewell, Hunterdon County, New Jersey where a Dutch clergyman from Bucks County, Pennsylvania, baptized six of his grandchildren in 1710 and 1712, which indicates that the family still maintained the Dutch religion and language. On February 12, 1729, at the age of 78 years, Johannes Opdyck made his will, leaving his estate to be equally divided among his eight living children. The next generation shifted the surname from Opdyck to Updike. When the executors of Johannes' estate, son Lawrence and grandson Eliakim Anderson, submitted their final bills on April 7, 1731, they listed the refreshments for the funeral; rum, sugar and spice, a barrel of cider and biskakes, all good food and drink in true Dutch fashion.

Summarized by Dr. Evelyn Ogden from records submitted by Beverly June Ellison Nelson #352

References:

Riker, David M. *Genealogical and Biographical Directory to persons in New Netherlands*, Supplement, p. 300, 2004.

Opdyke, Charles Wilson, *The Opdcyk Genealogy*, Weed, Parson & Co. Albany, NY, p. 152, 1889.

Van Laer, A.J. F., trans. "Minutes of the Court of Fort Orange and Beverwyck," SUNY Albany, 1920-23, p. 88.

Van Laer, A.J. F., trans. "Minutes of the Court of Rennsselaerwyck," SUNY, Albany, NY, p. 103. 1922.

Nelson, William, Documents of the State of New Jersey, Vol. XXIII, Calendar of New Jersey Wills, Vol.1, 1670-1730, Press printing & Publishers, Patterson, NY, p. 347, 1901. (Internet archive).

LUBBERT GYSBERTSEN VAN BLARICUM (c.1601 - c.1655)

Lubbert Gysbertsen, wheelwright and wagon maker, was born c. 1601 in Blaricum, District of Gooiland in the Netherlands. He married there Divertje Cornelis. He died c. 1655 in Bergen Neck, New Jersey, probably killed in an Indian raid.

On 15 April 1634 Lubbert signed a contract with Killaen VanRensselaer, the Patroon of Rensselaerwyck in New Netherland near Fort Orange (now Albany, New York). He and his wife and their three children sailed on the ship de Eendracht which sailed from the Texel in May 1634. The Patroon advanced the expense of his passage to the West India Company, for which Lubbert would reimburse him over a three year period by working for him. Lubbert's account was opened in Rensselaerwyck on 20 July 1634, indicating that the trip took about two and a half months. His account with the Patroon was cleared in 1647. In 1648 his wife Divertje witnessed a baptism in New Amsterdam.

On 5 December 1654, Lubbert was given a Dutch patent for 50 morgens (100 acres) in Bergen Neck, New Jersey, below Cavan Point, in the area south of present Jersey Cityr. His son-in-law, Jan Cornelis Buys, had 25 morgens just south of his land and beyond that his son, Jan Lubbertsen, also had 25 morgens. Farther south, his sons Lubbert and Gysbert Lubbertsen, each had 25-morgen farms. It is not known when these farms were first occupied, but Lubbert's granddaughter, Tryntje Oosteroom, according to her marriage record, was born in New Jersey. She was baptized in New Amsterdam 16 August 1654.

In September 1655, an Indian was killed for stealing fruit from an orchard in New Amsterdam. In retaliation, a large Indian war party terrified the residents of New Amsterdam and then crossed the Hudson River to New Jersey, burned the Dutch bouweries and plantations, killed or captured anyone who had not fled. Lubbert may have been killed in this raid. An entry in the Minutes of the Court of Schepens and Burgomasters of New Amsterdam dated 1 May 1656 shows that Jan Corns. Buys, alias Jan Damen and Lubbert Gystertse's widow requested permission to trap as they "have been driven from their houses by the last trouble with the Indians;." the request was granted.

Dorothy J. Maxon #123

Hudson River Painting by Charles Wilson; source www.pixabay.com

References:

New York Genealogical and Biographical Record, Volume 99, July 1968. (Internet archive).

Zabriskie, George Olin. The Van Blarcom Family of New Jersey, 8 Generations, (Internet archive).

JACOB VAN DOORN (bef. 1655–abt. 1720)

Jacob VanDoorn was born in Gowanus, Long Island, NY, before 1655. In 1690 he married Maria Bennet. Between 1697 and 1701 he became the sole owner of 675 acres in what is now Holmdel and Marlboro Townships; and in about 1698 he moved the family from Long Island to the Monmouth County, New Jersey. Jacob Van Dorn built his first house, probably initially a log cabin, on a knoll on the property, near the families Schencks, Couwenhovens and Hendricksons. The family traveled every Sunday to attend services at the first Dutch Church.

As early as 1714, Jacob built a dam and erected a grist mill, a great convenience to the settlers within four or five miles around. Jacob died abt. 1720; his will divided his estate between his oldest and fourth sons, directing that they pay £75 to each the other children, with an additional £37 to the youngest. His wife Mary survived him by many years.

Summarized by Dr. Evelyn Ogden from documents submitted by #387 Arthur Howell Johnson, Jr.

References:

Beekman. George. *Early Dutch Settlers of Monmouth County, NJ*, Moreau Bros. Publishers, Freehold, NJ 1901.

Honeyman, A Van Doren. *Van Doorn Family in Holland and America, Vol. I.*, Plainfield, NJ 1909.

Footnote to History

By 1699 there were enough Dutch settlers in Monmouth County to have a regular preaching service; and a congregation was organized in that year. Services were conducted in Dutch by three ministers from Brooklyn, on a rotating schedule. They travel in small boats a cross the great bay. Church records of 1709, record in low Dutch, that Rev. Joseph Morgan was installed as pastor of the "Reformed congregation of Freehold and Middletown."

BALTUS BARENTS VAN KLEECK (1645-abt.1717)

Baltus Barents VanKleeck was baptized on 6 Aug. 1645 in Haarlem, The Netherlands. His father was Barent Baltus who was from Lipstadt in Westphalia, and who on 18 May, 1631, had married Sara Peters in Haarlem. Less than five years later, on 29 January, 1636, Barents now a widower married Mayken Quiters of Haarlem. They had seven children, including Baltus and Elsie.

Barents Baltus emigrated to America; he first appears in the New Netherland records in Flatbush on 8 July, 1654. He married the first time a woman whose name is unknown and who was buried in 1676 in Flatbush. He married second Tryntje Jans Buys daughter of Jan Cornelis Buys (alias Damen) and Ybetje Lubberts (daughter of Lubbert Guybertsen) in 1657 or 1658.

Baltus Van Kleeck moved first to Albany to be near his sister Elsie who had married the large landholder Robert Sanders. This is where their daughter Sara was born.

In about 1683, Baltus Van Kleeck purchased land in Bergen. The three tracts, known as lot No. 49, lot No. 67 and lot No. 156 and so marked on the map of the "Bergen Common Lands" in the County Clerk's Office at Hackensack, N.J. Lot No. 49 was a tract of upland. Lot No. 67 was a piece of meadow. Lot No. 156 was a lot in the town of Bergen. In total they comprised 36 and a half acres of farmland and a lot in the village. The family then moved to Bergen where his wife's relatives had returned after the Indian uprising in 1655. On 2 July 1683, Baltus Barens and wife Tryntie Jans joined the Bergen Dutch Church. Their son Peter was baptized there on 2 April 1688.

Baltus sold the Bergen property 8 May, 1697 and on 3 June, 1697 bought a large parcel of land at Poughkeepsie, where the family settled permanently. Baltus Van Kleek is considered to be the founder of Poughkeepsie and in turn Dutchess County. In 1702 he built the first stone house there with a lintel stone that contained the initials of Baltus and Tryntie. Baltus VanKleeck also donated land for the building of the first church. In later years Baltus VanKleeck was very prominent in the affairs of Poughkeepsie. He was a Captain of the Militia of Ulster and Dutchess County in 1700, and in the 16th Colonial Assembly in 1715, he represented Dutchess County. He died between 1 Sept. 1716 and 9 April 1717. His stone house remained standing in Poughkeepsie until well into the Nineteenth Century with an adjacent family graveyard.

Craig Hamilton Weaver #370

References:

A.S. Van Benthuyson, A.S. Van Kleek Genealogy

Bennett, Bruce. Pierre Parmentier of New Amsterdam and Descendants. (Internet archive).

Holland Society Yearbook "Records of the Bergen Dutch Church" 1915 (Internet archive).

Kingston Dutch Church Marriage Records (Internet archive)

NYG&B Record Vol 138. (Internet archive).

PETER VAN NEST (c 1625 - aft. 1709)

Peter VanNest was born c. 1625 in the Netherlands; he emigrated from Utrecht, arriving in the colonies in 1647 and settling in Brooklyn. He married about 1652 Judith Jorise Rapalje, born 5 July 1635. She was the daughter of Joris Jansen Rapalje and Caralyna Trico Rapalje; first settlers of New Amsterdam. Peter and Judith were the parents of eight children: Catalyna, Pieter, Sitje, Jeronimus, Jacomyntje, Sara, Joris and Marritie. Peter was a carpenter by trade.

The second land title in Somerset County, New Jersey was dated 12 December 1681; and signed by four Indians in consideration of 120 pounds. Among the earliest permanent settlers in this section of East Jersey was Peter Van Nest, who purchased land there in 1681/2. He added to his land holdings on 26 Oct 1693, when James Graham, conveyed to him a large track of land. In 1693 VanNest was appointed by Somerset for the purpose of raising soldiers to "defend the Province" and in 1694, he was appointed along with J. Tunison, Commissioner of Highways.

One of their daughters, Catalina, married Derrick Middagh and on 1 May 1709, Peter VanNest of Somerset County, yeoman, and his wife, conveyed to Derrick Middagh, of the same place, yeoman; land originally purchased from James Graham in 1693.

Laura Carolina Jennings Fafeita #398A

References:

Early Church Records of Somerset County New Jersey. Colonial Roots, Lewis, Delaware 2002. (Internet archive).

"First Things in Old Somerset." A Collection of Articles:24, Brooklyn Museum,1899. (Internet archive).

Genealogy of NJ Families Vol. I:889, 1996. (Internet archive).

Sisser, Fred III. *Somerset County Genealogical Quarterly, Vol. 2* #1 March 1984.

Snell, James P. *History of Hunterdon and Somerset Counties, New Jersey*. Philadelphia 1881.

Somerset County Historical Quarterly, Vol. VI- 1917:115.

PENELOPE VAN PRINCIS (KENT, STOUT) (c. 1622 –1732)

Penelope VanPrincis is considered the first white woman in New Jersey. The daughter of Baron VanPrincis (a.k.a. Van Prinzen), she was born in Amsterdam, the Netherlands, in 1622. After her marriage to John Kent c.1640, bride and groom set sail for New Amsterdam; near the end of the journey their ship ran aground near what is now Highlands in Monmouth County, New Jersey.

Penelope, with her husband and others made it to shore; however, her husband was too ill to travel with the rest of the survivors who headed on foot toward New Amsterdam. Penelope and her husband stayed behind in the Navesink woods and it was not long before they were attacked by hostile Indians. John was killed and Penelope, partially scalped, horribly cut and left for dead. She survived for a week before she was found by two friendly Indians. She begged to be put out of her misery and the younger one was willing to oblige, but the elder one stopped him. He threw her over his shoulder and took her to their camp. There he sewed her up with fish bone needles and vegetable fiber. She lived with the Indian until she recovered and eventually made it to New Amsterdam.

In 1642, Penelope met Richard Stout who had left Nottingham, England, to serve in the British navy. At the end of his seven-year enlistment, he had left his ship in New Amsterdam. Penelope married the English-born colonist, in 1644, when she was 22 and he was 40. They settled at Gravesend, Long Island on a plantation, which he had been allowed to purchase from the Dutch. Stout prospered and became a large landowner.

After the English took over the rule of New Amsterdam in 1664, Penelope persuaded her husband and a number of their neighbors at Gravesend to move across the Lower Bay to what is now eastern New Jersey, near the village of the Indian chief who had saved her life. John Stout became one of the original Monmouth Patent purchasers.

After their move to Middletown in Monmouth, the elderly Indian who had rescued her was a frequent visitor to the Stout home. Penelope is considered the "mother of Middletown."

The Stout's were Baptists and in 1668 Richard and others met to organize the first Baptist Church in New Jersey. Richard and his son John were among the eighteen male charter members and for twenty years they met at the homes of the members until a log church could be built.

Richard Stout's will was written on 9 June 1703 and proved before Governor Lord Cornsburg, on 23 October 1705 at Perth Amboy. In it he left his orchard, all the land he owned and home to his wife and left one shilling each to his sons and daughters. He also left one shilling each to his daughter-in-law, Mary Stout and her son John.

Penelope lived to the ripe old age of 110. While the exact location of Penelope's grave is unknown, both she and her husband were buried in Middletown, Monmouth County.

Children of Richard and Penelope Van Princis (Kent) Stout:

1. John Stout (1645 - 1724)*
2. James Stout (1648 - 1715)*
3. Mary Stout Bowne (1650 - 1675)*
4. Alice Stout Throckmorton (1652 - 1703)*
5. Sarah Elizabeth Stout Pike (1656 - 1714)*
6. Jonathan Stout (1665 - 1722)*
7. David Stout (1667 - 1732)*
8. Benjamin Stout (1669 - 1734)*

Compiled by Evelyn Ogden from documents submitted by # 400 Richard Charles Burd

Image: Penelope VanPrincis; Commemorative Coin shows her being saved by Indians

References:

Baer, Mabel Van Dyke. *National Genealogical Society Quarterly*, *Vol.*52. Pt 1, No.2 June 1964.

De Burton, Maria Ruiz. *History of American Women*, Posted 2014. (Internet Archive)

Stillwell, John E. Historical and Genealogical Miscellany: Early Settlers of New Jersey and their Descendants, New York 1916. (Internet archive).

Wills of New Jersey, Liber, pg. 120. Will of Richard Stout, Trenton, New Jersey. (Internet archive).

CLAES JANSEN VAN PURMERENT (abt. 1655- aft. 1690)

Claes Jansen VanPurmerent was born in Holland, probably at Purmerend, date unknown. He first appears in the records as the purchaser on 20 August 1655 of a tract called Pembrepock, along the side of the Hudson River, which he subsequently sold in 1658. On 11 November 1656, Claes Jansen married at the Reformed Dutch Church in New Amsterdam, Annetje, daughter of Cornelis VanVoorst and Vrouwtje Ides.

Claes Jansen VanPurmerent (Cuyper) purchased on Aug 20, 1655, a tract called Pembrepock, along the Hudson River. On Nov 11, 1656, Claes Jansen married at the Dutch Church in New York, Annetje, daughter of Cornelis VanVoorst and Vrouwtje Ides. In 1659, Claes Jansen VanPurmerent, wheelwright, wife, servant and child returned to Holland on the Beaver.

It is not known how long he remained in Holland; however, on Jan 31, 1662, he obtained a patent for land at or near Horsimus, now a part of Jersey City. Annetje was listed in 1664 as belonging to the Bergen Church. Claes Jansen was elected schepen for Ahasymus in the Bergen Court, Aug 31, 1674, and was appointed a surveyor of highways in 1682. The couple had twelve children. The name of at least one son appears in the records as Cornelis Claessen Cuyper.

Claes Jansen died intestate Nov. 30, 1688, at Ahasymus. His wife, according to Bergen church records, died July 12, 1725, as Annatje Stoffels, listed as widow of Claes Jansen Kuyer.

David Stringfellow #364

NJ Palisades and Hudson River; source www.uniquelyminnesota.com

References:

Cook, Richard W. "The Cuyper Family", *The Genealogical Magazine of New Jersey, Vol. XXXVIII, No. 3*, pp. 97-100, Sept. 1963.

Cook, Richard "The Cuyper Family," *The Genealogical Magazine of New Jersey, Vol. XXXVIII*, 1996.

Records of the Reformed Dutch Church in New Amsterdam and New York, Marriages from 11 December 1639 to 26 August 1801, p. 21. (Internet archive).

Records of the Reformed Protestant Dutch Church of Bergen in New Jersey, 1666 to 1788, pp. 27, 35, (Internet archive).

CORNELIS VAN VOORST (c. 1580 – 1638)

Cornelis (Cornelius) VanVoorst, son of Hendrick van Voorst and his wife Anna Cornelis Frans de Bure, was born about 1580; married 1) on 15 June 1607 in a civil ceremony at Utrecht, Holland, Beatrix van der Laen, daughter of Cornelis Thijsz van der Laen. She died before 1628 when he married Vrouwtje Ides, who died in Ahasymus (Pavonia, New Jersey) in 1641. He died 1 July 1638 during a visit to his sister and her husband in Holland.

Cornelius was a woodcarver and cabinet maker who was banished from the Netherlands as the result of his participation in an aborted uprising in 1610 over the local government of Utrecht. He went to Italy and learned the language. In 1619, as part of a general amnesty he was free to return to Holland, but did not do so immediately. On 26 April 1626 he made a statement before a Notary that he had been "engaged by the Directors of the West India Company to go to New Amsterdam" for the collection of certain debts owed him. He sailed soon after on The Amsterdam Arms.

In New Netherlands the family lived in Ahasymus (Pavonia), in the southern part of present Hoboken, New Jersey. In 1632 Cornelius was appointed superintendent of the colony, the civil and judicial head. He was acting as the agent for Michael Pauw.

By 1662 one of Cornelius' two surviving children, son Ide Cornelissen van Voorst, received deeds for about 150 acres of land at Ahasymus that probably had been his father's. Annken, the other child by Vrouwtje, married Claes Jansen van Purmerant.

Robert J. Hardie, Sr #C97

References:

New York Genealogical and Biographical Society Record, Vol. LXVI: "An Armory of American Families of Dutch Descent -Van Vorst"; also pp. 27-30, 1935.

Harvery, Cornelius Burnham, Editor. *Genealogical History of Hudson and Bergen Counties, New Jersey*, p. 244, "The Van Vorst Family".1900.

Winfield, Charles H. *History of the County of Hudson, New Jersey*. Chap. XIII, "The Van Vorst Family", pp. 424-431,1874.

WALING JACOBSE VAN WINKLE (c.1650 - c.1729)

Waling Jacobse VanWinkle, son of Jacob Waling VanWinkle and Tryntie Jacobs was baptized at the Dutch Reformed Church in New Amsterdam on 10 October with no sponsors, only his father present. He was married 15 March 1671, by the court at Bergen, New Jersey, to Catharyna Michielse, with banns published 26 February and recorded with the marriage date and place at the Bergen Reformed Dutch Church. Catharyna was a daughter of Michael Jansen Vreeland baptized at the New Amsterdam church 24 October 1649. On 15 August 1674, Waling Jacobse was nominated to the office of Schepen (judge) of the "Court of Justice at Bergen" and received his commission on 31 August 1674.

Waling Jacobse was one of fourteen purchasers of the Acquackanonk Patent, acquired from the Indians in 1679 and ratified by the Lord Proprietors of New Jersey in 1684. The area includes present-day Passaic, Paterson and vicinity.

As early as 1682, Waling Jacobse had an extensive farm at Barbadoes Neck, now Rutherford. On 2 March 1692, and again on 30 June 1695, he was elected a member of the General Assembly of New Jersey, representing first Acquackanonk and then Barbadoes Neck. A founder of the Acquackanonk Church, he was elected elder in May 1696 and re-elected in May 1701.

Eight children were born between 1672 and 1690 to the VanWinkles: Annetje, Jacob, Michael, Trintje who died in infancy, Johannis, Trintje Sarah and Abraham. Waling died between 1 November 1727 and 12 September 1729, at Acquackanonk, then in Essex County, New Jersey. His wife Catharyna was the sole executrix.

Julia VanRiper Dumdey #C72

References:

Lee, Francis B. *Genealogical and Memorial History of New Jersey*. 172,173, 1910. (Internet archive).

Nelson and Shriner. *Paterson and Its Environs*, (The Silk City) Vol. 2, p. 6 , 1910. (Internet archive).

Scott, William. *History of Passaic and Its Environs*, pp. 55-65, 1922.

Van Winkle, Daniel A. *Genealogy of the Van Winkle Family, 1630 - 1913*, Jersey City, 1913.

HARTMAN (MICKIELSEN) VREELAND (1651-1707)

Hartman Mickeilsen Vreeland (later the name was changed to Vreeland from Mickeilsen) was baptized Oct 1, 1651 and married Matje Braecke in 1672. He was a wheel wright by trade, and lived first at Rechpokus on part of his wife's inheritance. He then purchased 270 acres of land including "Stoffel's Point", and an island in the Passaic River near Acquackanonck called Hartman's Island (Dundee Island). He died on January 18, 1707 in Bergen County.

He made the first land transaction in the area known as Acquackanock, when he purchased from an Indian chief Dundee Island in the Passaic River, later called Hatman Island. Michielsen then induced others from Bergen to join in the purchase of a large tract of land (5500 acres) along the river up to the falls, from the Indians paying coats, blankets, kettles, powder and other goods. On March 28 1679, the associates received a patent from the Proprietors of East Jersey

Hartman and Matje had 13 children, his first-born was Claus who married Annetje Harmanse; (2) Aeltje; (3); Michael, who died at the age of 14; (4) Dirck, who married Margrietje Diedricks Banta; (5) Fitje, who married Dirck Paulusen; (6) Syntje; (7) Aagtje, who married Cornelis Blinkerhoff; (8)Dedricksje; (9) Marietyje, who married Thomas Fredericks; (10) Jannetje, who married, Gerrit Van Ripen; (11) Michael, who married Elysabet VanRipen; (12) Arriantje, who married Zacharias Sickles; and lastly (13) Enoch, who married Jannetje Van Blerkum. Subsequent generations changed the name from Mickeilsen to Vreeland.

Constance Doreen Trimmer Lucy #330

References:

Vreeland, Nicolas, Editor. *History and Genealogy of the Vreeland Family*, 1999.

Winfield, Charles. *History of the County of Hudson*, 1874. (Internet archive).

Footnote to History

The municipality of Acquackanock (City of Passaic) was established in 1693 in Essex County. The original Acquackanock included parts of Essex and Passaic Counties, and parts of the City of Paterson and the Township of Little Falls.

First Settlers, Colonists and Biographies by Descendants

JOHN WARD (16xx - 1684)

John Ward, a turner (dish turner, his trade) was born in England and came to New England in the 1630's. He married Sarah Lyman, date and place unknown. John Ward, turner, as he was known to differentiate between him and the other John Wards, became active in affairs of Newark where he was chosen cattle brander 1668-77, Constable 1670, Townsman 1675/6, Warner of Town Meeting 1676 and 1684, Grand Juryman 1677, and fence viewer 1678. In 1673 he and his cousin John Catlin were on a committee to agree on money to send a messenger to England and also to go to New Orange (New York City) to a part of the Neck, as cheaply as possible.

In 1679, John Ward, turner was granted the remainder of the Elder's Lot on which one of his sons could build. He received 44 acres beyond Second River, which was bounded by property of his aunt, Widow Ward, wife of Lawrence Ward. His land is now the center of Bloomfield. It is uncertain whether he moved to this land or stayed in Newark until his death and that of his wife in 1684.

Robertson D. Ward #C83

Property allotted to John Ward

Drawing prepared for the bicentennial of the Newark by Samuel Conger and William Whitehead for the New Jersey Historical Society.

References:

New Jersey Historical Society. *Records of the Town of Newark 1666-1836*, 1864. (Reprint 1966).

Bloomfield Historical Society. Bloomfield, Old and New. (Internet website).

Cunningham, John T. *Genealogical and Memorial History of the State of New Jersey Newark*. 2002.

JOHN WARD SR. (c. 1625 - 1694)

John Ward, Sergeant (or Senior) son of Richard and Joyce (-) Ward, was born in England. In a sworn affidavit in 1661 he stated his age as about 36 years which means he was born c. 1625.

John Ward was brought to New England, after 1635, when his father died in Stretton, England. He was apparently in Wethersfield, Connecticut, in 1640 when his mother's will was probated. In 1646 he moved from Wethersfield to Branford, where he married, Sarah, last name unknown, in 1646. Their first child was born in Branford in 1647.

On 30 October 1666, John signed the Fundamental Agreements of the new colony of Newark, New Jersey and moved there in the spring of 1667. His wife Sarah died prior to 1690, when he then married his second wife, Hannah Crane Huntington, the widow of Thomas Huntington.

John's name appeared frequently in the Newark town records. He was chosen to arbitrate disputes, elected surveyor of the highways and drew several lots of land. In 1673 he was chosen one of a group to negotiate with the new Dutch rulers. That same year he was elected lieutenant of the militia. From 1676 to 1680 he was a magistrate. He was on a committee in 1679 to curtail travel to New York City on account of a smallpox epidemic in that city. Finally, in 1692 he was on a committee formed to encourage John Prudden to become the new minister. John died in Newark, New Jersey, his will dated 31 October 1694, was proved 5 December 1694.

Karen Hand Wolzanski #112

Property Allotted to John Ward, Sr.

Drawing prepared for the bicentennial of the Newark by Samuel Conger and William Whitehead for the New Jersey Historical Society.

References:

Cory, Charles H. Jr. *Lineal Ancestors of Captain James Cory and of his Descendants*, 1937.

New Jersey Historical Society. *Records of the Town of Newark 1666-1836*, 1864. (Reprint 1966).

Simonds, J. Rupert. *A History of the First Church and Society of Branford, CT*, `1919. (Internet archive).

Trumbull, J. H. Public Records of the Colony of Connecticut, 1850. (Internet archive).

White, Lorraine Cook (Compiled by). Branford Vital Records.

THOMAS WARNE (c. 1652 - 1722)

Thomas Warne, son of Stephen Warne of Plymouth, England, was born c. 1652. Thomas Warne was one of the twenty-four Proprietors of East Jersey, after the death of Sir George Carteret, and the sale of New Jersey by the trustees of the estate. In 1682 John Heywood, citizen and skinner of London, one of the original twelve Proprietors purchasers of the state, sold half of his share to Thomas Warne, merchant of Dublin, Ireland. Unlike many Proprietors, Thomas actually came to the new province with his father in his 31st year, in March 1683, bringing with them 11 servants.

Thomas was unmarried when he arrived in New Jersey and remained a bachelor until he was about 50 years of age. He married Mary Lord Carhart, between 1698 and 1700, she was the widow of Thomas Carhart of Woodbridge. Mary was a daughter of Robert Lord of Cambridge, Massachusetts and the grand-daughter of Thomas Lord, an original proprietor of Hartford. Mary brought with her into the marriage three sons by her former husband, who were brought up by their step-father. Mary and Thomas Warne had five sons and one daughter.

In a grant of land to the new Proprietors in 1686, Thomas received land on the south side of Mittevang Creek (Matawan Creek) containing 400 acres and called Warne's Neck, now part of Matawan Borough. He owned 1000 acres on the north side of the creek, most of it in what is now Old Bridge Township, Middlesex County, New Jersey. He is reported to have had a wigwam in that area about 1685, while he was surveying his land. He also owned land on what became the Princeton Battlefield.

Frequently mentioned in the public records of the time in Monmouth and Middlesex Counties, he attended at least 88 meetings of the Board of Proprietors between 1685 and 1705; was commissioned a Justice of the Court of Common Right, now Court of Chancery; member of the Governor's Council 1683-1699; and member of the Council for the Management of Public Affairs for the Province of East Jersey in all Debates, Consultations, Resolutions and Procedures.

Thomas Warne's will dated 1722, listed his personal estate at his plantation as 2 negro men, 2 negro boys, 1 negro woman and 2 children. He died in 1722 and was buried in the Topanemus Burying Ground at Marlboro, New Jersey, with his wife.

Marian L. Smith #C21 and James P. DeSalvo   # 341A

The Thomas Warne History Museam and Library is in Olde Bridge, New Jersey

References:

Ellis, Franklin. *History of Monmouth County*, reprint 1974.

Labaw, George Warne. *A Genealogy of the Warne Family in America*, 1911.

Pomfret, John E. *N.J. Proprietors and Their Lands*, 1964.

BARTHOLOMEW WEST (16xx - c.1674)

Bartholomew West was probably the son of Matthew West, who first appeared in Lynn, Massachusetts as early as 1636 and removed to Newport, Rhode Island about 1646. Bartholomew married there Catharine Almy, daughter of William and Audrey (Barlow) Almy.

While living in Portsmouth, Rhode Island, Bartholomew West purchased 70 acres of land on 23 February 1661. He was one of the original purchasers from Rhode Island of land in Monmouth County, East Jersey, in 1665. He was one of the Deputies from Shrewsbury to the General Assembly of East Jersey 14 December 1667. The family lived on land on the corner opposite Christ Church in Shrewsbury.

Bartholomew West died in Shrewsbury, New Jersey, before 1675. His widow Catharine married second, Nicholas Brown, Jr.; she died in Shark River, New Jersey in 1703.

Sally Graham #C43

New Jersey Wildlife

References:

Horner, William S. *This Old Monmouth of Ours*, p. 203, 1932.

Sinnott, Mary Elizabeth. *Annals of the Sinnott, Rogers, Coffin, Corlies, Reeves, Bodine and Allied Families*, pp. 225 - 228

Salter, Edwin. *History of Monmouth and Ocean Counties, New Jersey*, pp. 28, 29, xiii, 1890. (Internet archive).

The Genealogical Magazine of New Jersey, Vol. 19, p. 58.

JOHN WINANS (WYNANTS) (1640 - 1694)

John Winans was born in Watertown, Holland in 1640. He was the son of famous Dutch landscape painter Jan Wynants, by his first wife. After his father's second marriage, he left home to become an apprentice to Gobelin a weaver. In 1653 he came to New Netherlands to live with a relative.

He married his first wife, Susannah Melyn in 1664 at New haven, Connecticut. She was the daughter of Cornelius Melyn, the legendary Patroon of Staten Island, New Amsterdam from 1640 to 1660. The Winans had nine children (John, Susannah, Elizabeth, Samuel, John II, Joanna, Conrad, Jacob, Isaac). His second wife was Ann Robertson, they had three children (William, Phebe, Experience).

John Winans was one of the original "80 Associates" who founded and settled Elizabethtown, New Jersey in 1664-65, after the English took the Dutch colony. He was Burgess in 1668. In 1673, when the Dutch had reclaimed the colony, he was a delegate to negotiate with the authorities for the submission of the town to the Dutch. He was well educated, as was indicated by the books that he owned and his use of a Coat-of-Arms with origins back to the 1100's.

John Winans died in Elizabethtown, New Jersey in December 1694. The family plot is in the First Presbyterian Church in Elizabeth.

#356 Kenneth Winans

References:

Baskas, Richard Scott. *Cornelius Melyn*, 2008.

Groome, Edythe D. Winans. *Jan Wynants, the Weaver*. 1980.

New York: National Americana Society 3 volume set. *American Families of Historic Lineage: Being a Genealogical, Historical, and Biographical Account of Representative Families of Eminent American and Foreign Ancestry, Recognizing Social Standing and Distinguished Achievements*, 1910.

The New York Genealogical and Biographical Record, Vol. LXVIII, 1937. (Internet archive).

Winans, Orin. *History and Family Trees*. 1978.

BARNABAS WINES (1628 – 1715)

Barnabas Wines, son of Barnabas and Anne (Eddy) Wines, was baptized 15 May 1628, St. Clemens Church, Ipswich, County Suffolk, England and died in the fall of 1715 in Southold, Long Island, his will proved 29 September of that year. He married Mary, probably daughter of John Mapes, who survived him, dying 13 June 1717 at 89.

Barnabas' parents, his sister Anna and he came to Watertown, Massachusetts, where his father was made a freeman 6 May 1635. The family moved to Southold, Long Island, where, by 1659 young Barnabas is recorded as owning extensive property. In May 1659 he appeared as a witness against the Quaker, Arthur Smith, in New Haven court. He was admitted a freeman of the Connecticut Colony 12 May 1664, Southold having gone under the jurisdiction of New Haven two years before.

In 1663 he started selling off his Southold property, the last being his home lot and home after he had become one of the 80 founders of Elizabethtown, where he took "The Oath of Alleagance and Fidelity" on 19 February 1665. He was a member of the first jury drawn there in May 1671. His application for a survey for 240 acres was filed 9 May 1676, but the patent issued 22 October 1678 was for only 164 acres.

It is not known when he left Elizabethtown; we merely know that in 1683 he was assessed on Pounds 122 at Mattituck, Southold Township, Long Island. He had not disposed of his Elizabeth property, however, for on 21 April 1708 he sold, for ten *shillings together with the reall love, good will and effection I have for my daughter Sary ye wife of 1 Eliazar Luce...for the more comfortable support of them and their children* 200 acres of woodland in Elizabethtown *entered in ye sd Town Book of Records Number B p.20*. Later, Barnabas's widow and his son Barnabas sold other property there.

Kenn Stryker-Rodda #C5

References:

Hatfield, Rev. Edwin F. *History of Elizabeth, New Jersey*, East New Jersey Property Index, Liber 2, folios 22, 90, 110, 1868. (Internet archive).

Elizabethtown Records, Book B

Salmon Records, Sulfolk County, NY. (Internet archive).

Southold Town Records l:81f, 285, 352; 2:166, 211; et passim (Internet archive).

JOSEPH WOODRUFF (1676-1742)

Joseph Woodruff was born in 1676 in Southampton, L.I. He migrated to New Jersey as a young man, leaving behind, his parents, John and Hannah Newton Woodruff and siblings, John, Samuel, Benjamin, Nathaniel, Isaac, Sarah, Hannah, Abigail and Elizabeth.

Just before 1700 Joseph Woodruff married Hannah (surname unknown) and as a newly married couple, they arrived in New Jersey and settled on 100 acres of land in Essex County, "a cros Rahway river at a great bend a mile below stream from Crane's fod" (now Cranford, three miles south of Westfield). *They lived on the border of civilization ... in 1665 land sold for 10 acres for a penny... wolves and Indians were in abundance... they took muskets to church* (Woodruff 1908). Court records show that their land deed was called into question in 1718.

Joseph and Hannah were the parents of thirteen children. On 15 January 1742 Joseph Woodruff made his will and died 2 February of the same year. He named his wife Hannah as executor, along with son Thomas and friend, William Miller. To his widow he left "the best room in my dwelling house, one third of improvements of all my land and one third of all movable estate". All of his children were named in his will: John, Jonathan, William, Samuel, Abigail Woodruff Gold, Thomas, Hezekiah, Joseph, Nathaniel, Isaac, Benjamin, Sarah and Joanna.

Joseph Woodruff and his wife Hannah are buried in Westfield, New Jersey. His tombstone reads, Departed this life 2 February Anno Domini 1741 in the 65th year of age. Hannah Woodruff's tombstone reads, *Hannah Y wife of Joseph Woodruff Died August the 14th. Anno Domini 1742 in ye 58th year of her age.*

Mary Ellen Ezzell Ahlstrom #304

References:

Townley, C. E. "Woodruff Notes," 1967.

Woodruff, Frances E. *A Branch of the Woodruff Stock*, Grafton Press Publishers, NY, 1908.

Woodruff, Ceylon Newton. *Woodruff Chronicles, Volume I*, 1967..

WILLIAM WOOLMAN (c.1625 – 1692)

William Woolman was born in the British Isles c. 1625. He left Gloucester England, in the early fall of 1678 on the English ship, "Shield", with his only son, John. The ship made landfall at the mouth of the Delaware River and William made his way upstream to the Burlington settlement.

By March 1681 Woolman was settled on "Rankokus alias Northampton River" where the neighboring farms were held by Waiter Humphrey and Bernard Devonish. His son John had given his father 150 acres in Northampton in settlement of arbitration between them. Seventy-five of these acres were left in appreciation to George Elkinton with whom William Woolman had lived during the latter years of his life.

This early settler is best remembered as the great-grandfather of the Reverend John Woolman, the famous Quaker preacher, sometimes known as the Quaker Saint of the eighteenth century, forever pleading the cause of abolition with the inherent evils of slavery and the plight of the American Indians. Reverend Woolman was born on October 19, 1720 at Rancocas, West Jersey, married on October 18, 1749 to Sarah Ellis, and died of small pox on 7 October 1772 at York, England, where he had gone to attend the quarterly meeting of the Society of Friends.

Paul Woolman Adams, #41

Rancocas Creek

References:

San Antonio Express, March 10, 1971, article: "Quaker Saint Devotes Time to Free Slaves" John Woolman, Quaker Social Prophet, Quaker Leader Series, California Yearly Meeting of Friends Church

Whitney, Janet. *John Woolman, American Quaker*, Little, Brown & Co., Boston, 1942

Woolman, Amelia Mott, editor. *Encyclopedia Britannica Journal of John Woolman*, printed 1922 from the original.

JOSHUA WRIGHT (before 1633-1695)

Joshua Wright, Sr. was born in East Riding, Yorkshire, England and baptized 4 October 1633. He married Elizabeth Empson, daughter of William Empson of Gowlefield House on *the 10 day of ye four month 1669*. The marriage was "contrary to discipline" of the Quaker faith. Joshua Wright died "ye 10th of ye 8 mo. 1695 and Elizabeth Wright died the 12th day of 1 mo. 1705/06.

In England in 1677 he acquired a one-sixth share of the Province of West Jersey. He was one of three brothers who emigrated to West Jersey from England. The family, including daughter Elizabeth and sons Robert and Joshua, left their home in Ashford-in-the-Water, Blakewell Parish, Derbyshire. They sailed from Hull ye 24 day of ye 6 mo. And came to ye fall of the Delaware River about ye 20 day of ye 10 mo. 1679. They settled on a tract of 400 acres in Nottingham Township, Burlington County (now Hamilton Township, Mercer County). Three sons were born in West Jersey: Thomas, Joseph and "Samll." There may also have been a fourth son, Richard.

Joshua Wright was one of the five original owners of the Trenton Area. He was a member of the West Jersey General Assembly from 1683 to 1685 and was a signer of the *Concessions and Agreements* of Proprietors, Freeholders and Inhabitants of the Province of West Jersey in 1676. This document, executed in London and attributed to William Penn, predates the Bill of Rights by 113 years. According to former Governor Edward C. Stokes, neither the Great Charter of Virginia nor the Mayflower Compact compare with them in liberality, tolerance and protection of individual rights.

Guy Franklin Leighton #319

References:

Klett, Joseph R. *Genealogies of New Jersey Families*. Baltimore: Genealogical Publishing Co. 1996.

Ristenblatt, Donna Spear "Joshua Wright, Sr." (Website).

Trenton Historical Society. *A History of Trenton*. Princeton: University Press, 1929.

(Wright Family Document, Rutgers University Library)

First Settlers, Colonists and Biographies by Descendants

ROBERT ZANE (1642-1694)

Robert Zane, Jr. was baptized on 29 March 1642 at the Church of St John the Baptist at Yarcombe, Devonshire, England. His family relocated to Ireland in 1656 following England's Civil War. As did many other families of the era, they moved to Ireland where they were able to enjoy religious freedom.

In 1664 Robert married Margaret Hammond in Dublin, Ireland. Margaret was the daughter of Thomas Hammond and Grace Midlem of Yorkshire, England. She traveled with her brother James to Ireland in or about 1661 where she met Robert. Together Robert and Margaret had three children, though only one son, Nathaniel would survive. With the Restoration of the monarchy in 1661, resurgence in persecutions of Quakers developed in both England and Ireland.

The Zanes sailed for America in 1673 on the Mary of Salem, probably as the advance guard for the Irish Tenth (or one tenth of all West Jersey), also called Fenwick's Colony of Salem, West Jersey. It is believed that Margaret died en route to America as there is no record of her death in Ireland or after arrival in America. Zane landed at Elsinburra later traveling up to nearby Salem, West Jersey with his young son. He eventually built a house in Salem, however within a few years' time, left to locate and settle land along Newton Creek, West Jersey.

In 1677 he became one of the Proprietors of West Jersey, listed as Robert Zane of Dublin, Ireland, serge maker. Two years later he married his second wife, Alice Alday, rumored to be of Native American descent. She died leaving no issue. By 1681, Robert had settled and built a home at Newton, New Jersey; in the following year, he was elected to the first Legislature of New Jersey, and re-elected in 1685.

Robert Zane died in 1694 leaving his third wife of thirteen years, Elizabeth Archer Willis (1658-1699) and three children with her in Newton, New Jersey. Descendants of those children, such as his great grandson, Isaac Zane were among the earliest settlers of the West. Isaac's son Ebenezer Zane built his cabin where Wheeling, West Virginia now stands. Another of Roberts descendants, his son Nathaniel's granddaughter, Ester "Hetty" Zane married Richard Collin at Christ Church in Philadelphia, merging two old New Jersey families of Zane and Collins.

Susan Jeanne Bakley Coxe #344

References:

Clement, J. Sketches of the First Emigrant Settlers Newton Township Old Gloucester County West Jersey, 2005.

Pennsylvania Magazine of History and Biography, Vol. XII, No 1, pg 124, 1888.

Pomfret, John E. *The Province of West Jersey 1609-1702*, p.123, 1956.

APPENDIX A

Concessions and Agreements

Excerpted by Evelyn Ogden from the Concessions and Agreements

Signed John Berkley and G. Carteret, 10 Feburary 1664

The CONCESSIONS and Agreement of the Lord Proprietors of the Province of New Cesaea or New Jersey to and with all and every of the Adventures and all such as settle or plant there.

Item make choice of twelve deputies or representatives from amongst themselves; who …with the…Governor and council for making of such laws, ordinances and constitution as shall be necessary…

Item that a chief Secretary or Registrar which we have chosen…shall keep exact entries in faire books of all public affairs…And to avoid deceits and Law Suites shall record…All grants of Land from the Lords to the Planters, and all Conveyances of Land house or houses from man to man…and all Leases for land house or houses made… by the Landlord to any Tenant for more than one year.

Item That the Surveyor General …shall have power by himself or Deputy to Survey lay out and bound all such Lands…granted from the Lords to Planters, and all other Land within the Province which may concern particular men…

Item That the Governor, Councilors, Assembly men, Secretary Surveyor and all other Officers of Trust shall swear or subscribe in a book…that they will bear true Allegiance to the King…be faithful to the interests of the Lord Proprietors…endeavor the peace and welfare of the Province. And that they will truly and faithfully discharge their respective Offices, and do equal Justice to all men according to their best skill and Judgement without corruption, favor or affection.

Item That all persons are or shall become subjects to the King of England and swear…Allegiance to the King and faithfulness to the Lords shall be admitted to Plant and become freeman of the said Province and enjoy the freedoms and immunities hereafter expressed…

Item …the General assembly….by Act to Constitute and appoint such and so many Ministers or Preachers as they shall think fit…Giving liberty besides to any person or persons to keep and maintain what Preachers or Ministers they please.

Item That no person qualified as foresaid within the said Province at any time shall be any ways molested, punished, disquieted or called in Question for any difference in opinion or practice in matters of Religious concernment…

Item … join with the…Governor and Council… for the making of such Laws Ordinances and Constitutions as shall be necessary for the present good and welfare of said Princince… as soon as parishes, divisions… or other distinctions are made, that then the inhabitants or freeholders of the several respective…divisions, do….meet on the first day of January, and choose freeholders for each respective division…... to be the deputies of or representatives of the same; which body of representatives or the major part of them, shall with the Governor be the General Assembly of the said Province, unless the Governor or his deputy willfully refuse, in which case

Part II: Which ASSEMBLIES are to have power:

To appoint their own times of meeting… and places they shall think convenient. …ascertain the number of their Quorum provided that number is not less than the third part of the whole…

To enact and make all such Laws, Acts and Constitutions as shall be necessary for the well Government of the said Province, and them to repeal; provided the same be consonant to reason, and as near as may be conveniently agreeable to the laws and customs of his Majesty's kingdom of England; provided that they do not be repugnant to the article for liberty of conscience...

By Act ...to constitute all courts, together with the limits, powers and jurisdictions of the same; as also the several offices and number of officers belonging to each court, with their respective salaries, fees and perquisites; their appellations and dignities, with the penalties that shall be due to them, for the breach of their several and respective duties and trusts.

By Act to lay equal taxes and assessments, equally to raise moneys or goods upon all land (excepting the lands of us the Lords Proprietors before settling) or persons within the several .... manors, divisions...hereafter be made and established in said Province, as oft as necessary shall require, and in such manner as to them shall seem most equal and easy for said inhabitants; in order to better supporting of the publick charge.... for the mutual safety, defence and security of said Province.

By Act to ...erect within the Province and so many Manors with their necessary Courts Jurisdictions freedoms and Privileges as to tem shall seem meet and convenient, and also to divide the Province into Hundreds Tribes Parishes or such other Divisions or distinctions as they seem fit...default such names as they please. Also to create and appoint Ports Harbors Creeks and other places seemed good and ....to fortify and furnish with Provisions...Ordinance powder...Armor and all other weapons...both offensive and defensive as shall be thought necessary and convenient for the safety and welfare of the Province...

By their enacting...to erect...fortresses Castles Cities Corporations Burroughs, Towns, Villages and other places of Strength and defense...

By act ...to constitute Trained bands and companies with the number of Soldiers for the safety strength and defense of said Province...

By Act...to give unto all Strangers as to them shall seem meet A naturalization, and all such freedoms and privileges within the Province...by swearing or subscribing as aforesaid...as the Kings natural subjects.

The general Assembly by act shall make provisions for the maintenance and support of the Governor...Constables of the Province shall Collect the Lords Rent...

Lastly to enact constitute and ordained all such other Laws Act and Constitutes as shall be necessary for the good property and settlement of the Province...

Part III: THE GOVERNOR with his Council...

To see that all Courts established by the Laws of the General Assembly and all Ministers and Officers civil and military do execute their several Duties and Offices respectively according to the Laws in force, and to punish them for Swearing from the Laws or acting contrary to their Trust, as the nature of their offense shall require.

According to the Constructions of the general Assembly to nominate and Commission the several Judges Members and officers of Courts...Provided that they appoint none but such as are freeholders the Province unless the general Assembly consents.

According to the Constructions of the general Assembly to appoint Courts and Officers in Cases criminal, and empower them to inflict penalties upon the offenders...

To place Officers and Soldiers for the safety, strength, and defense of the forts Castles Cities...according to the number appointed by the general Assembly...Provided that they appoint no military forces but are freeholders in the said Province, unles the General Assemby shall consent.

Where they see cause after Condemnation to Reprieve until the Case be presented, with copies of the whole Trial and proceedings and proofs the Lords who will accordingly either pardon or command execution of the sentence on the Offender who is in the meantime to be kept in safe custody till the pleasure of the Lords be known.

In case of death or other removal of any representatives within the year...the respective Division or Divisions to which he or they were chosen...the freeholders of the same to choose others in their stead.

To make Warrants and to Seale grants of Lands according to these our Concessions and the prescriptions by the advice of the general Assembly in such form as shall be at large set down in our Instructions of the Governor in his Commission, and which are hereafter expressed.

To Act and do all other thing or things that may conduce to the safety, peace and well Government of the said Province, as they shall see fit, so as they be not contrary to the Laws of the said province.

Part IV: For the better security of the Proprietors and all the Inhabitants

They are not to impose nor suffer to be imposed any Tax Custom Subsidy, Talladge, Assessment, or any other duty whatsoever upon any colour or pretense upon the said Province and inhabitants thereof other then what shall be imposed by the Authority and consent of the general Assembly and then only in manner as aforesaid.

They are to take care that Land quietly held planted and possessed seven years after its being first duly surveyed by the Surveyor General or his Order shall not be subject to any review re-survey or alteration of bounds on what pretense so ever by any of us or any officer or Minister under us.

They are to take care that no man if his Cattle Stray Range or Graze on any Ground...not actually appropriated or set out to particular persons shall be liable to pay any Trespass ...nor any person hindered from taking up and appropriating any Lands so grazed upon...and that no person do purposely suffer to graze on such lands.

And That the Planting of Said Province May Be More Speedily Promoted

We do grant unto all persons who have already adventured to the said Province of New Caesarea or New Jersey or shall transport themselves before the first day of January...six-hundred and sixty-five, these following proportions: for every freeman ho shall go with the Governor...or meet him at the rendezvous...for settlement of a plantation there, armed with a good musket, bore twelve bullets to the pound, with ten pounds of powder, and twenty pounds of bullets...and six months provision for his own person...one hundred fifty acres...for every able servant...armed and provided for...the like quantity of one hundred fifty acres...and for every weaker servant, or slave, male or female, exceeding the age of fourteen... seventy-five acres. And to very Christian servant, exceeding the age foresaid, after the expiration of their time of service, seventy-five acres of land for their own use.

To every master or mistress who shall arrive before the first day of January...six hundred sixty-five; one hundred and twenty acres of land. And for every able man servant,...armed and provided for, arriving within the time foresaid...one hundred and twenty acrers of land. And every weaker servant, or slave, male or female, exceeding the age of fourteen... seventy-five acres. And to very Christian servant, exceeding the age foresaid, after the expiration of their time of service, sixty acres of land for their own use.

To every free man and free women that shall arrive in the Province, armed…within the second year…first day of January…six hundred sixty-six; …ninety acres of land. And for every able man servant,…armed and provided for, arriving within the time foresaid…ninety acres of land.

And every weaker servant, or slave, male or female, exceeding the age of fourteen… forty-five acres. And to very Christian servant, exceeding the age

foresaid, after the expiration of their time of service, forty-five acres of land for their own use.

To every free man and free women that shall arrive in the Province, armed…within the third year…first day of January…six hundred sixty-seven; …thirty acres of land. And for every able man servant,…armed and provided for, arriving within the time foresaid…thirty acres of land….

Note: There is a complete copy of the Concessions and Agreements State Government Information Services, The New Jersey State Library

Genealogical Index of Names

Over 2000 names linked with settlement of New Jersey during the Proprietary Period

The Index of Names includes not only the names of founders, approved to date for membership in Descendants of Founders of New Jersey, but also more than a thousand of additional early settlers who are referenced in the biographies, such as spouses, members of subsequent generations; individuals recorded as founders of some of the earliest towns; grantors, grantees, deed holders and native American sellers of land who can be documented as founders of New Jersey.

Abbott, Thomas, 60
Abel, Ann[e], 153
Abington Friends Meeting, 180
Abraham Isaacsen Verplanck, 65
Achter Kol., 76
Achter Kull, 31
Ackerman, Abraham, 17
Ackerman, David, 17, 65
Ackerman, Laurents, 17
Ackerman, Louwerense, 64
Acquackanock, 203
Acton, Benjamin, 60
Adams, Alexander, 50
Adams, John, 47, 59
Adams, Thomas, 47
Albers, Hans, 55, 56
Alger, Mary, 66
Alger, Susanna, 66, 168
Alger, Thomas, 17, 66
Alger, Thomas Jr., 66
Alien, Judah, 44
Allen, Elizabeth,, 67
Allen, George, 124
Allen, Jedediah, 17
Allen, John, 17, 39, 47, 67
Allen, Judah, 44
Allen, Mary, 67
Allen, Mercy, 67
Allen, Priscilla, 67
Allen, Samuel, 67
Allmey, Christopher, 42, 43
Allways (Indian Sachem), 59

Almy, Catharine, 208
Almy, Christopher, 39
Almy, Elizabeth, 91
Almy, Job, 39
Almy, William, 208
Alrichs, Jacob, 80
Amboy Point, 46, 130
Anderson, Eliakim, 193
Andres, Joachim, 17
Andrews, Ephram, 47
Andros, Governor Edmond, 95
Andros, Sir Edmond, 190
Andross, Yokum, 33
Ann, Stanley, 47
Anthony, Annetje, 163
Applegate, Bartholomew, 17, 68
Applegate, Daniel, 44
Applegate, Thomas, 17, 44, 68
Aquackanonck (Passaic), 71
Arnold, Stephen, 40, 43
Ashton, James, 17, 40, 42
Assamhockin Creek, 59
Assembly of the Province of West New Jersey, 159
Assiscunk Creek, 159
Atkins, Jane, 121
Auger, Thomas, 47
Austin, Elizabeth, 17, 69
Austin, Francis, 69
Averill, John, 47
Ayers, Hannah, 70
Ayers, John, 70
Ayers, John, Jr., 70

First Settlers, Colonists and Biographies by Descendants

Ayers, Joseph, 70
Ayers, Mary, 70
Ayers, Obadiah, 17, 46, 47, 70
Ayers, Samuel, 70
Bacon, Elizabeth, 67
Bagwell, Eleanor, 132
Baily, John, 31, 32, 33
Bainbridge, John, 17
Baird, John, 17
Baker, John, 30, 31, 33, 155
Baker/Bacon, Samuel, 47
Baldwin, Benjamin, 17, 56
Baldwin, John Jr, 85
Baldwin, John Sr., 56
Baldwin, John, Sr., 17
Ball, Edward, 17, 55, 56, 107
Ballenger, Henry, 132
Baltus, Barent, 196
Banta, Epke Jacobse, 17
Banta, Margrietje Diedricks, 203
Baptist, 41, 101, 179, 198
Baptist Church, 183
Baptist Church of Middletown, 79
Barbadoes Neck, 202
Barber, Francis, 32, 33
Barclay, Col. David, 118
Barclay, Robert, 118
Barlow, Audrey, 208
Barnegat Bay, 38
Barnes, Thomas, 43
Barrett's Run, 82
Bartlett, Benjamin, 138
Bartlett, Thomas, 50, 51
Bateman (Family), 60
Bateman, Elizabeth, 145
Bateman, William, 145
Bauldwin, John, Jr, 55
Bauldwin, John, Sr, 55
Bayle John, 31
Bayonne, 26
Beach, Richard, 33
Beape, Sarah, 42
Beckly, Sergt. Richard, 54
Beere, Jonathan, 60

Bellier, Lysbeth, 64, 65
Benedick, Thomas, 31, 155
Benedict, James, 127
Benedict, John, 127
Benton, William, 178
Bergen, 108, 113, 196, 202
Bergen County, 65, 142
Bergen Neck, 25, 52, 87, 194
Bergen Reformed Dutch Church, 64, 113, 196
Berkeley, Lord John, 16, 22, 27, 155
Berry, John, 64
Bertholf Guiliam, 71
Bertholf, Cryn, 71
Bertholf, Rev. Guiliam, 17
Betterby, Joane, 95
Biddle, William, 17, 72, 167
Bilderback, Albert, 177
Bilderback, Peter, 176
Billinge, Edward, 58
Billow, Peter, 50, 51
Bingley, William, 47
Bird, John, 40
Bishop, Ann, 73
Bishop, David, 73
Bishop, Elizabeth, 73
Bishop, Hannah, 73
Bishop, Joanna, 73
Bishop, John Jr, 47
Bishop, John Sr., 73
Bishop, John, Sr., 17, 47
Bishop, Jonathan, 47, 73
Bishop, Noah, 73
Bishop, Rebecca, 73
Blackford, Daniel, 51
Blackford, Samuel, 51
Blackford, Thomas, 51
Blanchan, Catherine, 111
Blashford, Elizabeth, 101
Blatchley, Aaron, 55, 56
Blatchley, Thomas, 17, 54, 55
Blinkerhoff, Cornelis, 203
Bloomfield, 107
Bloomfield, Mary, 47, 112
Bloomfield, Thomas, 17, 46, 47, 112

Blossom, Elder Thomas, 119
Blossom, Elizabeth, 119, 162
Bodine, Sarah, 111
Bogaert, Tunis Gysbertse, 192
Bogaet, Neeltje, 191
Bogart, Catlyntje Tunisen, 192
Bogers, Benjamin, 44
Bollen, John, 33
Bond, Jane, 155
Bond, Joseph, 33, 75
Bond, Mary, 75
Bond, Robert, 17, 33, 75
Bond, Stephen, 55, 56
Bonham, Nicholas, 50, 122
Bonhamtown, 122
Bonnell, Benjamin, 76
Bonnell, Isaac, 76
Bonnell, Jane, 76
Bonnell, Lydia, 76
Bonnell, Nathaniel, 17, 33, 76
Bonnell, Nathaniel II, 76
Bonnell, Samuel, 76
Bonnell, Susanna, 76
Bonnell, William, 76
Boombaert, Jan Cornelisse, 17
Borden, Benjamin, 39, 78, 128
Borden, Francis, 43, 44, 78
Borden, John, 43, 44
Borden, Richard, 17, 39, 78
Borden, Samuel, 42
Bordentown, 23
Bound Brook, 149
Bourne, Gerrard, 39
Bowentown, 82
Bowne, Ann, 17, 79
Bowne, Gershom, 44
Bowne, James, 17, 39, 40, 42, 79
Bowne, John, 39, 42, 91, 137
Bowne, Mary Stout, 17
Bowne, Samuel, 17
Bowne, William, 17, 39, 40, 79
Bowne,, James, 43
Boyer, Alexander/Sander, 17, 80
Boyer, John/Jan, 80

Boyer, Joseyn, 80
Boyer, Peter, 80
Boyer, Samuel, 80
Brackett, John, 34
Bradbury, Edward, 17
Bradley, Joshua, 47
Branch, Long, 178
Brassey, Rebecca, 60
Bridlington, 93
Brinkerhoff, Hendrick, 17
Brinley, Francis, 39
Brinley/Brindley, Simon, 50
Brinson, Daniel, 51
Brockett, John, 17, 33, 81
Brockett, John, Jr, 33
Broer, Sinnick, 176
Brooks, Henry, 82
Brooks, John, 55, 56, 82
Brooks, Josiah, 82
Brooks, Timothy, Jr, 82
Brooks, Timothy, Sr., 17, 82
Broucard, Bourgon, 192
Brown, Abraham, 17, 40, 43
Brown, Andrew, 83
Brown, Christian, 83
Brown, George, 17, 47, 83
Brown, Grier, 83
Brown, James, 17, 83, 84
Brown, John, 39, 85, 107
Brown, John Sr., 56
Brown, Katherine, 42, 43
Brown, Martha, 130
Brown, Mary, 76
Brown, Nicholas, 17, 42, 43
Brown, Nicholas Jr, 208
Brown, Phebe, 107
Brown, Rev. Richard, 83, 84
Brown, Richard, 139, 140
Brown, Thomas, 83
Brown, William, 83, 84
Browne, John, 53, 55
Browne, John Jr, 55
Browne, Nicholas, 39
Bruen, John, 85

First Settlers, Colonists and Biographies by Descendants

Bruen, Obadiah, 17, 55, 56, 85
Bryan, Isaac, 44
Bryce, Joseph, 40
Budd, Mary, 97
Budd, Thomas, 97, 181
Budd, William, 17
Bull, Henry, 39, 42
Bunn, Matthw, 47
Burden, Benjamin, 40, 43
Burlington, 23, 72, 84, 89, 93, 97, 99, 102, 117, 121, 147, 164
Burlington County, 69, 99, 116, 123, 128, 132, 159, 168, 170, 172, 175, 181, 182, 213
Burlington County Assembly, 167
Burlington Monthly Meeting, 84, 93, 97, 121
Burlington., 95
Burr, Aaron, 37
Burwell, Ephram, 55
Burwell, Zachariah, 55, 56
Butler, Dorothy, 123
Butterworth, Henry, 96
Butterworth, Marie, 96
Button, William, 60
Buys, Cornelis, 87
Buys, Jan Cornelis, 17, 87, 194, 196
Buys, Tryntje Jans, 196
Byllyng, Edward, 97
Cabot, John, 24
Cackmackque (Indian Sachem), 53
Caleb, John, 89
Calkins, Hugh, 75
Calkins, Mary, 75
Calvinists, 60
Camfield, Ebenezer, 55
Camfield, Gregorie, 88
Camfield, Matthew, 17, 55, 56, 88
Camfield, Samuel, 56
Camp, William, 55, 56, 188
Canackawack (Indian Sachem), 49
Cape May, 59
Cape May County, 89, 131, 180
Captamin (Indian Sachem), 53
Carhart, Thomas, 206
Carle, Thomas, 51
Carman, Caleb, 17
Carr, Benjamin, 90

Carr, Governor Caleb, 90
Carr, Margaret, 133
Carr, Robert, 17, 39, 90, 133
Carter, Nicholas, 33
Carter, Timothy, 50
Carteret, Governor Philip, 22, 33, 34, 46, 47, 63, 74, 75, 76, 81, 85, 106, 146, 150, 155, 163, 184
Carteret, Sir George, 22, 27, 49
Carwithe, Caleb, 33, 92, 142, 169
Catlin, John, 55, 56, 204
Cawood, Sarah, 98
Cawood, Thomas, 47, 51, 98
Chamberlin, Henry, 91
Chamberlin, John, 17, 45, 91
Chamberlin, Louis, 91
Chamberlin, Rebecca, 91
Chambless, Nathaniel, 59
Chambless, Nathaniel Jr, 59
Chamlain, Sealy, 33
Champners, John, 43
Champney, Band Edward, 59
Chandler, Lydia, 136
Chapman, Jane, 159
Charles, John, 188
Charles, Mary, 188
Chechenaham (Indian Sachem), 59
Cheeseman, William, 40, 43
Chester Township, 147
Chesterfield, 175
Chestnut Neck, 176
Christ's Church at Shrewsbury, 91
Church of England, 58, 102
Chutte, George, 39
Clais, Jacob, 34
Clark, Elizabeth, 92
Clark, John, 17
Clark, Richard, 17, 92
Clark, Richard Jr, 17
Clark, Richard, Jr., 92
Clark, Walter, 39
Clarke, Benjamin, 50
Clarke, Faith, 109
Clarke, Walter, 39
Clarkson, James, 17, 47
Claws, Thomas, 51

Clayton, Honour, 84
Clayton, Joan Smith, 93
Clayton, Prudence, 93
Clayton, William, 84, 93
Clayton, William, Jr., 17, 93
Clement, John, 153
Clement, Jonathan, 94
Clements, Robert, 17, 94
Clements, Robert, Jr,, 47
Clift, Hannah, 95, 117
Clift, Joseph, 95
Clift, Samuel, 17, 95, 117
Clifton, Hope, 96
Clifton, Mary, 96
Clifton, Patience, 96
Clifton, Richard, 96
Clifton, Thomas, 17, 39, 96
Coddington, John, 17
Coddington, William, 39
Coggeshall, John, 39
Coggeshall, Joshua, 39, 44
Cohansey, 82, 111
Cohansey Creek, 60
Cole(s), Samuel, 17
Cole, Jacob, 40, 44
Cole, Mary, 44
Cole, Thomas, 182
Coleman, Joseph, 39
Colin, Nicholas, 177
Collins, Edward, 97
Collins, Francis, 17, 97, 99
Collins, Mary, 97
Colman, John, 22, 25
Columbus, 173
Compton, William, 17, 40, 42, 44, 47
Concessions and Agreements, 27, 28, 40, 46, 54, 97, 121, 175, 213, 215
Concklin, Benjamin, 34
Condit, John, 17
Conger, John, 17, 47, 98
Congregational Church, 54, 103, 144
Conklin, John, 39
Connecticut Farms, 76, 81
Connecticut Farms Presbyterian Church, 76
Cook, Anthony, 99

Cook, Hannah, 44
Cook, Henry, 17, 99
Cook, Joan, 178
Cook, John, 39, 43, 178
Cook, Thomas, 43
Cook, William, 99
Cooks, Abraham, 117
Cooper, Mary, 60
Coperen, Sara Guiliamse Van, 71
Corlies, George, 17
Cornelis, Divertie, 194
Cottrell, Ebenezer, 44
Court of Justice at Bergen, 202
Couwenhoven Family, 195
Couwenhoven, Cornelius, 100
Couwenhoven, Peter, 33
Couwenhoven, Rulif, 100
Couwenhoven, William, 100
Couwenhover, Cornelius, 17
Covert ,Elizabeth, 58
Covill, Rebecca, 187
Coward, Rebecca, 44
Cowescomen (Indian Sachem), 31
Cox, Rebecca, 60
Cox, Thomas, 17, 39, 40, 42, 43, 101
Coxe, Daniel, 17, 102, 111
Craft's Creek, 173
Craig, Andrew Sr., 17
Cramer, William, 32, 34
Cranbury Towne, 166
Crane, Alice, 103
Crane, Azariah, 17, 55, 56
Crane, Delivered, 55, 56, 103
Crane, Hannah, 205
Crane, Jasper, 17, 55, 56, 103
Crane, Jasper Jr., 185
Crane, John, 55, 56, 103
Crane, Joseph, 17
Crane, Stephen, 17, 33
Cranford, John, 44
Crawford, Jane, 99
Cripps, John, 117
Cromwell, John, 47
Cromwell, Oliver, 27, 58, 128, 145

Crosse, Thomas, 159
Crosswicks, 170
Cullpeper, Susanna, 144
Cumberland County, 58
Curtis, John, 55, 56
Curtis, Thomas, 159
Cuyper, Cornelis Claessen, 200
Daglesh, Robert, 55, 56
Dahlbo, Oele, 17
Dame Schools, 36
Damen, Hendrickje Jans, 87
Damen, Jan, 194, 196
Damen, Jan, 87
Daniel, Daniel Mc, 51
Dans, Richard, 43
Dare, Virginia, 164
Darking, Richard, 60
Davenport., John Jr, 161
Davidse, Joris Christoffelse, 104
Davis, James, 17, 104
Davis, John, 56
Davis, Nicholas, 39, 43
Davis, Stephen, 55, 56
Day, Dorothy, 162
Day, George, 55, 56
Dayton, Jonathan, 37
Deale, 44
DeBure, Frans Anna Cornelis, 201
Decent, John, 92
DeCou, Jacob, 164
Delaware River, 59, 116, 153
Demarest, David, 17, 105
Demarest, David Jr., 17
Demarest, Jean, 105
Demarest, Maria (DeRuine), 17
Demarest, Rachel (Cresson), 17
Demarest, Samuel, 17, 105
Denell, Benjamin, 40
Denison, Robert, 53, 55, 56, 85
Dennis ,Robert, 49
Dennis, James L., 106
Dennis, Jonathan, 47
Dennis, Mary, 106
Dennis, Robert, 17, 47, 106

Dennis, Samuel, 17, 47
Deuell, Benjamin, 40, 43
deVaux, Nicholas, 17
Devonish, Bernard, 212
Dickenson, John, 33
Dickenson, Rev. Jonathan, 37
Dikeman, Hugh, 43
Dille, John Sr, 17, 47
Dod, Daniel, 17, 56, 107
Dod, Samuel, 56
Dole, Richard, 150
Doremus, Cornelis, 17, 108
Doremus, Johannes, 108
Doremus, Thomas, 108
Dorset, James, 17, 43
Doty, Edward, 109
Doty, John, 51
Doty, Samuel, 17, 50, 109
Dowsett, Thomasine, 129
Drake, Capt. Francis, 17, 50, 51
Drake, Francis Jr, 51
Drake, George, 50
Drake, John, 50
Drake, Joseph, 51
Drake, Mary, 49
Droogestradt, Hendrick, 163
Drummond, Gavine, 17, 110
Drummond, Robert, 110
DuBois, Jacob, 111
DuBois, Louis, 111
DuBois, Sarah, 17, 111
Dun, Hugh, 47
Dungan, Rev. Thomas, 17
Dungan, Thomas, 40, 42
Dunham, Ann Stanley, 112
Dunham, Benajah, 50
Dunham, Edmund, 50, 122
Dunham, Elizabeth, 122
Dunham, Jonathan, 17, 46, 47, 112
Dunn, Hugh, 17, 46, 49, 50, 122
Dunn, Hugh Jr, 51
Dunn, Mary, 122
Dunn, Samuel, 51
Duokura, William, 44

Index

DuPui, Moses, 113
DuPui, Nicholas, 17, 113
Dutch East Indian Company, 24
Dutch Reformed Church, 113, 134, 195
Dutch Reformed Church at Hackensack, 64
Dutch Reformed Church of Bergen, 71
Dutch Reformed Church of Raritan, 191, 192
Dutch West Indies Company, 174
duTrieux, Jacob, 17, 114
duTrieux, Maria, 114
duTrieux, Philippe, 114
duTrieux, Philippe Jr, 114
East Jersey Proprietor, 110
Easton, Peter, 39, 44
Eaton, Michael, 59
Eaton, Thomas, 18, 44
Eckley, John, 102
Eckley, Sarah, 102
Eddy, Anne, 210
Eeape, Sarah, 43
Eleanor of Aquitaine, 111
Elizabeth and Anne (Ship), 184
Elizabeth River, 32, 76
Elizabeth Town Purchase, 27
Elizabethtown, 22, 23, 31, 32, 33, 34, 35, 36, 37, 46, 49, 52, 75, 76, 79, 81, 88, 92, 94, 104, 120, 134, 141, 145, 146, 155, 156, 157, 158, 163, 165, 170, 209, 210
Elizabethtown Associates, 33, 75, 76, 81, 92, 148, 155
Elizabethtown Code of Laws, 37
Elkinton, George, 212
Ellis, Roger, 39, 44
Ellis, Sarah, 212
Ellison, John, 18, 115
Ellison, Susannah, 115
Elmer, Daniel, 60
Ely, Benjamin, 116
Ely, Hannah, 116
Ely, Joshua, 18, 116
Ely, Ruth, 116
Emery, Stephen, 47, 140
Empson, Elizabeth, 213
Empson, William, 213
England, Christiana, 60
English, Elizabeth, 117
English, Hannah, 117

English, Joseph II, 18, 117
English, Rachel, 117
English, William, 117
Ericson, Leif, 24
Essex County, 85
Estell, Daniel, 40, 43
Evelyn, William, 159
Eves, Thomas, 18
Evesham, 69
Fairmount Cemetery, 184
Falconer, David, 18, 118
Farsworth, Thomas, 51
Fawne, Elizabeth, 47, 94
Femmetje, Tunison, 192
Fenick, John, 16
Fenwick, Anne, 59
Fenwick, Elizabeth, 59
Fenwick, John, 58, 59, 160
Fenwick, Priscilla, 59
Fenwick's Colony, 23, 58, 153, 160, 214
Field, John, 51
Finnish Settlers, 58
First Baptist Church at Middletown, 137
First Church of Newark, 161
First Presbyterian Church of Elizabeth, 35, 76, 134
First Presbyterian Church Woodbridge, 48
Fithian, John, 60
Fithian, Samuel & Priscilla, 60
Fitz-Randolph, Benjamin, 50, 119
Fitz-Randolph, Dinah, 122
Fitz-Randolph, Edward, 18, 119, 162
Fitz-Randolph, John, 50, 119
Fitz-Randolph, Joseph, 119
Fitz-Randolph, Nathaniel, 18
Fitz-Randolph, Thomas, 50, 119
Fletcher, Alice, 175
Fletcher, Elizabeth, 175
Fletcher, Richard, 175
Folkerson, Rebecca, 191
Fordham, Florence, 89
Fort Casimir, 80, 176
Fort Elfsborg, 22
Fort Nassau, 80
Fort Trinity, 80

Fouike, Thomas, 18
Fowie, Joane, 78
Fowie, Richard, 78
Fox, Anne, 85
Fox, George, 41, 90, 133
Fox, John, 187
Frampton, William, 18
LeMaistre,, 43
Frazee, Christopher, 43
Frazee, Joseph, 18, 33, 120
Fredericks, Thomas, 203
Freeborn, Gideon, 40, 44
Freehold, 23, 130
Freeman, John and Hannah, 47
Freeman, Stephen, 54, 55, 56
French Burying Grounds, 105
French Patent, 105
French, John (Mason), 47
French, Sara, 121
French, Thomas, 18, 121, 173
Friends Meeting at Shrewsbury, 130
Friends School, 60
Fuller, Dr. Samuel, 122
Fuller, Edmund, 122
Fuller, Hannah, 18, 122
Fuller, Mary, 122
Fuller, Nicholas, 122
Fuller, Samuel, 122
Fullerton, James, 141
Fundamental Agreements, 54, 55, 85, 144, 152, 169, 190, 205
Gaillard, Alice, 190
Gaillard, Hugh, 190
Gannet, Rehoboth, 47, 50
Gardiner, Richard, 44
Gardner, John, 56
Gardner, Lyon, 165, 184
Garrett, Annanias, 44
Gauntt, Hananiah, 18, 123
Gauntt, Israel, 123
Gauntt, Peter, 124
Gauntt, Zachary, 39
Gavine, Robert, 110
Gaylord, Alice, 190
Gaylord, Hugh. See Gaillard, Hugh

General Assembly of East Jersey, 190
General Assembly of New Jersey at Elizabethtown, 41, 46, 74, 75, 76, 81, 112, 145, 156, 183, 184
Genung, Jeremiah, 18
George Fox, 180
Gibbons, Mordecai, 44
Gibbons, Richard, 39, 43
Gifford, Annaniaih, 44
Gifford, Christopher, 44, 124
Gifford, Hannaniah, 43
Gifford, William, 18, 40, 124
Giles, James, 50
Giles, Matthew, 50
GillJohnson, Ann Philpot, 176
GillJohnson, Sarah, 176
Gillman ,John, 49
Gilman, Charles, 49
Gilman, Charles, 50
Gilman, John, 50
Gilman, Mary, 47, 66
Gloucester, 23, 138, 147, 181
Gloucester County, 97, 167, 182
Godfry, James, 50
Gold, Abigail Woodruff. See Woodruff, Abigail
Goldingand, William, 43
Goldsmith, Ralph, 39
Gordon, Annabel, 47, 83
Gordon, Charles, 18
Gordon, Thomas, 50, 150
Gosling, Dr. John, 97
Gould, Daniel, 39, 44
Goulding, William, 39
Governor Barclay, 46
Gracey, Matthew, 18, 126
Gracey, Parthenia Bethany, 126
Graham, James, 197
Gransden, Alice, 131
Grasie, Daniel, 47
Graues, Zackery, 34
Gray, John, 33
Greater Egg Harbor, 117, 180, 181
Green, Henry, 91
Greene, Thomas, 117
Greenland, Henry, 50
Greenwich, 23, 82

Gregory, Jacim, 127
Gregory, John, 18, 127, 184
Gregory, Joseph, 127
Gregory, Judah, 127
Gregory, Phoebe, 127
Gregory, Sarah, 127
Gregory, Thomas, 127
Gretson, Henry, 51
Griffin (Ship), 59, 153
Griffin ,Robert, 59
Griffith, Benjamin., 51
Griffith, Robert, 153
Griscom, Benjamin, 60
Grover, Abigail, 78, 128
Grover, James, 18, 39, 128
Grover, Rebecca, 18
Grover, Safety, 18, 44
Grover, Thomes, 43
Grubs, Thomas, 51
Guy, Richard, 60
Hackensack, 26, 54, 65, 71, 105
Hackensack Indians, 52, 85, 184
Hackensack River, 105, 108
Haddonfield, 97
Haines, Amos, 69
Haines, Ann, 69
Haines, Daniel, 69
Haines, Deborah, 69
Haines, Elizabeth, 69
Haines, George, 69
Haines, Jane, 69
Haines, John, 18
Haines, Margaret, 69
Haines, Richard, 69
Haines, Thomas, 69
Haines, Thomas II, 69
Hains, William, 18
Hale, John, 139, 140
Hale, Mary, 129, 171
Hale, Samuel, 18, 47, 129, 171
Hale, Sarah, 129
Hale, Thomas, 129
Half Moon (Ship), 25
Hall, John, 40

Hall, William, 18, 60
Hamilton, Alexander, 37
Hamilton, Robert, 44
Hammond, Margaret, 214
Hammond, Thomas, 214
Hampton, Andrew, 130
Hampton, David, 130
Hampton, Elizabeth, 130
Hampton, Janett, 130
Hampton, John, 18, 130
Hampton, Jonathan, 130
Hampton, Joseph, 130
Hampton, Lydia, 130
Hampton, Noah, 130
Hance, John, 18, 39, 43
Hancock, Isabel, 175
Hancock, John, 18
Hancock, Sarah, 60
Hancock, Timothy, 147
Hand, Alice, 131
Hand, Benjamin, 131
Hand, Deborah, 131
Hand, George, 131
Hand, Jeremiah, 131
Hand, John, 131
Hand, Katherine, 131
Hand, Prudence, 131
Hand, Recompense, 131
Hand, Shamgar, 131
Hand, Thomas, 18, 131
Handcock, Richard, 59
Handson, Tobias, 39
Hannson, Eichard, 44
Hanoe, John, 43
Harbert, Thomas, 43
Harding, Eleanor, 132
Harding, Hope, 132
Harding, Rebecca, 132
Harding, Thomas, 18, 60, 132
Hardington, Martha, 90
Harish (Indian Sachem), 53
Harlow, Gregory, 132
Harmanse, Annetje, 203
Harmon, Jane, 109

First Settlers, Colonists and Biographies by Descendants

Harris, Daniel, 34
Harrise, 60
Harrise (Family, 60
Harrison, John, 51, 55, 56
Harrison, Richard, 18, 54, 55
Harrison, Robert, 56
Harrison, Samuel, 56
Hart, Thomas, 40
Hartman Mickeilsen Vreeland, 203
Hartman's Island, 203
Hartshome, Richard, 45
Hartshorne Burying Ground, 133
Hartshorne, Hugh, 133
Hartshorne, Kathrine, 133
Hartshorne, Richard, 18, 43, 133
Hatfield, Matthias, 18, 32, 33, 134
Hatton, Samuel, 44
Havens, Ann, 135
Havens, Dionis, 135
Havens, John, 18, 40, 43, 135
Havens, William, 135
Hawes, John, 40
Haynes, Charles, 42
Haynes, Jonathan, 47
Hazard, Robert, 40
Headley, Leonard, 33
Heard, James, 40
Hector (Ship), 81
Hedge, Samuel, Jr., 59
Heilson, Ann, 119
Hempstead, 89
Henaminkey (Indian Sachem), 59
Hendricks, Daniel, 50
Hendricks, John, 50
Hendrickson Family, 195
Hendrickson, John Jr., 176
Henry, Jasper, 47
Heritage, Richard, 18
Herman, Augustine, 75
Heyden, William, 43
Heywood, John, 206
Hibbs, William, 18
Hicks, Gabriel, 43
Higgins, Anne, 166

Higgins, Benjamin, 136
Higgins, Eliakim, 136
Higgins, Jediah, 50
Higgins, Jonathan, 136
Higgins, Mary, 50, 136
Higgins, Richard, 18, 136, 166, 179
Higgins, Thomas, 50
Hill, William, 32
Hilliard, T., 60
Hillitt, George, 43
Hindes, John, 33
Hinds, James, 92
Hirbert, Francis, 43
Hixson, William, 18
Hoboken, 26
Hodgkin, Hannah, 180
Hoge, William, 18
Holder, Mary, 178
Holeman, Samuel, 40, 43
Holland, Thomas, 18
Holmdel Cemetery, 174
Holmes, Jonathan, 39, 42, 143
Holmes, Obadiah, 60
Holmes, Obadiah Jr., 137
Holmes, Rev. Obadiah, 18, 39, 42, 137, 143
Homdell, John, 42
Hooglandt, Christopher, 18
Hopewell Township, 172
Hopewell, Hunterdon County, 193
Hopkins, Samuel, 33
Horabin, John, 39
Horner, John, 51
Howell, Ann, 168
Howell, Daniel, 138
Howell, Katherine, 138
Howell, Mordecai, 138
Howell, Priscilla, 182
Howell, Thomas, 18, 138
Howell, Thomas and Catherine, 182
Hudson River, 155
Hudson, Henry, 22, 24
Huet, Joseph, 40, 42, 43
Huet, Kandall, 44
Huet, Randall, 40, 42

Index

Huet, Thomas, 44
Huguenot, 105, 111, 114, 126, 140, 149
Hulett, George, 40
Hulit, George, 18
Hull, Hopewell, 49
Hull, Benjamin, 18, 49, 50
Hull, Hopewell, 50
Hull, Samuel, 50
Humphrey, Waiter, 212
Hunloke, Edward, 102
Hunterdon County, 167
Huntington, Thomas, 18, 55, 103, 205
Hutchinson, Ann, 135
Hutchinson, George, 123
Hyde, Edward -3rd Earl of Clarendon, Lord Cornbury, 133
Hyde, Katharine, 137
Hyst, Reyneer Van, 60
Ides, Vrouwtje, 200, 201
Ilsey, Elisha, 47
Ilsley, John, 47
Ilsley, Mary, 150
Ilsley, Sarah, 129, 171
Ilsley, William, 129, 150
Indian War, 87
Inquehart, John, 37
Jackson, Francis, 44
Jacob, Thomas, 43
Jacobs, Tryntie, 202
Jacques, Abigail, 140
Jacques, Anne, 150
Jacques, Daniel, 139, 140
Jacques, Elizabeth, 140
Jacques, Hannah, 139, 140
Jacques, Henry, 18, 46, 47, 139
Jacques, Henry Jr, 47, 150
Jacques, John, 139
Jacques, Jonathan, 139
Jacques, Mary, 47, 139
Jacques, Richard, 139
Jacques, Ruth, 140
Jacques, Sarah, 139, 140
Jacques, Stephen, 139, 140
James, Benj., 51
James, William, 39, 42, 43

Jans, Femmetje, 87
Jarvis, Elizabeth, 173
Jasper (Indian), 139
Jeffrey, Francis, 44
Jeffrey, John, 60
Jenkins, Job, 44
Jenkins, John, 39
Jennings, Governor Samuel, 97, 168
Jeppes, Jenti, 18
Jersey City, 87, 113, 194
Jerson, John, 44
Jewel, George, 50
Jobs, George, 43
Jobs, John, 40, 43
Jobstown, 123
Johnson ,Thomas, 54
Johnson, John, 55, 56
Johnson, Joseph, 56, 161
Johnson, Richard, 60
Johnson, Thomas, 55, 56, 185
Johnson, William, 33, 142, 160
Jones, Benj., 51
Jones, Jeffery, 18, 141, 142
Jones, Jeottry, 33
Jones, Robert, 40, 43
Joris, Janneke, 108
Joy, Hannah, 44
Keen, Gertrude, 181
Keith, George, 173
Kelly, Mary, 47, 98
Kempe, Sarah, 72
Kent, 164
Kent (Ship), 84, 93, 95, 117, 132, 147
Kent, Stephen, 47
Kent, Stephen Jr, 47
Kief's War, 26
Kieft, Governor Wilhelm, 89
Killigsworth, Thomas, 60
King,, John, 44
Kingsland, Edmund, 142
Kingsland, Elizabeth, 142
Kingsland, Isaac, 18, 142
Kingsland, Nathaniel, 142
Kinsey, John, 18

First Settlers, Colonists and Biographies by Descendants

Kinsley, Eldad, 82
Kirk, Gabriel, 40
Kitchell, Robert, 18, 55, 56
Kitchell, Samuel, 18, 53, 54, 55, 56, 85
Klauw, Wyntje (Winifred) Franse, 99
Knight, Ann, 139
Knight, Ann and Richard, 47
Knight, Benjamin, 140
Knight, Joanna, 97
Knight, Richard, 139, 140
Knox, William, 83
Kogers, Benjamin, 44
Kuyer, Claes Jansen, 200
Labour Point, 117
LaFetra, Edmond, 18
Lafetra, Edmund, 39
Lafetra, Edward, 43
Laing, William, 51
Laiton, William, 40
Lambert, Robert, 33
Lampson, Eleazer, 185
Lanckford, Prudence, 84
Lane, Margaret, 97
Langstaff, John, 50
LaRue, Sarah, 114
Laurence, Richard, 55, 56
Lawrence, Abraham, 33
Lawrence, Hannah, 43
Lawrence, Thomas, 51
Lawrence, William, 18, 40, 43, 44
Lawrie, Governor Gawen, 142
Lawton, Anne, 178
Layton, Mary, 110
Layton, Thomas, 91
Layton, William, 40, 43
Layton, William and Violet, 110
Lee, Rachel, 116
Leeds, Daniel, 43
Leeds, Thomas, 18, 43
Leeds, William, 43
LeFevre, Catherine, 192
Lefevre, Hypolit, 60
Lenni Lenape, 22, 24, 31, 52, 167, 184
Leonard, Henry, 18, 43

Leonard, James, 42
Leonard, John, 44
Leonard, Nathaniel, 44
Leonard, Samuel, 44
Leonard, Thomas, 44
Lepinton/Lippington, Daniel, 50
Leprary, Mr., 33
Lessenby, Henry, 47
Liang, John Jr, 51
Liming, John, 18, 143
Liming, John Jr, 143
Liming, Thomas, 143
Liming, William, 143
Lincoln, Mordeaci, 143
Lindsley, Francis, 18, 56
Linle, Benjamin, 144
Linle, Deborah, 144
Linle, Ebenezer, 144
Linle, Francis, 55, 144
Linle, John, 144
Linle, Jonathan, 144
Linle, Joseph, 144
Linle, Ruth, 144
Lippencott, Abigail, 44
Lippencott, Bestue, 44
Lippencott, Jacob, 44
Lippencott, John, 43
Lippiencott, Richard, 39
Lippincott, Bartholomew, 40
Lippincott, Remembrance, 18, 44
Lippincott, Richard, 18, 43
Lippitt,, Henry, 39
Little, George, 47
Lonestaff, John, 51
Longfield, Cornelius, 51
Lopers, Janetje Johanna, 104
Lord, Mary, 206
Lord, Robert, 206
Lord, Thomas, 206
Lothrop, Jane, 122
Lowry, Thomas, 50
Lubberson, Abraham, 134
Lubberts, Eybe, 87
Lubberts, Ybetje, 196

Lubbertsen, Gysbert, 87
Luce, Eliazar, 210
Ludington, Thomas, 56
Luke Watson's Point, 92
Lyman, Sarah, 204
Lymon, Robert, 55, 56
Lyon (Ship), 89
Lyon, Benjamin, 145
Lyon, Ebenezer, 145
Lyon, Henry, 18, 33, 55, 56, 127, 145
Lyon, John, 145
Lyon, Joseph, 145
Lyon, Mary, 145
Lyon, Nathaniel, 145
Lyon, Richard, 145
Lyon, Samuel, 55, 56, 145
Lyon, Thomas, 55, 56, 145
Lyons Farm, 148
Lysbeth, Elizabeth, 114
Maddox, John, 60
Mahawskcy (Indian Sachem), 59
Mahoppony (Indian Sachem), 59
Maidenhead Township, 99
Makany, David, 47
Malster, William, 60
Manamowaone (Indian Sachem), 31
Manasquan, 133
Maning, Ann, 50
Maning, Jefrey, 50
Manning, James, 51
Manning, John, 51
Manning, Joseph, 51
Mansfield Township, 99, 117
Mansson, Hans, 181
Mansson, James, 181
Manustome (Indian Sachem), 53
Mapes, John, 210
Mapes, Mary, 210
March, George, 47
March, Hugh, 47
Marcus Hook, 93
Marie Sohier, 105
Markham, William, 93
Marsh, Henry, 43

Marsh, Mary, 146
Marsh, Samuel, 18, 33, 146
Marsh, Samuel, Jr, 146
Marshall, Grace, 161
Martin ,John, 49
Martin, Benjamin, 18, 51
Martin, Capt. Jacob, 122
Martin, John, 50, 122
Martin, John , Sr, 18, 47
Martin, John, Jr., 50
Martin, Jonathan, 51
Martin, Joseph, 18, 50
Martin, Margaret, 149
Mary of Salem (Ship), 214
Masters, Clement, 18
Masters, Francis, 18, 39
Masters, Pauline, 43
Matawan, 206
Matje, Braecke, 203
Matlack, William, 18, 147
Mattano (Indian Sachem), 31
Mattox, Lewis, 40, 44
Mayham, Richard, 97
Mayham, Sarah, 97
McPherson, Robert D., 103
Mecum, William, 177
Meeker, Benjamin, 148
Meeker, John, 148
Meeker, Joseph, 33, 148
Meeker, Mary, 148
Meeker, Sarah, 148
Meeker, William, 18, 33, 148
Mellot, Jean Pierre, 18, 149
Melvine, Isabel, 110
Melyen, Jacob, 33
Melyn, Cornelius, 134, 209
Merlet, Gideon, 149
Meter, John Jansen Van, 111
Meter, Joosten Jansen Van, 111
Mey, Cornelis, 22, 80
Michielse, Catharyna, 202
Middagh, Derrick, 197
Middlesex County, 74, 109, 110, 130, 191, 206
Middleton, Hugh, 60

First Settlers, Colonists and Biographies by Descendants

Middletown, 23, 38, 40, 41, 90, 100, 101, 126, 128, 133, 137, 183, 187, 198

Midlem, Grace, 214

Mifflin, John Sr, 18

Miller, William, 211

Millison, John, 50

Mills, John, 60, 124, 167

Mills, Mary, 124

Mills, Sarah, 124

Misgacoing (Indian Sachem), 38

Mitchell, Richard, 146

Mohut (Indian Sachem), 59

Moleing, Jacob, 142

Molleson, Gilbert, 118

Molleson, Margaret, 118

Monfoort, Jannetije, 174

Monmouth, 22, 23, 39, 41, 45, 68, 78, 79, 90, 91, 96, 101, 114, 123, 124, 126, 128, 133, 137, 143, 151, 170, 174, 189, 195, 198, 206, 207, 208

Monmouth County, 38, 41, 115, 130, 178, 187

Monmouth Patent, 39, 67, 79, 90, 96, 100, 101, 124, 128, 137

Moor, Thomas, 33, 39

Moore, Elizabeth, 158

Moore, Matthew, 47

Moore, Samuel, 18, 47, 50, 150

Moorestown, 23, 182

Morford, Thomas, 18, 43

Morgan, Elizabeth, 68

Morris, Col. Lewis, 68, 91

Morris, Elizabeth, 152

Morris, George, 33

Morris, John, 56, 91, 152

Morris, Lewis, 18, 43, 151

Morris, Rebecca, 91

Morris, Richard, 151

Morris, Thomas, 18, 54, 55, 151, 152

Morss, Peter, 33

Morss, Robert, 33

Moss, Mary, 188

Mott, Gershom, 45

Mott, Jacob, 178

Mount Holly, 168

Mount, George, 18, 39, 40, 43, 44

Mount, Matthias, 18

Mount, Richard, 18

Mowry, Mehitable, 82

Mundaye, Nicholas, 50

Mundie, David, 51

Mundy, Nicholas Jr, 51

Munroe, Alex, 56

Musgrave, Lydia, 129

Myhoppon (Indian Sachem), 59

Myhoppony (Indian Sachem), 59

Naversink River, 130

Navesink, 38, 42, 68, 96, 133, 135, 151

Necomis (Indian Sachem), 59

Nesmith, John, 18

Nevis Merchant, 143

New Barbadoes, 142

New Beverly, 93

New Brunswick, 49

New Eason, 123

New Sweden, 22, 176, 177, 181

Newark, 23, 52, 85, 88, 103, 107, 127, 144, 152, 161, 169, 184, 188, 204, 205

Newbold, Ann, 164

Newbold, James, 164

Newman, William, 40

Newsego (Indian Sachem), 59

Newton, 214

Newton Monthly Meeting, 97

Nicholson, Samuel, 18, 60, 153

Nicolls, Governor Richard, 22, 30, 31, 34, 38, 67, 76, 90, 158

Noble, Richard, 60

Noiret, Jacquemine, 114

Norris, Henry, 18, 33

North, Agnes, 132

Northampton, 132

Norton, Nathaniel, 33

Nyssen, Teunis, 191, 192

Obama, President Barack, 112

Obama, President Barack, 47

Oele, Dahlbo, 18

Oelsons, Hans, 93

Ogden, Benjamin, 156

Ogden, David, 33, 54, 156, 185

Ogden, Jane Bond, 156

Ogden, John, 18, 31, 32, 33, 34, 35, 46, 60, 155, 156

Ogden, John, 142

Ogden, John Jr., 33, 156

Ogden, Jonathan, 33, 156
Ogden, Joseph, 156
Ogden, Mary, 156
Ogden, Rebecca, 156
Ogden, Richard, 60, 155
Ohanuelhouse, Adam, 44
Old Bridge, 206
Olden, William, 51
Oliver, William, 33, 92
Oman, Benjamin, 33
Oosteroom, Tryntje, 194
Osborn, Joseph, 33
Osborn, Mary, 120
Osborne, Caleb, 18
Osborne, Jane Curtis, 130
Osborne, Steven, 120
Osbourne, Jeremy, 34
Osbourne, Stephen, 33
Ouge, Isaac, 43
Pack, George, 18, 33, 158
Page, Anthony, 40
Painter, Richard, 33
Pancas, John. See Pancoast, John
Panckhurst, John. See Pancoast, John
Panckhurst, Joseph, 159
Panckhurst, Rev. Samuel, 159
Pancoast, Ann, 160
Pancoast, Elizabeth, 159
Pancoast, James, 159
Pancoast, John, 18, 159
Paradys, Maria Melyn, 134
Pardey, 33
Pardon, William, 33
Parker ,Elisha, 46
Parker, Benjamin, 47
Parker, Elisha, 47
Parker, George, 18, 44, 175
Parker, John, 33
Parker, Joseph, 40, 43
Parker, Nathaniel, 44
Parker, Peter, 40, 43, 44
Parker, Sarah, 175
Parkhurst, Benjamin, 33
Passage Point, 91, 151

Passaic, 203
Passaic River, 155, 184, 203
Passaquenecqua Lands, 91
Paterson, 108
Patrick, Hannah Annet je, 68
Patterson, Edward, 18, 39
Patterson, John, 18
Paulusen, Dirck, 203
Pauw, Michael, 201
Pavonia, 26, 201
Peach Tree War, 26
Peck, George, 18
Peck, Jeremiah, 33, 55, 56
Penn, William, 93, 95, 117, 118, 130, 132, 133, 182
Penn, William Jr, 72
Pennington, Ephraim, 55, 56, 188
Pennsauken, 147
Perawae (Indian Sachem), 53
Percy, Henry, 40
Perine, Joshua, 50
Perkins, Lydia, 72
Perrin, Daniel, 18
Personage Home Lot, 56
Perth Amboy, 23, 42, 75, 149, 183
Peters, Sara, 196
Petersen, Laurens, 193
Peterson, Christiern, 177
Peterson, Moses, 34
Pewtinger, Richard, 163
Philip (Ship), 163
Philpot, Maria, 177
Pickard, Clarence Mott, 133
Pierce, Daniel, 46, 47, 49, 139
Pierce, Joseph, 46
Pierce, Joshua/Joseph, 47
Pierson, Abigail, 161
Pierson, Abraham, Jr., 161
Pierson, Rebecca, 161
Pierson, Rev. Abraham, 18, 55, 56, 161, 184
Pierson, Thomas, 161
Pierson, Thomas Sr., 18
Pierson, Thomas, Jr., 56
Pierson, Thomas, Sr, 55
Pieters, Stijntje (Christina), 193

Pike, Andrew, 70
Pike, Ephraim, 70
Pike, Hannah, 70, 162
Pike, John, 18, 46
Pike, John (Captain), 47, 70, 119, 162
Pike, John, Jr, 47
Pike, John, Jr., 162
Pike, Joseph, 162
Pike, Ruth, 162
Pike, Thomas, 47, 162
Piles, William, 33
Pilesgrove, 104
Piscataway, 23, 49, 109, 119, 122, 136, 149, 150, 166, 179
Pittenger, Richard, 18
Planken, Abigael Ver, 64
Pledger, John, 59
Plum, Elizabeth, 156
Plum, Samuel, 55
Plummer, Deborah, 140
Plummer, Ephraim, 47, 139
Plummer, Francis, 150
Plummer, Hannah, 150
Plummer, Ruth, 140
Plummer, Samuel, 140
Plumstead, Clement, 72
Pontony, Henry, 149
Poole, Thomas, 159
Pope, John, 33
Popomora (Indian Sachem), 38
Portland Point, 40, 79, 100
Potter, Marmaduke, 47
Potter, Rebecca, 47, 98
Potter, Samuel, 18
Potter, Thomas, 18, 39, 44
Poulson, Margaret, 176
Poulson, Paul, 18
Pound, John, 18, 51
Powell, Elizabeth, 18, 164
Powell, Prudence, 164
Powell, Robert, 164
Powell, Roderick, 34
Praire, Robert La, 47
Predmore, John Jr, 166
Presbyterian Church of Woodbridge, 83, 98

Preston, Sarah, 148
Price, Benjamin, 18, 33, 165
Price, Benjamin, Jr, 33, 165
Pridmore, Ino, 51
Pridmore, John, 18, 166
Princeton, 37
Proprietor, 47, 93, 118, 121, 214
Proprietors, 22, 28, 46, 49, 59, 97, 167, 184, 206
Prudden, John, 205
Puritan, 52, 75, 144, 152, 188
Purmerland Church, 149
Purmerland Church (Ship), 113
Pyatt, Jacob, 51
Pyatt, Rene, 51
Quaker, 37, 58, 78, 93, 95, 97, 102, 130, 133, 159, 189
Quaker Meeting at Bordentown, 123
Quaker Meeting at Crosswicks, 170
Quaker Meeting at Little Egg Harbor, 123
Quaker Meeting at Manasquan, 143
Quakers, 40, 41, 52, 58, 60, 67, 72, 84, 96, 118, 121, 123, 124, 130, 132, 143, 153, 164, 170, 173, 175, 189, 214
Rahway, 46, 73, 146
Rahway River, 98
Rancocas, 121, 164, 168
Rancocas Quaker Burying Ground, 132
Rankokus, 212
Rapalje, Judith Jorise, 197
Rapalje, Sarah Joris, 192
Raritan River, 25, 31, 38, 46, 49, 155, 166, 192
Rawles, John, 68
Reading, John, 18, 167
Reading, John, Jr, 167
Reape, Sarah, 18, 43
Reape, William, 18, 39
Rechpokus, 203
Reeve, Walter, 18, 168
Reformed Dutch Church at Hackensack, 65
Reformed Dutch Church at Raritan, 191
Reformed Dutch Church of Freehold and Middletown, 195
Reid, James, 18
Reid, John, 130
Richardson, Richard, 39, 40, 41, 43
Ridder, Peter, 80
Riggs, Edward, 18, 54, 55, 56, 169
Riggs, Joseph, 55, 56

Ripley, Jeromus, 192
Rising, Governor, 80
Roberts, Hugh, 55, 56
Roberts, John, 147
Robertson, Ann, 209
Robins, Daniel, 47, 170
Robins, Joseph, 18, 170
Robinson, John, 192
Robinson, Walter, 50, 51
Rogers, John, 55, 56
Rogers, William, 40
Rognion, Vincent, 50
Rolfe, Appiah, 171
Rolfe, Easter, 171
Rolfe, Elizabeth, 171
Rolfe, Henry, 171
Rolfe, John, 171
Rolfe, Jonathan, 171
Rolfe, Moses, 18, 129, 171
Rolfe, Nathaniel, 171
Rolfe, Richard, 171
Rolfe, Robert, 171
Rolfe, Samuel, 171
Roosa, Elizabeth, 169
Rose, Samuel, 55, 56
Ross, George, 18, 33
Rounsavell, Benjamin, 172
Rounsavell, Hannah, 172
Rounsavell, Martha, 172
Rounsavell, Richard, 18, 172
Rouse, Simon, 33
Royce, John, 51, 192
Roysefield, 192
Ruckman, John, 18, 39, 40, 43
Rudderow, John, 182
Rumsey, William, 60
Runyon, John, 51
Runyon, Vincent, 51
Runyon, Vincent Jr, 51
Runyon, William, 51
Russell, Patience, 124
Rutherford, 202
Sacunck, 109
Saddock, Thaomas, 39

Sadler, Richard, 40, 68
Salem, 23, 58, 60, 82, 84, 93, 111, 153, 214
Salem County, 72, 82, 176
Salem Monthly Meeting, 153
Sales, Phebe, 192
Salsbury, Evan, 33
Samuel.Hedge, Jr., 59
Sanders, Robert, 196
Sandford, Elizabeth, 104
Sandy Hook, 25, 38, 183
Sanford, Sanford, 142
Sarah,Tunison, 192
Sayre, Joseph, 18, 33
Sayre, Mary, 165
Sayre, Thomas, 165
Scattergood, Benjamin, 173
Scattergood, Elizabeth, 173
Scattergood, Hannah, 173
Scattergood, Joseph, 173
Scattergood, Sarah, 173
Scattergood, Thomas, 18, 173
Scattergood, Tomsin, 173
Schenck Family, 195
Schenck, Altje, 174
Schenck, Annetje, 174
Schenck, Antje, 174
Schenck, Jan, 174
Schenck, Jannetje, 174
Schenck, John, 18, 174
Schenck, Leah, 174
Schenck, Maria, 174
Schenck, Peter, 174
Schenck, Rachel, 174
Schenck, Roelof, 174
Schenck, Roelof Jr., 174
Schenck, Sarah, 174
Schenck, William, 174
Schenck., Margaretta, 100
Schooley, Alice, 175
Schooley, Elizabeth, 175
Schooley, John, 175
Schooley, Mary, 175
Schooley, Robert, 175
Schooley, Samuel, 175

Schooley, Sarah, 175
Schooley, Thomas, 18, 175
Scullard, Mary, 171
Scullard, Rebecca Kent, 73
Seals, Phebe (Femmetje), 191
Seargeant, Jona., 55
Seasson (Indian Sachem), 53
Seeley, Robert, 18
Seeley, Sarah, 85
Senecke, Andrew, 18
Senior, Mary, 116
Sergeant, Jonathan, 56
Serrah, Nicholas, 44
Seuakhenos (Indian Sachem), 31
Shaberly, William, 39
Shacanum (Indian Sachem), 59
Shackerly, William, 40
Shaddock, Samuel, 40
Shaddock, William, 39
Shadock, William, 44
Shamquesque, Bartholomew, 40
Shattoek, William, 43
Shattuck, William, 18
Shearman, William, 40
Sheppard, David, 60
Sheppard, James, 60
Shield (Ship), 116
Shield (Ship), 212
Shiloh, 82
Shinn, Clement, 43
Shinn, George, 43
Shinn, John Sr, 18
Shortwood, Elizabeth, 95
Shotwell, Abraham, 18, 33
Shrewsbury, 22, 38, 42, 68, 72, 90, 91, 96, 100, 110, 115, 128, 130, 135, 151, 189, 208
Shrewsbury Baptist Church, 41
Shrewsbury Quaker Meeting, 41
Shrife, Caleb, 43
Shuccotery (Indian Sachem), 59
Sicer, Samuel, 39
Sickles, Zacharias, 203
Sidler, Richard, 43
Siliver, Archibald, 44
Simmons, Michael, 50, 51

Simpkin, Michael, 34
Sinnickson, Anders, 18, 176
Sinnickson, Andrew, 177
Sinnickson, Broer, 176
Sinnickson, Catharina, 177
Sinnickson, Dorothea, 177
Sinnickson, Ingrid, 176
Sinnickson, John, 176
Sinnickson, John Jr., 176
Sinnickson, Margaret, 177
Sinnickson, Sarah, 176, See GillJohnson, Sarah
Sinnickson, Sinnick, 176, 177
Skillman, Thomas, 18, 34
Slater, Edward, 50
Slocum, Giles, 18, 90, 178
Slocum, John, 40, 43
Slocum, Nathaniel, 18
Smalley, John, 18, 50, 179
Smalley, John Jr., 50
Smalley, Joseph Jr, 51
Smart, Isaac, 59
Smith, Arthur, 210
Smith, Barbara Carver, 150
Smith, Edward, 39, 40, 42
Smith, John, 18, 40, 43, 49, 60
Smith, John (Wheelwright), 47
Smith, Richard, 50
Smith, Samuel, 47
Smith, Thomas, 19, 160
Snowden, Ann, 159
Society of Friends at Burlington, 95
Somers Point, 180, 181
Somers, John, 19, 180
Somerset County, 111, 192, 197
Somerville, 191
Speare, Benjamin, 42
Spicer, Samuel, 39, 40, 43
Spinning, Humphrey, 19, 33
Springfield, 123
St. Jean Baptist (Ship), 111
Stacy, Mahlon, 116
Stacy, Rebecca Ely, 116
Stanborough, Sarah, 120
Stanley, Oney, 177

Stannard, Anna, 135
Stanton, Elizabeth, 121
Staples, Thomas, 56
Steelman, James, 19
Steenmen, Cornelius, 44
Stelle, Gabriel, 43
Stevens, Barbara, 129, 150
Steward, John, 51
Steynmets, Casper, 19
Stiles, Martha, 182
Stiles, Robert, 19, 182
Stiles, Robert Jr, 182
Stille, Ella, 181
Stockton, Richard, 51
Stokes, Ann, 96
Story, Kobert, 44
Story, Robert, 39
Stout, Alice, 42, 183
Stout, Benjamin, 183
Stout, David, 183
Stout, James, 42, 183
Stout, John, 40, 42, 183
Stout, Jonathan, 183
Stout, Mary, 42, 43, 79, 183, 198
Stout, Peter, 42, 183
Stout, Richard, 19, 38, 39, 40, 79, 183, 198
Stout, Richard Jr., 43
Stout, Sarah, 42, 183
Straatemaacker, Dirck, 19
Stratton, Benjamin, 60
Stuyvesant, Governor Peter, 27, 80, 108, 176
Stuyvesant, Margarita, 163
Sussell, Richard, 39
Sutton, Amy, 122
Sutton, William, 19, 50
Swaine, Abigail, 184
Swaine, Christiana, 184
Swaine, Daniel, 184
Swaine, Elizabeth, 54, 184, See Ward, Elizabeth Swaine
Swaine, Joanna, 184
Swaine, Mary, 184
Swaine, Phoebe, 184
Swaine, Samuel, 19, 54, 55, 56, 184
Swaine, Sarah, 184

Swaine, William, 184
Swedesboro, 22
Swedish Settlement, 59
Swiney, Thorlogh, 43
Sylvester, Nathaniel, 19, 39, 43
Tallman, Douwe Harmense, 19
Tapp, Anna, 190
Tapp, Edmond, 190
Tapp, Jane, 190
Tartte, Edward, 40
Tarville, Mary, 162
Taylor, Edward, 19
Taylor, John (Blacksmith), 47
Taylor, Robert, 39
Terhund, Albert Albertse, 19
Tewman, John, 47
The Corn Mill, 56
The Elder's Lot, 56
The Meeting House Lot, 56
The Seaman's Lot, 56
The Tailor's Lot, 56
Thingorawis (Indian Sachem), 49
Thompson, Andrew, 19
Thompson, Hur, 19, 33
Thompson, Isabella Marshall, 60
Thompson, John, 60
Thompson, Moses, 33
Thompson, Thomas, 33
Thorne, Israel, 47
Throckmorton, Job, 19, 40, 42, 187
Throckmorton, John, 19, 39, 40, 42, 43, 187
Thurston, Edward, 39
Thurston, Mary, 178
Thyssen, Willemetie, 87
Tichenor, Abigail, 188
Tichenor, Daniel, 55, 188
Tichenor, Hannah, 188
Tichenor, John, 188
Tichenor, Jonathan, 188
Tichenor, Martin, 19, 55, 56, 188
Tichenor, Samuel, 188
Tilton, John, 39, 189
Tilton, John Sr., 19
Tilton, Peter, 19, 40, 43

First Settlers, Colonists and Biographies by Descendants

Tindal, Richard, 60
Tinicum Island, 80, 176
Tinton Manor, 151
Tomkins, Jona., 55
Tomkins, Jonathan, 56
Tomkins, Michael, 54, 56, 85
Tomkins, Nathan, 39
Tomkins, Seth, 56, 188
Tompkins ,Michael (Micah), 53
Tompkins, Nathaniel, 43
Tomson, John, 40
Tooker, Charles, 33
Toppan, Abraham, 47
Toppan, Isaac, 47
Toppin, Abr., 162
Torucho (Indian Sachem), 59
Tospaininkey (Indian Sachem), 59
Town Bank, 23, 89
Townsend, John, 39
Toy, Susannah, 181
Treat, Ensign John, 188
Treat, John, 56
Treat, Richard, 88, 190
Treat, Robert, 19, 52, 54, 55, 56, 88, 103, 127, 152, 161, 184, 188, 190
Trenton, 102, 116, 193, 213
Trotter, William, 19, 33
Truex, Jacob, 44
Tunisen, Jan, 19, 192
Tunison, Cornelius, 19, 191, 192
Tunison, Cornelius Jr, 191
Tunison, Teunis, 192
Tunisons, Tunis Gysbert, 191
Turril/Tarville, Mary, 47
Turrill, Mary, 162
Tuttell, Nathanael, 33
Updike, Catherine, 193
Updike, Johannes, 19, 193
Updike, Laurens Janszen, 193
Van der Laen, Beatrix, 201
Van der Laen, Cornelis Thijsz, 201
VanBlaricom, Jan Lubbertsen, 19
VanBlaricom, Lubbert Gysbertsen, 19
VanBlaricom, Magdaleentje Theunis, 19
VanBlaricum Gysbertsen, Lubbert, 194

VanBlaricum, Gysbert Lubbertsen, 194
VanBlaricum, Jan Lubbertsen, 194
VanBlaricum, Lubbert, 194
VanBlerkum, Jannetje, 203
VanBoskerk, Jannetje (Jans) (Van Horn), 19
VanBuskirk, Lourens Andriessen, 19
VanCouwenhoven, Neeltje, 174
VanDoorn, Jacob, 195
VanDoorn, Walling Jacobse, 19
VanHorn, Barent Christian, 19
VanHorn, Cornelius Christiansen, 19
VanHorn, Jannetje, 19
VanHouten, Helmigh Roelofs, 19
VanHouten, Klaes, 19
VanHouten, Roeloff Cornelissen, 19
VanHouten, Theunis, 19
VanKleeck, Baltus Barents, 19, 196
VanKouwenhoven, Gerret Wolphertse, 174
VanKouwenhoven, Sarah Willemse, 174
VanKouwenhoven, William, 174
VanLaer, Adrian, 19
VanLaer, Aeltie, 64
VanNest ,Peter, 197
VanNest, Pieter Jr, 19
VanPrincis, Baron, 198
VanPrincis, Penelope, 19, 38, 79, 183, 198
VanPurmerent, Claes Jansen, 19, 200, 201
VanQuellen, Robert, 46, 47
Vanquellin, Robert, 34
VanRensselaer, Killaen, 194
VanRipen, Elysabet, 203
VanRiper, Jurian Thomassee, 19
VanVoorhees, Albert Stevense, 19
VanVoorst, Annetje, 200
VanVoorst, Annken, 201
VanVoorst, Cornelis, 200, 201
VanVoorst, Cornelius, 19
VanVoorst, Henrick, 201
VanVoorst, Ide Cornelissen, 201
VanWestervelt, Lubbert Lubbertson, 19
VanWinkle, Abraham, 202
VanWinkle, Annetje, 202
VanWinkle, Jacob, 202
VanWinkle, Jacob Waling, 19, 202

Index

VanWinkle, Johannis, 202
VanWinkle, Michael, 202
VanWinkle, Sarah, 202
VanWinkle, Trintje, 202
VanWinkle, Waling Jacobse, 19, 202
Vaughan, John, 43
Vermeulen, Martyntje Hendrickse, 71
Vermeulen, William, 71
VerPlanck, Abraham Isaacsen, 19
VerPlanck, Hillegont, 65
Verrazzano, Giovanni, 24
Verrazzano, Giovanni, 22
Vickery, Thomas, 177
Vincents, 120
Vreeland, Hartman (Michielsen), 19
Vreeland, Michael Jansen, 19, 202
Waddington, William, 19, 60
Wade, Edward, 60
Wade, Robert, 60
Wade, Samuel, 59
Wainright, Thomas, 43
Wainwright, Patience, 143
Waiters, Elizabeth, 59
Walden, Ann, 179
Walker, Elizabeth, 60
Walker, Samuel, 50
Wall, Garret Sr, 19
Wall, John, 39
Wall, Walter, 43
Wall, Walter, 19, 39, 40
Walland, Jarret, 44
Walters, Joseph, 55, 56
Wamesane (Indian Sachem), 53
Wansick, Thomas, 40
Wapamuck (Indian Sachem), 53
Wapamuk (Indian Sachem), 85
Ward, Elizabeth Swaine, 156
Ward, Joannah, 184
Ward, John, 205
Ward, John, 19, 55, 56, 204
Ward, John, Sr., 55
Ward, Josiah, 54, 55, 56, 184, 185
Ward, Joyce, 205
Ward, Laurence, 55, 56

Ward, Lawrance, 204
Ward, Marmaduke, 42, 43
Ward, Nathaniel, 107, 185
Ward, Richard, 205
Ward, Thomas, 43
Wardell, Eliaikim, 44
Wardell, Eliakim, 19, 39, 43, 72
Wardell, Lydia, 72
Ware, Joseph, 59
Warne, Stephen, 206
Warne, Thomas, 19, 43, 206
Warren, Richard, 124
Warren, Sarah, 124
Waterford, 147
Watkins, John, 47
Watson, Luke, 19, 30, 31, 33, 46, 155
Watson, Luke,, 32
Webb, Edward, 59
Webb, George, 39
Webley, Thomas, 45
Webster, Nathan, 47
Weehawken, 26
Weinam, Maria, 177
Wekamuck (Indian Sachem), 53
Wells, John, 117
West India Company, 64, 194, 201
West Indian Company, 25
West Jersey, 58, 102
West Jersey Assembly, 168
West, Ann, 91
West, Audry, 42, 43
West, Bartholomew, 19, 39, 43, 208
West, Joseph, 44
West, Matthew, 208
West, Nathaniel Jr, 19
West, Robert, 39
West, Stephen, 44
Westcott Family, 60
Wester, Thomas, 51
Westfield, 211
Wetherill, Christopher, 19
Weymoers, Martyntje, 71
Whaling, 89, 92, 131, 141, 142, 156
Wharton, Edward, 43

First Settlers, Colonists and Biographies by Descendants

Wharton, Edward, 39
Wheeler, Nathaniel, 55, 56
Whitacar, Richard, 60
Whitaker, John, 46
Whitaker, John, 47
White, Christopher, 60
White, Denis, 33
White, Peter, 19, 44
White, Robert, 33
White, Samuel, 44
Whitehead, Isaac, 19, 32, 33
Whitehead, Issac, 76
Whitehead, Sarah, 156
Whitehead, Susanna, 76
Whitelock, John, 43
Whitelock, William, 43
Whitlock, Thomas, 19, 40
Whitlook, Thomas, 42
Wickof, Peter, 174
Wilants, John, 32
Willett, Samuel, 44
Williams, George, 91
Williams, Mary, 140
Williams, Mathew, 56
Williams, Thomas, 44
Willis, Daniel, 147
Wills, Daniel, 164
Willson, Great John, 33
Willson, Robert, 19
Wilmont, Ann, 76
Wilson, (Little) John, 33
Wilson, John, 39, 40, 43
Winans, John, 19, 33, 209
Winckfield, George, 50
Windfield, George, 51
Windham, Robert, 59
Winds, Barnabas, 33
Wines, Anna, 210
Wines, Barnabas, 19, 210
Winkle, Jacob Waling Van, 19
Winterton, Thomas, 39
Winthrop Fleet (Ships), 119
Wolverson, Peter, 32
Wood, John, 19, 39

Wood, Jonas, 33, 92
Woodbridge, 23, 46, 48, 64, 66, 73, 74, 79, 83, 94, 98, 106, 112, 129, 136, 139, 150, 162, 166, 171, 206
Woodbridge Patent, 73
Woodbridge Town Meeting House, 48
Woodbridge,, 70, 112
Woodbury, 23
Woodruff, Abigail, 211
Woodruff, Benjamin, 211
Woodruff, Elizabeth, 211
Woodruff, Hannah, 156, 211
Woodruff, Hannah Newton, 211
Woodruff, Hezekiah, 211
Woodruff, Isaac, 211
Woodruff, Joanna, 211
Woodruff, John, 33, 156, 211
Woodruff, John Jr., 211
Woodruff, Jonathan, 211
Woodruff, Joseph, 19, 211
Woodruff, Nathaniel, 211
Woodruff, Samuel, 211
Woodruff, Sarah, 211
Woodruff, Thomas, 211
Woodruff, Timothy, 19
Woodruff, William, 211
Woodward, Rev. John, 46
Woolcott, Samuel, 44
Woolley, Emmanuel, 19, 39
Woolley, John, 19, 43
Woolman, John, 212
Woolman, Rev. John, 212
Woolman, William, 212
Woolman, Willman, 19
Woolurson, Peter, 34
Worden, Andrew, 50
Worledge, John, 60
Worth, Joseph, 51, 59
Worth, Morris, 43
Worth, Richard, 46, 47
Worth, William, 19, 43
Worthley, John, 19
Wright, Elizabeth, 213
Wright, Joshua, 19, 213
Wright, Robert, 50, 51
Wright, Thomas, 43

Index

Wynkoop, Maria, 113
Yates, Mary, 136, 166
Young, Christopher, 34
Young, Joseph, 34

Young, Thomas, 33
Zabriskie, Albert, 19
Zane, Robert, 19, 214